3703549848

CW01390692

Ethics and Organisational Politics

For Dorothy and Franklin

Ethics and Organisational Politics

Chris Provis

University of South Australia

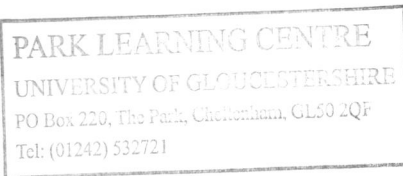

Edward Elgar
Cheltenham, UK • Northampton, MA, USA

Published by
Edward Elgar Publishing Limited
Glensanda House
Montpellier Parade
Cheltenham
Glos GL50 1UA
UK

Edward Elgar Publishing, Inc.
136 West Street
Suite 202
Northampton
Massachusetts 01060
USA

A catalogue record for this book
is available from the British Library

ISBN 1 84376 784 8

Material from *Moral Mazes: The World of Corporate Managers*, by Robert Jackall, copyright 1989 by Oxford University Press, used by permission of Oxford University Press, Inc.

Printed and bound in Great Britain by MPG Books Ltd, Bodmin, Cornwall

Contents

Acknowledgments

Like anyone who prepares a work of this sort, I have debts that run back over many years, and more of them than I can acknowledge in a brief space. To identify some individuals for thanks is inevitably unfair to others. However, I have no hesitation in expressing thanks to several academics from whom years ago I learned technicalities of philosophy and principles of intellectual work: in particular, to Brian Medlin, Greg O'Hair, Michael Stocker, Gerald Cohen and Stanley Benn. I must also give recognition to several mentors and guides who supported and assisted me as I subsequently worked in industrial relations. They included especially Sue Ohanian, John Cunningham, John Sanderson, Lachlan Riches and Michael Grimes. Over the years there have been various others whose timely words have in one way or another provided me with encouragement when it was important, and I particularly thank William Brennan, Celeste Galton, John Kleinig and Keith Hancock.

In recent times I have received various forms of assistance and support from colleagues at the University of South Australia, and I hope that the many others whom I might refer to will forgive me if I mention only Howard Harris, Sue Stack and Ian Richards as individuals with whom I have had extended relevant conversations, and Chris Leggett as someone from whose insights into organisational sociology I have certainly benefited. I am grateful also to members of I-Shou University in Kaohsiung, Taiwan, for their wonderful hospitality during a period I spent there which proved to be important in allowing me to work out some of the ideas of the book, and to members of the Philosophy Department at the University of Adelaide for stimulating discussions during two periods I spent as their guest. I am especially grateful to Garrett Cullity of that department for comments on a number of matters. For discussion and assistance with various other points I must thank Di Kelly, Lindy McAdam, Mike Metcalfe, Shoma Roy, Andrew Stewart and Alan Strudler, and I benefited from Saadia Carapiet's work as a research assistant in the early stages of writing. In more down-to-earth matters, I am grateful to James, at Charlie's Place, for much good coffee.

In addition, I express my gratitude to my friend Alan Lee, for stimulating intellectual exchange over many years, and perhaps most of all to my friend Rob Neurath, for reading through the whole of this book in draft and making incisive and valuable comments on it. The reviewers for Edward Elgar also gave me valuable assistance in that way.

At several places in the book I draw on material that has been published elsewhere in journal articles. In a number of cases, the articles and points I have drawn from them have benefited from comments and advice from editors and reviewers; I this context I note in particular the assistance I have received in regard to articles in *Business Ethics: A European Review*, the *Journal of Business Ethics*, and *Reason in Practice*, as well as a forthcoming article in *Business Ethics Quarterly*.

It will be clear to readers that I have debts to a number of other authors. C.P. Snow's novels are sources both of examples and insights. I have drawn heavily on Robert Jackall's *Moral Mazes* for examples and for comments on them. Another similar source which has been valuable is *The Whistleblowers*, by Glazer and Glazer. Acknowledgment of many other sources on which I have drawn will be found throughout the book.

Lastly, but above all, I express appreciation for the many forms of support given to me by my family.

Introduction

Why examine the ethics of organisational politics? One answer is that there are some theoretically interesting questions in the area. Our life in organisations occupies a sort of theoretical middle ground between our personal relationships and our wider social life as citizens of states and societies. Friendship and personal loyalties confront requirements of efficiency and good governance. Concrete statements by specific individuals interact with abstractions like group norms and official authority. Certainties about the words people use meet ambiguities about their meaning and purpose.

Another answer is that there are also some recurring practical questions that confront people who find themselves involved in organisational politics and who wish to act in an ethical way without at the same time conceding everything to opponents. We face situations where we see risks to aims and ideals we value, and wonder whether we can defend them through courses of action that themselves maintain those same ideals. We ask ourselves what others mean, we wonder how much to say, we hesitate over how much we are committing ourselves. We lie awake at night, considering options and looking for a way forward.

This book is motivated both by theoretical and practical concerns. It attempts to cast light on some ethical issues of organisational politics by identifying some important and common dynamics of political processes within organisations, and by showing how some general principles can guide us as we confront those processes. At the same time, it suggests that the theoretical and the practical are interwoven. Where the concrete meets the abstract, or the personal meets the social, there are some acute practical dilemmas. Sometimes, our practical concerns are straightforward: whether to sacrifice our own interests for others, or how to convince others about the best course of action. Then we may have to make a decision, but there are no complex theoretical questions to consider. In other cases, however, we have to juggle with conflicting loyalties and ambiguous information and others' chicanery, and it is not easy to see what matters most. We are uncertain what considerations we should pay attention to, and what weight we should give them. The aim of this book is to identify some of those considerations more clearly and to propose some general ways to approach them.

In this introductory chapter, I outline the structure of the book in general terms, and then comment briefly on some preliminary considerations.

THE STRUCTURE OF THE BOOK

The first two chapters of the book aim to set the scene for the discussion to follow. Chapter 1 canvasses different points of view about organisational politics, including some to the effect that organisational politics is inherently problematic, at odds with the unity and harmony to be hoped for in all effective and productive organisations. That view is hard to sustain, on any grounds. At most, it shows how definitions and formulations can themselves play a part in political processes: one person's politics can be another person's discussion and consultation. That view also fails to deal with the point familiar to most of us, that political tactics vary in how ethical and acceptable they are. Explaining how some can be more acceptable than others is an objective of this book. Subsequent chapters discount some explanations: for example, the view that what is acceptable is what is sanctioned by official organisational authority. In many cases, we can apply principles of fairness or harm avoidance, and we can also gain assistance from a principle to the effect that we ought to allow others to make responsible decisions.

However, that idea, that we ought to allow one another to make responsible decisions, has to confront the fact that we clearly depart from ideal, rational decision-makers in many respects. We are subject to many sorts of influence, and many which can play an important role in organisational politics. Chapter 2 discusses some of the most salient of these, as part of an argument that although we are subject to such influence, we can treat one another as autonomous decision-makers provided we are realistic about one another's capacities and circumstances. The limits on our capacities that we need to be aware of include the tendencies for our perceptions and expectations to be shaped by schemas and scripts, powerful social conformity effects and our tendency to accept shared group perceptions of what is legitimate, together with quasi-automatic responses to certain other influence mechanisms.

Those first two chapters aim to set the scene for a case study at the start of the second part of the book. Tricia is a manager in an organisation, who finds herself confronted by a complex mix of pressures when probationer Jennifer comes with a story of misconduct by Tricia's friend Simon. Discussion of this case in Chapter 3 raises several issues to be examined in subsequent chapters. One is the significance of personal relationships in organisational politics. Another is the 'dirty hands' problem: the extent to which effective political action may require us to set aside ethical principles. Yet another is the extent to which official authority and roles in organisations can show us ways out of ethical problems.

One approach we may consider to help us with decisions is to distinguish ethical considerations from others that may also weigh with us in various circumstances: considerations such as personal relationships or our commitments to ideals. However, I argue in Chapter 3 that such a distinction is not of great assistance. Those and other different sorts of considerations may often be sources of obligation. Such considerations may conflict with one another and when they do there is not necessarily any rule about how to arrive at a decision. Although none of them may be ignored or routinely subordinated to others, that is something we live with in a great deal of our decision-making.

If we are uncomfortable with that conclusion then we might seek guidance about what to do by reference to prescribed roles and legitimate organisational authority. This sort of approach to grounding ethical behaviour in organisations is examined in Chapters 4 and 5. In Chapter 4 we consider two ideas. One is that organisational authority may derive moral legitimacy from the institutions of the surrounding society, on the basis that if those institutions are themselves legitimate, they may transmit their legitimacy on to duly constituted organisations within the society. The second idea is that internal organisational norms create legitimate requirements on organisational members.

Neither of those ideas is finally satisfactory. The first suggestion encounters the difficulty that organisational rules and roles are too specific for all their content to be given legitimacy from surrounding institutions. The second meets the problem that some internal norms may contravene general moral principles. That is an issue we shall look at again later, in Chapter 10, as we see how processes of social impression management can generate norms out of people's mutual expectations, but there will still be no general presumption that local norms always create legitimate requirements. We all doubtless tend to succumb to pressure for conformity, but that is just one of the sorts of influence on us that may be at odds with responsible decision-making.

Thus, in Chapter 5 we move on to consider whether the sorts of factors that theorists have suggested may ground legitimate authority in nation-states may directly ground legitimate authority in organisations. One possibility is that members of an organisation may have an ethical obligation to comply with its demands and arrangements because they have consented to those arrangements.

Just as in nation-states, there are often difficulties with claiming that individuals have given their express consent. While tacit consent can ground obligations, there are on many occasions some difficulties with claiming that individuals have given even tacit consent to arrangements. Consent may be counterfeited when people are not given an opportunity to consider arrangements in a way that takes realistic account of their capacities, but that merely shows that we can be influenced by an appearance of legitimacy. In any event, there are many cases where it will be necessary to look for other explanations of ethical requirements. One possibility is that people may have obligations to comply with organisational arrangements to the extent that they might fairly be asked for consent to them. However, that will not provide a useful criterion for deciding when authority is legitimate.

It therefore does not seem as though an appeal to organisational authority can be used as a general basis for resolving ethical problems in organisational politics: there will always be some issues that require us to turn to other considerations. We shall need to look at the details of particular situations to see what is relevant to our decisions in those situations. In Chapter 6 we begin to examine some of the sorts of considerations that often are salient.

Prominent amongst those considerations are our loyalties to other individuals. While accepting the ethical force of friendships and other personal relationships may seem to run counter to requirements of impartiality and fairness, it seems necessary to recognise that such relationships have genuine ethical force, given that our friendships are so important for living full human lives. On the other hand, the same does not seem to apply to relationships with organisations or abstract groups, and so it is questionable whether loyalty to an organisation can reasonably be given any independent moral weight, or whether it can justify our tendency to favour members of abstract social groups we identify with.

Recognising the ethical significance of friendship does not mean that it necessarily outweighs other ethical considerations, but only that it may justify some special attention in ethical decision-making. In particular, for example, there may be grounds on some occasions to be especially slow in coming to adverse conclusions about our friends. That point takes us on to Part Three of the book. In Chapter 7 we turn to a range of ethical issues that arise about weighing evidence and drawing conclusions in organisational politics. Some of these issues are to do with drawing conclusions about technical matters, but many have more to do with attributing beliefs and intentions and actions to others.

In much of organisational politics, communications and actions are likely to be ambiguous, and we can have obligations not to go too far in the beliefs we come to, lest we be led astray, like Othello. At the same time, there is also a question about how much evidence it is reasonable for us to seek about an issue. That is partly a matter of our own resources, but partly also a matter of what the issue is. Requirements of confidentiality may need to be considered. In some cases, we may be precluded from exploring private matters. In other cases, people may be in the throes of working out positions on some question, and trying to obtain information about the process can be disruptive or give misleading conclusions. Sometimes, too, we should be alert for self-fulfilling prophecies, where our beliefs about others' intentions prove correct, but only because we have made them so.

The other side of the ambiguity that we confront in drawing conclusions is the ambiguity that people may deliberately impart to communications, and in Chapter 8 that point takes us on to issues of deception, concealment and impression management.

In deciding what is reasonable, we need to be realistic in our assessment of situations, particularly in regard to others' intentions and expectations. In cases of mistrust, it does not seem as though we should act deceptively on the basis of general assumptions about what others may do or expect, if at little cost we can obtain some evidence about their actual intentions and expectations.

There are methods of deception and influence which trade on our finite capacities and known predilections, and it is not always clear what ethical principles bear on such conduct. Sometimes it may be wrong because it is unfair or harmful. On at least some occasions the operative factor seems to be the extent to which it precludes us being held responsible for our decisions. Even where others are responsible for their decisions, we may still be culpable if we lead them into demonstrable error, even if we do so by using subtle techniques of impression management or linguistic formulation.

Bearing that in mind, we turn in Chapter 9 to consider some issues that arise about processes of 'framing' and of directing others' attention in one direction or another. Both can be means of persuasion, and neither seems to lead others to false conclusions. Nevertheless, such a tactic as distracting or redirecting others' attention clearly seems to be questionable to the extent that it inhibits others from making responsible decisions. It will not always be wrong, and neither will framing things in one way rather than another, but it will be necessary to consider the actual effects such tactics have on others.

The extent to which impression management may consist of framing things or directing attention one way rather than another takes us on to consider impression management as a process of joint social performance. This is the sort of social impression management described in many contexts by Erving Goffman, where people respond to one another's expectations, in conformity with some jointly accepted 'script'. In Chapter 10 we consider some ethical issues about the way that such social performances can be used as means of influence, particularly through manipulation of people's expectations about one another. What we lead others to expect of us can be an important source of obligation, and we also ought to take some account of expectations others have even where we have not ourselves induced those expectations in them. Sometimes, people's shared expectations constitute social norms, and may establish what is legitimate in a certain social environment. However, as we noticed in Chapter 4, group norms can sometimes be ethically problematic. We now see how the problems can go beyond straightforward conflict between local norms and general moral principles. People's expectations can be manipulated as means of influence and control. The result may be to place people in an ethical dilemma, where they have real obligations to others but these are exploited by third parties. A kind of 'dirty hands' problem can occur, and only sometimes will people have a way out through exposure of the tactic and revision of one another's expectations.

That discussion about the significance of the expectations people have of one another in organisations then leads us on in Chapter 11 to consider the effects of people's group allegiances; in particular, to note that allegiances to groups are often associated with commitments to particular beliefs and positions, and that others can trade on this to influence people's commitments. There are ethical questions about such influence. One approach is to deplore party alignments in organisational politics, but it is unrealistic to imagine that group commitments can always be avoided. Accepting that they are unavoidable, we need to consider ethical issues about the interplay between beliefs and group alignments. One point to bear in mind is that group conformity can lead our beliefs awry; another is that espousal of norms and values to signal commitments to groups can amount to hypocrisy, and undermine authentic commitments.

PRELIMINARY COMMENTS

Parts of the book draw attention to some analogies between issues that arise in organisational politics and issues that have been discussed about the politics of nation-states, while concentrating on matters that are particularly salient in organisations. It does not focus unduly on dirty tricks of office politics. The book seeks some general principles that give some basis for a realistic ethical approach. It especially considers how we can respect people as autonomous decision-makers while still recognising their finite capacities and susceptibility to influences of various sorts. Some readers will be surprised that certain ideas receive little treatment. 'Transparency', for example, is a term not used. 'Accountability' is another. The explanation is primarily that to weave these and some other important ideas into the argument would lengthen the discussion significantly. I have tried to focus on ideas that are keys to analysis, with wide application and the least possible technical usage. Thus, the concepts I try mainly to use are ones like 'responsibility', 'consent', 'expectation', 'obligation', and the like. This reflects an effort to relate issues about organisational politics to more general issues and to identify as clearly as possible what the similarities and differences are between processes in organisations and other social processes. It is not to say that other ideas are unimportant, but only that they do not add to the argument as I have found myself developing it. Ideas like transparency and accountability are important and useful, but I believe that it is not difficult to see how they might be incorporated into the general account given here.

Equally, it will be clear to many readers how the discussion might be linked to the work of such theorists as Weber and Giddens. Weber's account of legitimate authority and his discussion of 'personalism' both are relevant to parts of this book, and Giddens' 'structuration theory' might also be linked to some of the discussion below which alludes to situations where people have mutually intertwined expectations. The book could be expanded to analyse ideas of these and other theorists, and relate them to the line of argument here. However, I do not believe that the analysis would ultimately change the direction of the argument, and I hope that it may be possible to explore the relationships elsewhere.

On the other hand, I recognise that some of the ideas that do play an important role in the argument may invite more critical scrutiny than I give them: perhaps especially the ideas of 'responsibility' and 'expectations'. These ideas have both a descriptive and a normative element. To be responsible for something is to have played a causal part in bringing it about, but also in many circumstances to merit praise or blame for it. For something to be expected is for it to be anticipated or predicted, but also in many circumstances for it to be proper or appropriate. It may be contended that parts of the argument in the book rest too much on running together those dual elements of the ideas.

While the discussion touches on that issue here and there, it does not try to confront it in full detail. Here, I can only acknowledge that further detailed exposition of those parts of the argument could be worthwhile, but again would go beyond what is possible here. For the purposes of this discussion, I believe that the use I make of those notions is consistent with their use in other wider contexts. If I am correct then it is at least true that the argument here shows how we can reduce some of the issues and problems about the ethics of organisational politics to some other more general issues and problems about ethical action in general. That is my primary aim, to show how ethical problems that we encounter in organisations can be related to other ethical problems we encounter. Organisational processes throw some issues into sharp relief, but we can hope that the solutions to those problems are not ultimately more difficult than the solutions of other ethical problems we confront, even though they call forth some need for close attention and analysis.

At the same time, it is part of the argument here that the ethical issues we confront in organisations are not made simpler because that is where we confront them. Organisations often function to bring order and efficiency to dealing with classes of problems; often, that is why we maintain them, whether they are banks, schools, or armies. We may then be lured into thinking that they necessarily bring order and simplicity to dealing also with ethical problems. It is certainly true that processes in organisations can make it easier to act in an ethical way. However, they can also make it harder. At the very least, I shall argue, they cannot displace the need for us to make our own individual ethical choices and decisions.

PART ONE

Issues and Processes

1. Politics, Definitions and Ethics

Many of us spend a lot of time in organisations, and often encounter their politics. As we do so we are likely to find ourselves dealing with certain recurrent and distinctive ethical problems. We have to come to conclusions and make decisions in an environment which is fluid or ambiguous; we are subject to conflicting demands which all seem to have some legitimate call on us; we have to persuade others without misleading them; we have to convey information in ways that are honest but which guard us against chicanery and exploitation; we have to deal with expectations others have of us which we do not regard as reasonable. These and a variety of other problems are endemic to organisations and may give pause to anyone who wishes to act in an ethical way. They are political problems to the extent that they arise especially in situations where organisation members compete for power and resources. None of the problems is confined to life in organisations, but there they may come to special prominence.

This chapter sets the scene for our later more detailed discussion about these sorts of ethical problems. We note some reasons why they have not been much discussed. One is that traditional political theory has focussed primarily on the politics of nation-states. Another reason is a prominent contemporary strand of management theory which suggests that organisational politics is inherently unethical: there is then little scope for examination of specific ethical problems within organisational politics. That line of thought leads us to note that argument about the ethics of organisational politics can itself be part of organisational politics, and takes us on to some general problems of approach.

ORGANISATIONAL POLITICS AND POLITICAL THEORY

For several hundred years the central preoccupation of political theorists has been the politics of nation-states. There has been a special preoccupation with the rights and obligations of citizens and the state, whether the state has been conceived as the person of the monarch or an abstract constitutional authority. Hobbes, Locke, Rousseau and others grappled with issues about the source and extent of political authority within the nation-state. These are problems of ethics, insofar as they concern the question of what moral obligations we have to comply with that authority.[1] Perhaps the explanation for the emphasis on nation-states has been the assumption that they alone may use physical coercion to enforce their authority, but whatever the explanation, the emphasis has been clear.

This is not to say that political theory has confined itself only to the relationship between the citizen and the state. In the twentieth century, much attention was given to the relationships amongst individuals and groups of citizens, in matters like discrimination and disadvantage. Even here, however, the debate was often an outgrowth of concern that the state ought to treat its citizens equally, and to that extent still revolved about the idea of politics as fundamentally something to do with states and national governments.

It is true that other political environments have been examined in academic study. Anthropologists have studied power arrangements in small communities (e.g. Gluckman 1965), sociologists and psychologists have studied power dynamics within families (e.g. Laing 1971) and other social groupings, and management theorists have considered power within work organisations (e.g. French and Raven 1960, Bacharach and Lawler 1980, Pfeffer 1981 and 1992). But by and large these studies have been descriptive rather than normative. That is, they have focused on the causal dynamics, the factors that have explained how things have happened one way rather then another, and not on what ought to happen, on how individuals ought to cope with the dilemmas and ethical difficulties that arise for them.[2]

In some ways, this emphasis on the empirical reminds us of Machiavelli's work. In the Italian city-states, modern empirical study of politics began as Machiavelli wrote *The Prince* by way of advice to political actors about the best ways for them to conduct themselves. For Machiavelli, empirical descriptive study was crucial, and normative conclusions followed straightforwardly. He was impatient with ethical qualms that might detract from effectiveness, and explicitly argued that the political leader could not afford traditional virtues (Hampshire 1989, pp. 162–7). In this, he was aided by a limited conception of what is good for people: 'glorious worldly achievements which will be recognised in history' (Hampshire 1989, p. 165). It was only later that political theorists were bemused by such questions as the extent to which ends can justify means, or whether individuals have rights that may not be infringed for the good of the state.

The present situation in the study of organisational politics is rather similar to the study of the politics of nation-states in Machiavelli's time. Antony Jay wrote a book titled *Management and Machiavelli*, in which he noted that 'Machiavelli ... is in fact bursting with urgent advice and acute observations for top management of the great private and public corporations all over the world' (Jay 1967, chap. 1). Machiavelli's great achievement was to articulate some of the causal relationships that are important in political life, and Jay has pointed out how some of them are as significant for modern corporate political life as they were for the politics of Italian city-states. For us, however, it may be a concern that often normative inferences that have been drawn by theorists about organisational politics have been as straightforward and uninhibited as Machiavelli's.[3] There has been much less attention to normative issues in organisational politics than has been given to normative issues in the politics of the nation-state since Machiavelli's time. Mediaeval Christian theorists had tried to articulate principles of political actions and political arrangements that were systematic and consistent with their theology, but in doing so they neglected empirical detail. Machiavelli focussed on the empirical detail but pushed aside ethical reservations or dilemmas. Subsequent theorists restored some balance, in studying the politics of nation-states, but theorists have only recently started to consider ethical dilemmas in the politics of organisations.

ETHICS AND DEFINITION

One inhibition on writing about organisational politics is that a good deal of literature still contains the suggestion that organisational politics is inherently unethical. This provides one of the biggest obstacles to constructive discussion of ethical issues in organisational politics. Drory and Romm (1990) found definitions that relied on reference to outcomes that are 'self-serving' and 'against the organization', and which had a variety of other adverse connotations. Cropanzano, Kacmar and Bozeman say that we use the term 'organisational politics' to refer to influence attempts that are 'covert, crafty, and behind the scenes' (1995, p. 17). Their statement is prompted by definitions of organisational politics found in various authors, where in addition 'the idea that these behaviors are designed to promote or protect one's own self-interests is continually noted' (p. 7).

This conception of organisational politics has some clear shortcomings. It can lead to circularity, for example. When Kacmar and Baron say by way of definition that 'organizational politics involves actions by individuals which are directed toward the goal of furthering their own self-interests without regard for the well-being of others or their organization' (1999, p. 4), then it is hardly surprising that later they find that 'politics appears to be a negative force in organizations. That is, many of the consequences of organizational politics are negative for the individual and the organization' (p. 21). The approach also seems unduly restrictive. If we build into our definition of organisational politics that it is 'covert and crafty', then consider the situation where a boss says quite openly, 'Do this, or I'll fire you!' The definition excludes it from being considered 'organisational politics'.

More generally, such approaches to definition have two defects. One is that they are problematic as a basis for analysing the dynamics of organisational politics. If organisational politics must by definition be self-interested then we are impeded from seeing similarities and differences amongst pieces of behaviour which embody varying degrees of self-interest. For a manager to require his own signature on all outgoing correspondence may be a self-interested effort at maintaining his own position, or it may be an attempt to counteract the unprincipled behaviour of an underling. In either case, it is a way of managing power, and its dynamics may be similar. Certainly, there may also be differences. What his intentions and motives are will affect our explanations and predictions, and to the extent that they are accurately discerned by others around him they may respond differently and the whole course of events may be different. But there will be a whole series of possibilities, affected in part by the whole range of motives and intentions he may have. If we wish to understand the dynamics of such processes, we are not assisted by an attempt to quarantine just a few of them as 'organisational politics'. The same problem occurs if we include a requirement like 'covert and crafty' in a definition: there is a wide range of possibilities about how covert or open, how crafty or straightforward, actions are, and to draw an arbitrary line does us no good as students or theorists of organisational processes.

One requirement of a good definition is that it will help us to see similarities and relationships between processes that may on the surface seem different, or at least will not mask such similarities and relationships. A satisfactory definition of organisational politics would leave it open to us to see similarities and relationships with other political processes. There is plenty of scope for that. Jay's book is a quite explicit effort to show the similarities between the politics of corporate organisations and the politics of nation-states. Political anthropologists have examined the political processes in tribes, villages and other small communities, which show similarities in their political processes both to modern western organisations and to traditional monarchies or feudal empires. Gluckman says of such communities that 'the unifying force of ritual symbols is most important' (1965, p. xxii), just as other writers have emphasised the importance of such things in modern organisations (e.g. Deal and Kennedy 1988). Gluckman notes the interaction between politics and means of production, the way in which organisational structures can be in conflict with a principle of government, and how 'palace intrigues become more isolated from the main mass of people' (1965, p. xxii). Any of these might equally well be a possibility worth considering in corporate politics or the politics of nation-states. The sorts of factors that may figure in causal explanations may be similar in the different sorts of case, and if they are then that casts light on them all.

This is not to suggest that there are no differences amongst political processes in different contexts. For example, background culture and belief can play an important part in people's behaviour, and in their political activities. Gluckman notes that in the communities of which he is writing,

> Not all disturbances of social relations arise from open breaches of rules of right conduct. A marked characteristic of tribal society is that 'natural' misfortunes are ascribed to the evil wishes of witches or sorcerers, to the anger of spirits affronted by neglect of themselves or of the sufferer's obligations towards kin, to breaches of taboo and omission of ritual, and to rightful curses by appropriate persons. (1965, p. xxiii)

While 'rightful curses by appropriate persons' may often play a part in modern western organisational politics, probably there is less belief in witches, sorcerers or spirits. (Perhaps it has been replaced by belief in the gurus and wizards of information technology and their associated hardware or software gremlins.)

There may be these and other differences amongst political processes in different contexts, but the key point is that we are ill advised to adopt any definition of organisational politics that would hinder us from observing similarities or differences relative to other forms of politics. It is potentially useful to accept with Miller that 'There is politics in the board room, in the inter-departmental conference, in the school staff meeting, and in the annual conference of the dog-lovers' association' (1962, p. 15). If we do, we are better placed to develop our theoretical understanding of such processes. We can hope to see just how far background beliefs and culture affect such processes, and how much they are affected by the type of community or association in which they occur. It is not useful to give 'organisational politics' a more restrictive definition than we give to other types of politics.

The second general defect of such definitions is that they obscure genuine ethical dilemmas and problems. Labels such as 'self-interested' or 'covert and crafty' suggest that it is straightforward to discern what is ethical. Those phrases have clear negative overtones, and suggest that it is unproblematic what ethical stance to adopt toward episodes of organisational politics. In fact, though, there are many cases where things are not so simple.

One sort of example that has become well known is where an individual in an organisation sees a technical or moral problem about a decision or line of conduct that has become part of official organisational policy. In his extended study of several US corporations, Robert Jackall recounts a number of cases of political conflict within organisations. One is that of 'Joe Wilson', an engineer who was eventually fired after his increasingly forceful opposition to the ways his organisation was going about cleanup after the 1979 Three Mile Island nuclear accident (Jackall 1988, pp. 112–19). Wilson's dilemma was at least partly how to act in a way that he could accept as ethical where there were conflicts between organisational decisions and what he took to be wider values, as well as conflicts between obligations he had to his own staff and obligations to other managers in the organisation. Other managers in the organisation felt that Wilson's perceptions and priorities were awry. One of the points of conflict with other managers was their view that

Authority has the prerogative to resolve technical disputes. Whether Wilson liked
it or not, Bechtel had won the power struggle and they had the right, that is the
power, to call the shots on the cleanup. (Jackall 1988, p. 118)

In other words, the issue was one about the scope of legitimate authority, and
an individual's right to dissent. These are matters that have preoccupied
political theorists in other contexts from the Lutheran Reformation, through
the English Civil War and the American War of Independence to the Campaign for Nuclear Disarmament and the Vietnam Moratorium Campaign.

This issue of legitimacy is an important point in considering possible
definitions of organisational politics. Just as some definitions may build in
ideas of self-interest, or of covert, crafty behaviour, a related approach is to
build into the definition the idea that organisational politics is illegitimate.
Mintzberg says that

politics refers to individual or group behavior that is informal, ostensibly
parochial, typically divisive, and above all, in the technical sense, illegitimate –
sanctioned neither by formal authority, accepted ideology, nor certified expertise.
(1983, p. 172)

Like some of the other definitions, the idea that politics in an organisation
is necessarily illegitimate is conceptually a very difficult one to sustain. What
about lobbying before a meeting? It may not be until a decision is taken at the
meeting that there is any policy or behaviour that is 'sanctioned' on a particular matter.[4] Referring to 'accepted' ideology begs the question: accepted by
whom? It is circular to say: 'by legitimate authorities'. Similarly for 'certified' expertise: certified by whom? These are exactly the sorts of questions
that theorists about state authority have grappled with for many years.

A further problem with such a restriction is that when people in an organisation take opposed courses, we would sometimes have to say that one side
was but the other was not engaged in organisational politics. In Wilson's
case, he and his opponents in the organisation took different points of view
and pursued opposed courses of action. It is hard to see how we could say
that his opponents' actions were organisational politics while his own were
not, or vice versa: they were interacting with one another in the same environment, actions on each side responding to the others.

Legitimacy is one example where an issue about the politics of nation-states carries over to the politics of organisations. Another issue that does so
is the problem that has recently concerned theorists of politics and the ethics
of politics under the title of the 'dirty hands' problem: the idea that 'the vocation of politics somehow rightly requires its practitioners to violate important
moral standards which prevail outside politics' (Coady 1991, p. 373). That
idea is clearly reminiscent of Machiavelli, and we have already noted that
Machiavelli's idea of what is good for people is echoed by some modern
management writers. The idea that the vocation of politics requires practitio-

ners to get their hands dirty is equally echoed by the idea that the vocation of management does so also, when managers have to engage in organisational politics.[5] Jackall notes the view of Joe Wilson's ex-colleagues that 'Sunday school ethics – the public espousal of lofty principles – do not help managers cut the sometimes unpleasant deals necessary to make the world work' (1988, p. 118). The suggestion has been made more formally that 'managers, consultants, and organizational interventionists may have to adopt behaviours towards others which initially could be distasteful to them, but may in the long term prove to be an effective approach to achieving their goals' (Kakabadse and Parker 1984, p. 101, attributing the suggestion to Pettigrew 1975 and Schein 1977). Like the issue of legitimacy, questions about whether otherwise culpable actions can be acceptable because of the political context in which they occur are questions that may be salient in organisational as in other politics. There can be differences that affect the answers, but the questions are discernibly similar.

A DISTINCTIVE FEATURE?

So far, we might accept Aristotle's view, as put by T.A. Sinclair in his introduction to Aristotle's *Politics*. He says 'Aristotle calls the state the supreme form of human association, not the only one', that 'when Aristotle calls man "a political animal" he has in mind all aspects of life in humane society, all that contributes to "the good life"', and that according to Aristotle 'it is legitimate to take the general principles governing the larger associations as applicable also to the smaller' (Sinclair 1992, pp. 24–5).

On the other hand, however, Aristotle contends that 'the state has a natural priority over the household' (1992, p. 60; Book I, chap. ii), since 'the whole must be prior to the part', and goes on to argue that the virtues that people ought to have as household members are essentially derivative from virtues that they ought to have as members of the wider community (1992, p. 97; Book I, chap. xiii). This contention at least needs qualification.

One reason for care is that it is less clear than once it may have been that organisations are 'parts' of nation-states: trans-national corporations create problems for national governments (and for the international community), just because they can avoid straightforward subjection to national laws. However, there is another reason for care, here a more important reason. Even though we ought not define organisational politics in a way that presumes significant differences from other politics, nevertheless there may be some differences that we can identify fairly clearly. There is an aspect of politics in a household that is like much organisational politics: it often involves close personal relationships.

In discussing questions about what factors make state authority legitimate, or what the general human rights are of citizens within a state, or what obligations people have when they participate in the politics of nation-states, theorists have mostly been addressing issues about abstract relationships. That is, for example, the questions are not about what the state's relationship ought to be to Jane Smith, but what its relationship ought to be with any citizen, *qua* citizen, in abstraction from any of the qualities that distinguish Jane Smith from John Brown and other citizens. By contrast, within families, relationships are characteristically personal relationships, where people respond to one another on the basis of their concrete individual qualities. Admittedly, the matter is one of degree. I treat my mother as I do largely in response to her specific individual qualities and the specific relationship that she and I have developed over many years, but to some extent I am also guided by some abstract ideas about how sons ought to act toward mothers. Nevertheless, the difference is a real one: family life tends to involve more close personal relationships than the mass politics of nation-states. So, often, do organisational life and politics.

There is room for discussion of how the 'political' is related to the 'personal'. Feminists have questioned the extent to which discussion of personal relationships can be separated from political discussion (e.g. Okin 1991; Pateman 1983). It is certainly not the case that such issues have always been held separate. Mark Bloch paints a clear picture of how the politics of feudal societies was very much a matter of personal relationships: not only because of the family relationships amongst members of monarchic dynasties, but because feudal obligations were very much a matter of personal loyalty (1965, chap. 11). It is also plausible to suggest that parliamentary party politics often involves close personal relationships of loyalty and affection. Such relationships in parliamentary party politics cannot be quite dissociated from outcomes of elections, mandates given by voters, legitimate policy decisions, and so on. However, it is the latter sorts of questions that have most often been addressed in normative discussions about the politics of the nation-state.

For these reasons, we ought not assume that the sorts of questions that theorists have dealt with about 'public' politics are the only sorts of questions that may be relevant to organisational politics and the ethics of organisational politics. Jackall emphasises the significance in the organisations he studied of 'fealty' relationships (see 1988, e.g. pp. 18–21). These are closely analogous to the fealty relationships Bloch describes in feudal European society, and pose some significant ethical questions. Most of us will be aware of how personal relationships impact on the politics of organisations we have been involved in, and I shall argue that they give rise to some distinctive ethical obligations.

True, the possible tensions between abstract political obligations and concrete personal commitments pose ethical dilemmas on the level of national politics as well as within organisations. E.M. Forster wrote that 'if I had to choose between betraying my country and betraying my friend, I hope

I should have the guts to betray my country' (1965, p. 76). We can sympathise very strongly with that attitude when we read accounts of totalitarian dictatorships that use family members to inform on one another 'for the good of the state'. In other contexts, on the contrary, we may wonder whether abstract obligations may not have a stronger moral call on us than personal relationships. Consider the example of Dale Console: 'although the issue of loyalty to his former employers was still thorny, it did not prevent him from disclosing the unethical and illegal acts routinely perpetrated by the pharmaceutical industry' (Glazer and Glazer 1989, p. 44). A number of studies have noted the extent to which 'whistleblowers' have been torn by such conflicts (for some references and discussion see Provis, McKay and Tomaino 1998).

Ethical issues in organisational politics inevitably reflect some ethical issues of other politics, but we cannot say that the ethical issues that arise from organisational politics are just variant forms of the issues that political theorists have been addressing since the time of Machiavelli. There is at least some reason to believe that the issues of organisational politics will include more to do with personal relationships than did the political issues which preoccupied Hobbes and Locke and their successors.

UNITARISM, PLURALISM AND DEFINITION

Overall, we should not at the outset assume too much about the problems, but we should avoid any definitions that tend to foreclose options about the sorts of issues that we may wish to address. Thus, we do not want to assume that the problems are all ones of personal relationships, or that they are all ones of traditional political theory. Nor should we assume that all of the activities to be considered are self-interested, or covert and crafty, or illegitimate, because including those ideas in definitions may obscure things that are important.

We also want to avoid any assumption that the problems are primarily issues about efficiency or organisational effectiveness. There is a tendency by at least some theorists to make that assumption, rather like Machiavelli's assumption that worldly success is the criterion of value. Kacmar and Baron introduce their survey of literature about organisational politics with the comment that 'Virtually all human resources decisions (e.g., promotions, hiring) have the potential to be impacted by political actions and agendas. ... When this occurs, the best decisions are not always made' (1999, p. 1). Here is at least some orientation toward a 'unitary' conception of organisations: the idea that in general an organisation can be conceived of as a harmonious environment, with members united by common goals and values.[6] In such an environment, political activity can well seem aberrant and dysfunctional.

Such a unitary view of organisations has been common, often reflected in approaches to organisations that treat them as machines that ought to be made to function smoothly and effectively to produce good quality outputs at low cost and with little stress for the individuals who comprise them. The organisational machine will not function well if there are worn components, grit in the bearings, or parts out of alignment. Thus, Frederick Taylor's idea of 'scientific management' is sometimes taken as a good approach to organisations, to ensure that their machinery is as well designed as possible to process raw materials and turn them into goods and services.

Some academic writers seem to have accepted that ostensible organisational aims are a criterion of what should be accepted, even where behaviour seems ethically questionable: Schein suggested that in cases of information distortion and other covert means of influence, 'what needs to be investigated is whether the powerholder's intent is in line with organizational concerns' (1977, p. 67).[7] To many of us, it may seem problematic to make organisational concerns such a predominant criterion for ethical assessment.

Perhaps such academic writing is influenced by the popularity of the unitary view of organisations with managers who have been seeking compliance and consensus amongst their subordinates. The popularity with managers of that approach may remind us of similar attitudes that have been shown by some national leaders: for example, one of whom it has been written that 'the questioning of his assumptions or of his facts rattled him and threw him out of his stride ... The introduction of intellectual processes of criticism and analysis marked the intrusion of hostile elements which disturbed the exercise of this power' (Bullock 1962, pp. 372–3). There may be few organisational leaders who would go so far as Hitler in their suppression of dissent, but the unitary view of organisations can still be favoured because it functions to bolster the authority of incumbent leaders, and it is then associated with the idea that political activity within an organisation is necessarily dysfunctional, since it is inherently at odds with harmony and consensus. The fact that such ideas are common in practice emerges in the comment made by Glazer and Glazer that

> Several people in our study regretfully learned that their professional assessment sometimes had to be tempered or even submerged because opposition was not welcome in organizations largely characterized by hierarchy and the absence of a democratic culture. Their superiors had a tendency to define dissent as insubordination and disobedience as rebellion. (1989, p. 71)

The 'unitary' conception of organisations has been given other names, such as the 'rationalist' perspective. Bradshaw-Camball and Murray say that this 'simplifies and deemphasizes the structural dimension of politics by assuming that top management holds power based primarily on its legitimate and formal organizational authority and also, to some extent, on its expertise' (1991, p. 381). Like Alan Fox, they contrast this with other perspectives like the 'pluralist' perspective, which acknowledges interest group conflict as inevitable and acceptable within organisations (Bradshaw-Camball and

Murray 1991, p. 381; Fox 1974, pp. 255–70; see also Buchanan and Badham 1999, pp. 46 and 167–70).

The pluralist view that organisations are always a venue for interest group conflict is itself an echo of the approach to political theory that sees the wider society as equally an arena for contestation amongst interest groups. In the wider context, that view underpins the constitutional structures and political arrangements of many modern liberal democracies. In recent times, the general political theory of liberal pluralism has been questioned from a variety of directions, but generally in ways that continue to accept the necessity and importance of diverse opinions being respected in the community (see e.g. Offe 1985, Phillips 1993). If we agree that both societies and organisations ought to accept diversity of opinion, it is difficult to see how we can avoid accepting also that political activity is to be accepted and respected. Bernard Crick makes the point in his book *In Defence of Politics* that it has been in systems of tyranny and oppression that the term 'political activity' has most often been given pejorative usage (Crick 1964, e.g. p. 19; see also Crick 1967). Tyranny and oppression can have difficulty with diversity of opinions and views because respecting people's opinions seems to involve not only allowing them to hold those opinions, but also the political activity of putting the opinions to others and seeking agreement, contrary to the dominant regime.

Perhaps putting one's opinions to others and seeking agreement does not sound like the type of thing often connoted by 'politics', certainly not by 'organisational politics'. Here, again, however, we come to issues about the nature of satisfactory definition. The connotations of terms often may have to be ignored in order to give useful definitions of them. 'Flower' connotes something colourful and attractive, but plants may have flowers that are drab and ugly. 'Dinosaur' has the connotation of something large and unwieldy, but some dinosaurs were small and agile. And so on. Various studies have examined perceptions and attitudes about organisational politics (e.g. Kacmar and Ferris 1991, Ralston, Giacalone and Terpstra 1994), but care needs to be taken in assessing their implications. Learning about people's perceptions and attitudes towards flowers may be useful and informative for some purposes, but it may be possible to learn more about flowers by studying them directly.

The case of organisational politics is different from that of flowers or dinosaurs to the extent that a human social activity like organisational politics will be affected by the perceptions and expectations of the people who participate in it. We shall note further below how the work that social psychologists have done on 'scripts' and 'schemas' may be useful in helping us to understand political activity. For example, what people believe is normal and acceptable has a major influence on what they do and what they accept from others as 'legitimate' behaviour. But this is not to go so far as the suggestion that 'organizational politics is a subjective perception, not necessarily an objective reality' (Ferris et al. 1993, p. 86). If we accept that there is such a thing as political behaviour in general, we can expect it to occur in organisations. In pluralist organisations, it is likely to be more open than in unitarist organisations. In pluralist organisations, it may then be easier to scrutinise and easier to evaluate different political tactics as ethical or unethical. In unitarist organisations, it may be forced underground, harder to scrutinise, and more likely to be 'covert, crafty and behind the scenes'.

Because in unitarist organisations political activity is likely to be condemned as illegitimate, it follows that identifying some behaviour there as a piece of organisational politics is likely to delegitimise it, weakening support for those who do it and even rendering them liable to official sanction. It further follows, then, that in such a context to identify something as a piece of organisational politics can itself be a political tactic. Because the distinction between unitarists and pluralist organisations is not a perfectly clear and precise one, but in some respects a matter of degree, it will also be a matter of degree to what extent politics is openly accepted. This can result in complexity of political processes themselves, as actors assess what is and is not acceptable, and how it may be labelled. Buchanan and Badham devote a chapter to 'the terminology game' (1999, chap. 2). They note a variety of ways in which the terms used to describe organisational politics or to recommend approaches to it may serve political purposes or embody covert ethical judgements, and suggest that 'the essence of political behaviour thus lies ... in the ways in which it is represented by the players in the game' (p. 70).

DEFINITION AND CONTESTATION

The different attitudes pluralists and unitarists have towards organisational politics may reflect the fact that 'organisational politics', like 'politics' in general, is an 'essentially contested concept' (see Connolly 1993, chap. 1). In any event, we cannot hope here to give a precise definition that will gain universal acceptance. All we can do is try to make reasonably clear the general scope of our subsequent discussion. Above, it has been implied that organisational politics is a variety of politics more generally understood, albeit perhaps a variety that involves more personal relationships than the phenomena that have been the focus of political theorists since Machiavelli. It has been suggested further that putting one's views to others to elicit agreement is one example, and some other examples have been mentioned. For us it will suffice to conceive of organisational politics as political activity within organisations, so that the issue of definition is at least pushed back to the wider one of how to define politics in general.

We can assume that political activity typically involves attempts to influence others, as recognised by many definitions of organisational politics, that it has to do with power relationships (which is to some extent a corollary of the fact that it involves attempts to influence others), also recognised by a number of definitions of organisational politics, and that often it has to do with the distribution of resources. To assume these characteristics would achieve wide although not universal consensus, and is consistent with the idea Aristotle had of politics when at the outset of the *Nicomachean Ethics* he characterises it as the 'master-craft' (αρχιτεκτονικης) (1934, p. 5; Book I, chap. ii). This is a more exalted view of politics than ideas that it is necessarily 'covert, crafty, and behind the scenes', or the idea that it necessarily aims at furthering people's self-interest regardless of others.

Nevertheless, some problems still remain as the result of the contestability of specific terms and concepts in political processes. Even if we have some broad agreement on the overall scope of discussion, similar problems come up as we move to more detail. In broad terms, we may agree with Robert Solomon that 'the ideal is thus not to eliminate politics but to democratize and civilize our power relationships, to avoid jungle and battlefield metaphors and promote a culture in which politics is mutually supportive instead of antagonistic and destructively competitive' (1992, p. 131). We know there are difficulties of implementation in doing that: even when we know what to do, problems can arise in doing it, individual problems like weakness of will or communal problems like mistrust and suspicion. But there are also difficulties in getting clear about what to do, before we even start implementation. What, in practice, is it for politics to be mutually supportive? What, in concrete organisational terms, are democratic and civilized power relationships? These are the kinds of issues that our ensuing discussion will try to deal with. Even here, however, there are difficulties with terms and definitions. Cavanagh, Moberg and Velasquez noted the need to distinguish between forms of organisational politics that are ethically acceptable and others that are not, and suggested that the latter may include 'such Machiavellian techniques as "situational manipulation," "dirty tricks," and "backstabbing."' (1981, p. 364) Well, fine, but what tricks are dirty? What is the difference between 'situational manipulation' and 'organizing'? If I report your adverse comments to the boss, is that backstabbing? What if I report threats you have made, threats perhaps against me, as well as others? We may sometimes have clear intuitions when we are confronted with these in practice, but if we are trying to clarify underlying principles about ethics and organisational politics then it can hinder us if we build ethical presuppositions into the terms we use to refer to tactics and strategies.

Thus, we may expect that the sorts of examples of organisational politics that may be useful at this point will be ones which do not seem in their very description to carry overtones of moral condemnation or approbation. In their survey, Kacmar and Baron report a number of examples other authors have identified, which seem to satisfy that requirement. Thus, for instance, Allen and colleagues found that those most often mentioned by their respondents were: 'attacking or blaming others', 'selective use of information', 'impression management or image building', 'generating support for ideas', 'praising others and ingratiating', 'building powerful coalitions and strong allies', 'associating with influential others' and 'creating obligations and using reciprocity' (Kacmar and Baron 1999, p. 8). By and large, these do not seem to have too strongly built into them any presuppositions of ethical praise or blame. 'Attacking or blaming others' might seem to be something we generally ought to avoid, but it would be hard to suggest that blaming others is necessarily wrong: it seems as though that may depend on how, when and for what purpose it is done. 'Selective use of information' is hardly a description of something that is unethical in itself: selecting what information it may be relevant and appropriate to use for a particular purpose is often a key part of work, including managerial work. Again, the issue is how and for what purpose. Like some of the others, 'impression management' is an idea that we shall consider in more detail, but it seems clear that it is at least not straightforwardly unethical (see Moberg 1989, and Chapters 8–10 below). If it may seem that impression management has some connotation of unethical deceit or manipulation, 'generating support for ideas', on the other hand, appears to have a quite positive air: it is, after all, what academics and authors often make their primary task.

Overall, the sorts of tactics and strategies in the list are enough to show that there is room for serious discussion about what is ethical and what is not. Some of the difficulties we need to overcome emerge clearly in regard to the strategy of 'creating obligations and using reciprocity'. This builds on strategies of influence that have become well known in social psychology:

> A few years ago, a university professor tried a little experiment. He sent Christmas cards to a sample of perfect strangers. Although he expected some reaction, the response he received was amazing – holiday cards addressed to him came pouring back from people who had never met nor heard of him. The great majority of those who returned cards never inquired into the identity of the unknown professor. They received his holiday greeting card, *click*, and *whirr*, they automatically sent cards in return ...
>
> While small in scope, this study shows the action of one of the most potent of the weapons of influence around us – the rule of reciprocation. The rule says that we should try to repay, in kind, what another person has provided for us ... By virtue of the reciprocity rule, then, we are *obligated* to the future repayment of favors, gifts, invitations, and the like. (Cialdini 1993, pp. 19–20, citing Kunz and Woolcott 1976)[8]

It is important that at least on some occasions, reciprocity grounds genuine obligations, and is not just a mechanism of influence. On the other hand, it has limitations in that respect. Cialdini notes that sometimes people who want to influence others can trade on the mechanism of reciprocity (for instance, by the use of 'free samples'). In practice, what we want to say about the ethics of influencing people through reciprocity may again depend on the circumstances and manner in which the mechanism is used, but our attitude towards it can be embodied in terms we use. In one case, we may commend someone for accepting some ties of reciprocal obligation, by referring to the person's 'loyalty' to another. In another case we may condemn it, by referring to 'nepotism', when someone's appointment to a position is fulfilling an obligation or trying to create one.

Essentially the same reciprocity mechanism has been referred to as one person's 'squaring' another. Miller quotes F.M. Cornford's amusing account of this process, where amongst other things 'we shall emphasise the fact that there is *no connexion* whatever between my supporting your Job and your supporting mine. This absence of connexion is the essential feature of Squaring' (Miller 1962, p. 120, quoting F.M. Cornford's *Microcosmographia Academica*). The 'absence' is of course an ostensible but not a genuine absence. Here, as in much other organisational politics, some arrangements are made by 'a nod and a wink', using tacit understandings, paralanguage such as tone of voice or timing of utterance, and other mechanisms that leave no clear, reportable trace. Such concealment of the relationship between one action or another may go towards giving organisational politics a reputation for being 'covert' or 'crafty'.

At the same time, that example also brings us also to a complexity in the discussion of organisational politics which reflects similar complexity in politics generally (see Connolly 1993). It is sometimes very hard to discern people's real intentions and motives, and hard to determine whether actions are motivated by considerations like reciprocation of favours or authentic concern for common goals. An action by one manager which benefits another might be reciprocation of a favour, but it might also be justified by organisational purposes. If a manager appoints a protégé to a position, that might show favouritism, or it might show accurate perception of merit. That sort of ambiguity is common, and allows room for political tactics which consist of depicting actions in one way rather than another.

INTERPRETATION AND ETHICAL ASSESSMENT

As with so many other issues, in organisational politics and elsewhere, the fact that there are vague or ambiguous cases does not imply that there are no clear or well-defined cases. Nevertheless, even though in many cases there is some well-defined reality behind possible interpretations of people's motives and intentions, the frequent difficulty of identifying it has wide ramifications. As we have seen, just as it is difficult to give an uncontentious definition of organisational politics, so it may be difficult to give a comprehensive list of tactics or strategies of organisational politics, because whether or not something is a political tactic may be inherently contestable, and the contestation of the issue may itself be part of the political process.

It is not only with such *prima facie* questionable tactics like 'attacking or blaming others', 'selective use of information', and the like, that this point arises. Fairholm takes 'developing others' and 'training and orienting others' both to be strategies of organisational politics (1993, chap. 8). He says that they 'are the most effective tactics used with subordinates to get them to behave in desired ways' (p. 102). Clearly, though, they are often necessary and important activities which would be commended, and not categorised as organisational politics at all. They *may* be so categorised because they affect the distribution of power within the organisation. A manager who trains and develops others increases their skill and experience, but also enables them to increase their power. The manager's own power may be enhanced if they subsequently display loyalty in exchange for the training and development they have received. Others might accuse the manager of 'empire-building' (cf. e.g. Mintzberg 1983, p. 188). And so it might be. But it might also be aimed at the good of the organisation, or aimed at the good of the subordinates. It might even be all three.[9]

In a similar way, almost any activity within an organisation might be a tactic of organisational politics, given certain circumstances and participants' motives. Increasing the pay of an individual or group, purchasing new technology, allocating an order to one supplier rather than another, the list is endless. In this context just as elsewhere there will be a spectrum for the interpretation of events that ranges from cynicism at one end through realism to naïveté at the other end. As elsewhere, one's own interpretation of some particular set of events will be affected both by one's current personal situation relative to the events, and by one's generally charitable or suspicious inclinations. Once more, however, that does not entail that all interpretations are equally well grounded. That things' appearance is affected by the colour of one's spectacles does not entail that there are no optimal viewing conditions or that one can see things however one wishes.

What it does suggest is that there are problems with empirical research into organisational politics. Frans de Waal noted the difficulties that an ethologist confronts in studying political behaviour amongst chimpanzees, with the comment that 'to study animal behaviour is to interpret, but with a constant gnawing feeling that the interpretation may not be the right one' (1983, pp. 29–30). In studying human behaviour in organisations, one is assisted by the fact that unlike chimpanzees, human subjects can articulate their perceptions and explain their intentions. In studying political behaviour, however, this is a mixed blessing, since those labels and explanations play a part in the process, and actors often will not be open, frank, or correct in what they report about their perceptions, intentions and motives. They may distort their perceptions of political tactics depending on the extent to which they have themselves used such tactics or aspire to do so, and attitudes to tactics will be affected by the extent to which actors perceive them to be accepted or rejected by others. The result is that there are equal difficulties with useful measurement or quantification, despite many researchers' well-intentioned efforts. It seems to be this that has led researchers to the course noted above, forsaking organisational politics in favour of perceptions of organisational politics as a topic for research.

However, we have also noted that people's perceptions of the facts may be a causally important part of the facts. What is politically possible or necessary will often be determined by people's perceptions or expectations, but that does not mean that it is not really possible or necessary. The fact that people would perceive an appointment to be an act of nepotism might mean that it would be received with so much resentment that it is never made. It is not whether it is an act of nepotism that stops it being made, but the fact that it would be perceived so. But assuming that the resentment would be so great, it really is impossible, even though its impossibility is the result of people's perceptions.

This is not unique to organisational politics. It is a characteristic of politics in general. A political leader may appoint a member of a rival faction to a position in order to be seen by the faction as ready to compromise on other matters, or may refrain from doing so for fear of anger from members of the leader's own faction. Support for a particular bill, approval of some measure, alliance with some group, all might be effected or avoided in part because of the way the action would be perceived and the motives that would be seen to lie behind it, regardless of the action's inherent merits. Those perceptions could make passage of the bill inevitable, or impossible, the measure necessary or impracticable, the alliance unavoidable or unworkable, depending on the circumstances. That is sometimes the very thrust of the phrase 'politically impossible'. We have already noted cases where effects on people's perceptions can be important for political strategies and tactics. Unitarists may contend that what they are doing is not 'political', because it is just part of their organisational role (as though Prime Ministers might say that what they do is not 'politics', but 'Prime Ministering'). Not only in unitarist organisations, but in very many contexts, effective political action often will involve it not being noticed as such. No analysis of such situations is straightforward or easy, and that goes for ethical analysis, in organisational politics and other politics. At worst, for example, it can be hypocrisy or cowardice to accept something as necessary or impossible just because of people's widespread perceptions: sometimes, the ethical thing to do may be to embark on the impossible, for the sake of the future or one's own integrity.

How do we decide what is the ethical thing to do, in situations like that? We might turn to widely accepted approaches to ethics like utilitarian theory, theories based on human rights, or by theories of justice like the one put forward so persuasively by John Rawls in *A Theory of Justice*. Unfortunately, though, such theories are at odds with one another at significant points. We cannot simply accept any one of them as a full account that will deal satisfactorily with all the instances that confront us.

On the other hand, it can also be problematic to provide an account of the ethics of organisational politics which does not have a systematic underlying basis. A number of authors give accounts which provide plausible comments and worthwhile insights into such processes, but often those comments rest on direct and unconnected moral intuition, or resort to pointing out the imprudence or ineffectiveness of some arguably unethical behaviour. The absence of a systematic account of why the behaviour is unethical once again leaves the way open for disagreement, this time not so much because claims rest on some general theory as because they can seem like mere opinion.

We might try to proceed by a method of 'reflective equilibrium' (Rawls 1972, pp. 20–1), an iterative comparison of our ethical theory and our considered ethical judgements, aspiring to reconcile the two by gradual adjustments. Or we might fall back to the fact that agents in organisational politics characteristically share commitments at least to some norms and values.[10] Williams shows how these approaches might be combined, by considering the reflective equilibrium that may be reached by individuals who 'are irreversibly committed to living closely together in one society' (1985, p. 99). However, it is beyond us here to analyse and expound the underlying background assumptions that might justify the approach taken to arriving at views about what is ethical and what is not. Such an account would draw us much too far away from the specific ethical issues to be considered.

Certainly, in what follows I shall often call on a reader's intuitions about what is ethical behaviour and what is not. There will be room for differences of opinion. However, I shall try to knit together the suggestions that are put forward here by giving some explanations for the judgements which I claim to be intuitively plausible. These explanations will be in terms of some wider, more general principles, such as an ethical requirement to let others make responsible decisions, to avoid bad consequences, to be fair, and so on. If this approach is correct, there are a few such principles which do not constitute a general ethical theory, but which do provide a more systematic account of what is ethical than relying on separate, relatively disconnected judgements in different cases.[11] In the next chapter, I shall call attention to some aspects of human nature which are salient in parts of organisational politics and which are especially relevant to some of the principles that help to unify our intuitions about what is ethical in organisational politics. Ultimately I shall try to put together those points about human nature with some basic ethical principles in a way that is faithful to the realities of organisational politics: realities where we have to be aware that there can be an ethical dimension even to the conclusions we draw about others' motives and intentions, where people's impressions and expectations play an important part in making some of the realities what they are, and where the ways we create beliefs and impressions in others are a very important factor in affecting what they do.

It should be noted here that it is this effort to give an account of what is ethical that will be the focus of our discussion. The focus will not be so much on the other important question of how to support and encourage ethical behaviour. If a manager threatens subordinates with dismissal unless they support some personal aim of the manager's, that may be unjust, infringe their rights, and be against the long-term interests of the organisation and its stakeholders. That sort of case may be a hard one to deal with in practice if the manager has sufficient power, but it is not hard to deal with in terms of ethical appraisal: it is straightforwardly wrong, and that is all there is to it. The practical problem of how to deal with that and other unethical behaviour in organisations is a significant one, and one to which we ought to devote both intellectual and other resources.[12] However, it is not the only sort of question that is important. There are at least some cases where there are significant questions about what actually is ethical, and it is with that sort of question that I am primarily concerned. While the argument will rest on intuitions about some cases, my hope is that an account based on such cases will help illuminate others where intuitions are less clear.

SUMMARY

It may be worthwhile to consider whether political theory can address some of the normative and ethical issues in organisational politics in the same sorts of ways that it has addressed issues that arise in the politics of nation-states. To do so we must eschew definitions of organisational politics that incorporate some common negative assumptions, both because those assumptions are often questionable and contestable, and because they hinder us from full theoretical understanding of organisational politics, in particular from seeing similarities between organisational and other politics. The significance of personal relationships and loyalties may be a distinguishing mark of organisational politics, but the final terms of a definition are inherently liable to be contested, because the definition can itself play a part in political processes. For us, the main point is that any definition should leave the way open for a view of organisational politics as an important activity that is susceptible of ethical analysis but which can be important and praiseworthy.

In Chapter 2, we shall draw attention to some aspects of human psychology that are especially relevant for subsequent discussion. They remind us particularly of our limited and fallible capacities, and pave the way for discussion of how those limitations are relevant to specific issues. Although the sorts of issues that arise in organisational politics are not all quite the same as arise in the politics of nation-states, in Part Two we consider some that are broadly similar, like problems of 'dirty hands' and questions about what factors make authority legitimate. However, we also consider questions about the ethical implications of the many close personal relationships that we find in organisations. In Part Three, we shall move on to points about the ethics of communication, deception and 'impression management', and finally arrive at some issues about normative manipulation and group affiliations.

NOTES

1. I shall use 'ethical' and 'moral' more or less interchangeably, and will sometimes use the term 'normative' in a general way to embrace all matters of value and obligation, in contrast with 'descriptive'.

2. Admittedly, there are some notable exceptions. For example, in the 1960s and 1970s writers about industrial democracy addressed such issues: Pateman (1970) is one study that links general political theory to normative issues in organisations.

3. See, for example, Pfeffer (1992), pp. 7–8, where Pfeffer emphasises the importance of individuals understanding and using power if they are to gain success for themselves and their organisations.

4. Cf. Buchanan and Badham (1999), p. 102: 'Every change process requires the "management of meaning", and the delegitimation of opponents and opposing arrangements.'

5. The point is reflected in the title of McCalman's recent article (2001).

6. Alan Fox most clearly identified this 'unitary' conception of organisations and contrasted it with alternatives: here in particular see Fox (1974), pp. 249–50.

7. Cf. Drory and Romm (1990), p. 1133, who draw attention to how much 'the goal orientation of the firm' has tended to predominate over other considerations in much theorising.

8. Here and elsewhere in the book, italics in quotations are from the original unless otherwise specified. Cialdini's full account of reciprocity and other influence mechanisms is clear and useful, and will be alluded to at a number of points below. The extent to which reciprocity produces genuine obligations is discussed in Barry (1980). See also Aristotle (1934), p. 279; Book V, chap. iv.

9. It is not uncommon for actions to have more than one aim. Sometimes, then, there are difficulties in ethical evaluation: see, for example, Davis (1984).

10. Bailey says of political competition that 'the restraint upon manoeuvre which distinguishes a competition from a fight entails that the contestants have some values in common' (1969, p. 21).

11. A somewhat but not entirely different approach is taken by Velasquez, Moberg and Cavanagh (1983), where they consider the implications of different approaches to ethical theory for a variety of issues in organisational politics.

12. Two books that attempt to deal with some such issues are Treviño and Nelson (1995) and Nielsen (1996).

2. Human Nature, Behaviour and Ethics

The preceding chapter has contended that organisational politics ought to be accepted as a process that can be either constructive or destructive, depending upon details about how and to what ends it is conducted. It centrally involves some individuals influencing others. Views which condemn it out of hand may arise out of unitarist ideas that all significant influence within organisations ought to be grounded on legitimate authority. Those ideas are in turn likely to be built on a view that organisations can be constructed around rational authority and the belief that there are clear ways to distinguish legitimate from illegitimate authority.

I shall argue in the following chapters that we cannot generally base decisions on such a distinction, so that we are forced to look more closely at the specific dilemmas and tactics of organisational politics. Underlying a great deal of the discussion will be the view that ethical decision-making requires a realistic understanding of human nature. For example, we shall note some implications of modern cognitive psychology. Some findings cast light on ways that we may influence others. The argument will emphasise the fact that our cognitions and decisions are constrained by our finite psychological resources, and that the heuristics we often rely on to make judgements and decisions can be used to influence us.

The idea that sound political theory needs to be based on an understanding of human nature is not a new one, although it is plausible to suggest that often political theory has either used some idealised and optimistic view of human nature, or some unduly pessimistic one (cf. Duncan 1983, p. 6). In considering organisational politics we need to be on our guard from both directions. An unduly optimistic view might conceive organisations as arenas for the rational exercise of legitimate authority, into which any intrusion must be ill-conceived or morally bad. At the other extreme, a pessimistic view might imply that ethical analysis is a pointless waste of time in an environment where *Realpolitik* is a constant struggle for advantage.

We noted above that sometimes it may have potent force in the political process to identify and label some action or event. In broad terms, this is not new or surprising. To persuade people to see things in one way rather than another is often an important way to affect their decisions and actions. When lawyers act as advocates before a jury, after witnesses have been heard and all evidence presented, there may be matters of fact that are in contention – Was Smith telling the truth about what she saw? – but there may be no clear conflict about specific facts that were the subject of evidence. It may rather be that opposing lawyers try to get the jury to see the same facts in different ways. Did the defendant's actions conform to the legal definition of negligence? Did Green's admitted statements about Brown tend to harm Brown's reputation? We might say that each lawyer tries to get the jury to see the facts as fitting into one pattern rather than another. Such phrasing is consistent with modern psychology that sees human perception as essentially a matter of pattern recognition.

In this chapter we note some of the psychological mechanisms that seem important to political processes within organisations, starting with some such cognitive mechanisms, and proceeding to some related mechanisms to do with group processes. We touch on psychological mechanisms of influence, but also on aspects of group dynamics that have to do with influence, power, and conformity, including in particular the importance of group norms and perceptions of legitimacy.

This discussion does not purport to be an authoritative or a complete account, but only to identify and distinguish some mechanisms and processes that have specific relevance to our subsequent discussion of ethical issues. In the background is the belief that our neural systems have hard-wired into them some tendencies toward pattern-recognition both of objects and processes, and toward certain corresponding responses (see e.g. Margolis 1987 and Churchland 1995, especially pp. 104–21.) While these are enormously sophisticated and adaptable systems, nevertheless they are finite in capacity and subject to certain sorts of errors. One challenge for us is to recognise our special character as responsible agents while still acknowledging those limitations.

SCHEMAS AND SCRIPTS

Social psychologists often focus on people's cognitive states in explaining what they do (Fiske and Taylor 1991, p. 10), and in considering mechanisms which cast useful light on organisational politics, it is appropriate to start with cognition. For example, our perceptions and expectations about causal relationships are a very important type of cognition in our social life as elsewhere (see e.g. Lamb and Lalljee 1992). Examples we have given already suggest that this can be very important in organisational politics: Was John's promotion of Jean a reward for loyalty, an attempt to cement an alliance with an erstwhile foe, a response to the needs of the job, or a combination of all three? At the same time, of course, causal attributions are often very important in ethical analysis. Often, our attributions of blame revolve around our understanding and perceptions of how an action is caused. We excuse people for doing things when outside factors impact on their decision-making, and a lot of attention has been given to the idea of 'responsibility' in both law and morals (see Young 1991).

Sometimes we use quite familiar approaches to draw conclusions about causal relationships in social situations. Mill articulated principles of reasoning about causes that are still applicable to reasoning about social causation: we attend to what things occur together, what sorts of events occur separately, and so on.[1] We make use of what we know of a person's skills and capacities in determining whether they are responsible for a particular outcome, we consider what their knowledge or beliefs may have been, and what motives they have shown on other occasions.

Often, however, our inferences about what people do are underdetermined by the evidence we have. In *The Sussex Vampire*, Sherlock Holmes clears an innocent woman accused of vampirism by showing that what her husband had seen was equally compatible with her attempting to suck poison from a wound – which was, of course, the true explanation. But it was the idea of vampirism that had first presented itself to observers. That is an example of a cognitive 'schema': a way of seeing things that organises data into a pattern.

> A schema may be defined as a cognitive structure that represents knowledge about a concept or type of stimulus, including its attributes and the relations among those attributes ...
>
> Schemas facilitate what is called top-down, conceptually driven, or theory-driven processes, which simply means processes heavily influenced by one's organized prior knowledge, as opposed to processes that are more bottom-up or data-driven ... The basic message of schema research has been that people simplify reality by storing knowledge at a molar, inclusive level, rather than squirreling away, one-by-one, all the original individual experiences in their raw forms, which would be pure data-driven processing. (Fiske and Taylor 1991, p. 98)

A significant amount of work has been done on how schemas function to assist our cognitive processes. For example, there are 'person schemas', when we use our data about people to classify them as 'extroverted' or 'religious', and there are 'role schemas', which give us expectations about how a particular person is likely to act, whether the role be 'doctor', 'woman', 'manager', or the like. Related to these and very important for organisational politics are 'event schemas', also referred to as 'scripts'. These are sets of expectations about how people will act in specific situations, such as eating in a restaurant, a sports match or an interview for a job (Fiske and Taylor 1991, p. 119).

Ideas of scripts and schemas are associated with the 'cognitive miser' model, which has been the focus of a good deal of research in modern cognitive psychology. A central idea is that people perceive things and make inferences in ways that sacrifice some accuracy for improvements in efficiency (Fiske and Taylor 1991, p. 13).[2] The use of schemas in our cognitive processing can save us effort at the expense of accuracy, such as when we fail to notice details of a person or event, or when we recall only information that is relevant to the event schema. In organisational politics, we may recall the past association between the boss and the new appointee, and forget the good performance the appointee showed in a previous job. We acquire schemas partly through our own experience but partly also through stories. Some person schemas may be imparted through children's stories or common jokes ('stepmother' or 'mother-in-law', for example). Such schemas are not unchangeable, and as they get more experience people develop more detailed and sophisticated scripts and schemas. This is true in many areas. One, for example, is that of negotiation. Carroll and Payne note that:

> experienced negotiators are likely to have more schemas, more detailed schemas, more accessible schemas, and hopefully, more accurate and applicable schemas, than novices. For example, experienced negotiators would probably see negotiation possibilities in situations that others would take for granted, especially contexts in which they have previously negotiated. (1991, pp. 24–5; see also Thompson 1990, p. 88)

Research has also been done about the place of schemas in politics, and it seems that here as elsewhere experience and active involvement lead to more detailed and accurate schemas, amounting to 'expertise'.[3]

However, schemas and scripts have a place in politics that goes beyond the extent to which they organise and help observers' understanding of the process. Ernest Goffman's work preceded the modern social psychology theory of schemas, but largely revolved around the way people's actions often conform to social scripts. Not only do we perceive others' actions on the basis of schemas and scripts, we often decide on our own actions by reference to scripts that we take to apply to our current situation. A schema about a particular person or situation will affect others' perceptions and expectations, but to a significant extent can also affect the perceptions and expectations of the person in the situation (Fiske and Taylor 1991, chap. 6). Those expectations can then guide the individual's behaviour. Goffman presents many examples of people being led in their actions by such social scripts. Such scripts are associated with the sociological concept of a 'role', a set of prescribed activities for a person in a certain situation or set of relationships (see e.g. Emmet 1967, p. 140, Goffman 1972, pp. 75–82). The arrangement then is bolstered by the fact that people's expectations prove to be true because the individual acts so as to conform to these shared expectations. In this respect, social schemas go a step beyond the sorts of schemas that we have about parts of the natural world like flowers and rocks. On learning that a flower is a rose, we have expectations about what we shall see, but the rose does not share those expectations or act so as to confirm them.

On a cautionary note, though, we ought to bear in mind that it is a mistake to expect roles or scripts always to be clearly and explicitly defined. If people are priests or naval officers, there may be quite clear expectations about what they will do when they are saying mass or docking a ship, but if someone is a parent or a manager then expectations and schemas are less well-defined. Carroll and Payne seem to make this error in their discussion of 'negotiation' when they say that 'in order to negotiate, parties to a negotiation must perceive the situation they are in as a "negotiation"' (1991, p. 11). Observers might classify the process in which two people are involved as a negotiation whether or not they think of it in that way themselves. Because of such vagueness and ambiguity, people can have different and conflicting expectations about what is appropriate. Thus, people in the same situation may have different conceptions of that situation and of their roles. One participant might think of the process as a negotiation while the other is thinking of it as a discussion or even friendly banter. If so, they might have rather different expectations or perceptions about what is appropriate or proper. One of them might expect discretion and caution, the other, candour and openness. The fact that expectations are often shared can lead to all the more difficulty on the other occasions when they diverge.

That kind of problem can clearly arise within organisations. When people are negotiating, it seems that if one is aware of the possibility that different people are interpreting the situation in different ways then one should make some effort to ascertain what their expectations actually are.[4] Arguably, something similar is true in organisational politics when different people may have different expectations and understanding about the situation.

Thus, for example, it is quite possible that one person may see two actions as connected when another does not. Jones may think that his forthcoming promotion is contingent on his placing an order with a particular favoured customer. His boss may not see them as connected. It might well be wrong of his boss to make them connected, but it may also be important for his boss to ensure that Jones is under no misapprehension about the fact. More generally, the fact that people can have divergent expectations and understanding in a situation, and that some may possess a more sophisticated and detailed array of schemas, implies that often ethical political activity within an organisation may require participants to be aware of others' experience and understanding.

In summary, schemas about persons, events and roles can affect people's perceptions, expectations and actions. In regard to organisational politics, different people can have different and more or less sophisticated schemas. To that extent, I suggest, participants in organisational life have an obligation to take account of one another's understanding and expectations. An obligation along those lines seems to stem from requirements to respect others as responsible agents so far as we can; that requirement seems to imply an obligation to heed their perceptions, expectations and intentions.

In addition, such a policy seems wise because of what we know about specific psychological mechanisms that may affect our perceptions of others' actions. Sometimes, we are likely to attribute others' actions to shortcomings of character or questionable intentions, even when our evidence is inconclusive. An example is 'the Fundamental Attribution Error'. This is 'the tendency to attribute behavior exclusively to the actor's dispositions and to ignore powerful situational determinants of the behavior' (Nisbett and Ross 1980, p. 31; cf. Fiske and Taylor 1991 pp. 67–9). We all have a tendency to explain our own errors and failures by our circumstances, but other people's errors and failures to their character and personal shortcomings. On the other hand, we tend to explain our own achievements and successes by reference to our merits and skill, but others' to their circumstances and good fortune. In evaluating others and particularly in attributing responsibility or blame to them for what they do, it can be important to bear in mind these kinds of tendencies in our social cognition.[5] To the extent that they lead us to explanations that fail to deal with all aspects of the situation, it is important for us to consider different ways to see things not only by way of respect for others as moral agents, but also by way of trying to achieve accurate understanding.[6] (We might consider this a possible 'principle of charity' to invoke when explaining others' actions.[7])

Phenomena like the Fundamental Attribution Error are important also because some of the underlying causal mechanisms may be linked to various mechanisms of self-deception. That we often deceive ourselves in all sorts of ways is no new point, but ideas about schemas and related causal mechanisms provide some insights into how and why we do so (see Gilbert and Cooper 1985, pp. 77–81). They can be related to a 'conceptualization of the self as an information system that will sometimes distort information in order to maintain a coherent and stable view of the world' (Gilbert and Cooper 1985, p. 75, referring to Greenwald 1980). We shall not need to call on much by way of detail about these mechanisms, but we shall note on several occasions that particular situations can encourage us to deceive ourselves. Typically, these may be occasions where ambiguous evidence can be interpreted in more than one way or where we put ourselves in a position to acquire evidence that points in one way rather than another.

Those cases where we are selective in our acquisition or evaluation of evidence are complemented by feedback loops, where the evidence we acquire consists of facts that are created by our own behaviour. Sometimes, those kinds of feedback loops seem to be positive in their overall effects. For example, someone's confidence at some activity leads to success which renews and justifies the confidence. On the other hand, they can be negative in their effects, as the opposite sort of case shows, where someone's lack of confidence breeds failure that maintains the lack of confidence. Some of these kinds of mechanism we shall comment on further in the next section.

PRIMING AND SELF-FULFILLING PROPHECIES

Some of those points illustrate our limitations and shortcomings, but the view of human nature outlined at the start of the chapter rejects a cynical view of organisational politics in favour of one that accepts human frailty, arguing that we have a moral responsibility to take account of the realities of human behaviour both as observers of organisational politics and as participants in it. In this, our discussion tends to be at odds with accounts which emphasise the self-serving nature of people's behaviour. Those accounts imply that it is usually possible to give accounts of people's behaviour which identify self-interested motives coupled with deliberate efforts to conceal them and take advantage of others. It is possible to give some reasons against that cynical line.

To begin with we may note that the theory of 'psychological egoism' which suggests that all human behaviour is self-interested, seems to rest on confusion. It tends to argue that if we find a person acting in a way that is apparently altruistic – for example, making an anonymous donation to charity – then the individual is at least obtaining some covert psychological reward, such as freedom from guilt, ego-enhancement, increased self-esteem, reduction in tension from inconsistent beliefs, or the like. But if all behaviour is self-interested, we have blurred the distinctions that originally interested us between self-interested behaviour, and behaviour which achieves some psychological satisfaction only through helping others. In fact, that putative psychological satisfaction is nebulous and ill-evidenced, probably the result of assuming that since satisfying any motive results in some change in the agent, it must be aimed at that change. Psychological egoism was substantially discredited by earlier writers like Hume,[8] even though it still persists.

However, that it does persist can itself be explained by reference to some further psychological mechanisms that are relevant to organisational politics. Related to the idea of a 'schema' is the idea of 'priming':

> A phenomenon called *priming* describes the effects of prior context on the interpretation of new information. Priming is specifically a name for the fact that recently and frequently activated ideas come to mind more easily than ideas that have not been activated. (Fiske and Taylor 1991, p. 257)

The general effect has been studied since the nineteenth century. A simple example is that if we are presented with a red coloured patch and soon after with the word 'blood', we will recognise the word faster than if we had been presented with a green patch or no prior stimulus at all (Solso 1995, p. 104). Social psychologists have found some evidence of priming effects in a number of areas, such as gender-role stereotyping (Fiske and Taylor 1991, pp. 258–59). Some research has been done specifically into priming effects in people's political behaviour, and has found that self-interest can be 'primed': when people were exposed to stimuli like conversations that highlighted considerations of self-interest for those present, they were more likely later to cite self-interest as a reason for a particular political position (Young et al. 1991).

Priming effects can supplement imitation, which is well known as a way of prompting and maintaining particular sorts of behaviour. Bandura and Walters gave a good account of the fundamental part played by modelling and imitation in social learning (see Bandura and Walters 1963, chap. 2). They note the close relationship between imitative learning and role playing. When they and we refer to behaviour that people are 'expected' to display, there can be both a descriptive and a normative sense to 'expected'. To begin with, by seeing what some people do, we may come to expect them and others to act similarly on further occasions. Where subsequent observations allow it, priming effects are likely to confirm those expectations. To begin with, such expectations may be descriptive only: we do not necessarily think it improper or blameworthy when people fail to act as we anticipate. But after a time, in some circumstances, it may well be that our 'expectations' establish norms of behaviour, and failure to conform to expectations will attract censure.

Such mechanisms have been studied in great depth by psychologists, and in many respects they merit deeper and more qualified statement. For our purposes, however, the key point is that such mechanisms can establish the extent to which members of organisations display behaviour of a certain type. Claims that members of organisations always act in self-interested ways can be the result of perceptions that are shaped by expectations. To the extent that the perceptions are correct, that may still be because the behaviour is shaped by social learning. The perceptions, expectations and behaviour may form a self-sustaining loop.

Other 'self-fulfilling prophecy' effects can influence people to attribute self-interested motives to others. In general, these are cases where people's expectations elicit behaviour consistent with the interpretations. A particularly clear example emerged in a study by Kelley and Stahelski:

> Kelley and Stahelski presented subjects with a standard prisoner's dilemma game and explained the payoffs associated with various moves and countermoves. They then asked subjects to describe their understanding of the game and the appropriate strategy. Some subjects spontaneously expressed the view that the point of the game was to encourage the other player to adopt a cooperative strategy, so as to maximise the likelihood that the outcome would be a slow, steady payoff for both players. Other subjects thought that the point of the game was to *compete* with the other player. These subjects said that the appropriate strategy was to lure the other player into making the 'cooperative' move as often as possible and then to make the 'competitive' move so as to get the high payoff for themselves that would result from this pattern (and, incidentally, resulting in a large loss on that move for the other player).
>
> The experience of the cooperative players, when they actually came to play the game, was quite variable. If they were paired with a 'cooperator,' they quickly

settled into a mutually cooperative pattern. If they were paired with a 'competitor,' they were forced into a competitive strategy in order to avoid consistent, large losses. The experience of competitors, on the other hand, was uniform. If paired with another competitor, they settled quickly into the consistently competitive and ultimately mutually self-defeating strategy. If paired with a cooperator, their own behavior sooner or later forced the cooperator into a defensive competitive strategy also.

The intriguing point of the Kelley and Stahelski demonstration is that coopera-tors will learn, correctly, that the world contains both cooperators and competitors. Competitors, on the other hand, will learn, incorrectly, that everyone out there is a competitor. This is because competitors' own view of correct strategy will bias the behavior of others so as to produce evidence indicating that everyone shares their own strategy. (Nisbett and Ross 1980, p. 188, referring to Kelley and Stahelski 1970)

Both priming effects and self-fulfilling prophecies can help explain why people may tend to appeal to interpretations of others' behaviour as self-interested. In some circumstances people are induced to act in a self-interested way, and observers' explanations can be part of the mechanism that keeps the behaviour that way. The explanations will lead people to expect self-interested behaviour from one another, priming their own explanations and eliciting behaviour from them that compels self-interested behaviour from others, both by way of imitation and in self-defence. 'Imitation', because we look to others' behaviour for an indication of what is appropriate, and 'self-defence' because it is characteristic of self-interested behaviour that when others act in a self-interested way then as in the simulation by Kelley and Stahelski, one can suffer oneself if one does not take some defensive measures.

The fact remains, however, that such self-interested behaviour is not inevitable, and that there is no generally applicable presumption that people's behaviour is self-interested, in organisational politics or elsewhere. We have already argued against building presumptions of self-interest into any definition of organisational politics, and our discussion here suggests that there is no other general presumption of self-interest.

SOCIAL COGNITION AND GROUP DYNAMICS

This argument against unnecessary presumptions of self-interest in analysing organisational politics is based on our broader discussion of cognitive mechanisms and their function. Schemas, scripts and priming effects can elicit self-interested behaviour and so also explanations that unnecessarily presume self-interest. Such schemas and scripts can be maintained within organisations in various ways. The dynamics of such processes have been considered in some detail in the literature on 'organisational culture'.[9]

Organisational rituals, symbols and myths can maintain people's expectations, interpretations and understanding of what is appropriate. In particular, symbols and expressive behaviour in organisational politics can help promote or sustain scripts and schemas about social behaviour. We shall return to such matters later, for example in discussion about the idea of 'impression management'.

There are a number of other, related ideas about social cognition that have some part to play in discussions of organisational behaviour generally and organisational politics in particular. These include the idea of 'framing', a term that is given several meanings,[10] but is often referred to in discussion of experimental work done by Kahneman, Tversky and others which shows people's attitude to risk to be significantly influenced by how a situation is presented.[11] We are put in mind of this and other related effects by the old joke that the difference between an optimist and a pessimist is that an optimist's cup is half full, whereas a pessimist's is half empty. Messick and Bazerman (1996) have summarised a number of such effects and their implications for ethical decision-making in organisations. It is easy to see how framing can be used in techniques of influence and persuasion. Solso recounts the following story, which makes the point:

> Young Brother Gregory had been in the abbey only a few days when he innocently asked the head monk whether it was all right to smoke while saying his prayers. 'Of course not,' was the answer. A week later the young brother asked the monk, 'May I pray while I smoke?' (1995, p. 429)

Again, we shall return to some ethical issues in later discussion. Perhaps the most general point to bear in mind is that the psychological mechanisms in question are all-pervasive in our perception and decision-making (see Fiske and Taylor 1991, p. 391). They create efficiencies, but also have limitations and can lead to errors. I shall argue that we have some obligations to make allowances for others' limitations when we are trying to persuade them of a particular course of action.

Another particularly significant area where processes of social cognition mix with some other psychological processes is the area of group dynamics. A notable instance is the set of phenomena called to mind by the well-known terms 'in-group' and 'out-group'. They involve some significant cognitive effects, such as perception of oneself and one's own group as different from another group, and failures to notice variations within the other group (Fiske and Taylor 1991, p. 123). These and related processes of 'social categorisation' and 'social identification' include forms of misperception that can sustain group conflict.[12]

It came as something of a surprise to researchers to learn that inter-group rivalry and hostility did not arise only from competition for scarce resources or from incompatible goals. In 'minimal group' studies, they found clear tendencies for people to favour members of their own groups in matters of resource allocation, even when the 'group' in question was essentially a fictional construct. Our associated tendency to perceive members of other groups in over-simplified ways seems to be heightened when we are emotionally aroused, for example by fear or embarrassment or other kinds of emotions that are common in organisational life.

There are a number of mechanisms that seem to play a part in our tendency to favour members of our own group both in our evaluations and in our actions. One especially significant set of ideas comes together in 'social identity theory'. In particular, this suggests that our tendency to believe that we and other members of our own group are better than others is 'a powerful means of establishing or maintaining an adequate "social" identity for group members' (Baron, Kerr and Miller 1992, p. 142), including enhanced self-esteem. Intuitively appealing, this theory can help explain the significance of symbols and rituals for members of social groups.

Members of a group tend to favour members of their own group even when they are making some effort to be 'fair' in allocations or resources and rewards (Brown 1988, pp. 224–25). That can be added to the fact that even as individuals we tend to favour ourselves in assessments of what is fair and just (see e.g. Thompson and Loewenstein 1992, Messick and Bazerman 1996). Thus, there is clearly a potent basis for inter-group conflicts within organisations. In-group favouritism figures in organisational politics in a number of ways. One way is just to explain the causes of some political conflict. I have argued above that we should be wary of unnecessary assumptions of self-interest when we observe and interpret people's actions in organisational politics. The aspects of group dynamics we have just noted can take the point further, in that there will be many cases where we are likely to assume that others' behaviour is a deliberate attempt to pursue their interests at the expense of ours, that is to say, to take advantage of us, where in fact from their point of view they are seeking an outcome that is fair and reasonable.

In many ways, these points have been well known long before modern psychological research. But modern theory is making it clear that these aspects of our mental processing do not have to be construed as moral failings and that we shall not avoid them just by greater care or effort in our judgements. The processes are inherent to our mental functioning. As a corollary, we can often explain inter-group conflict without reference to covert self-interest or inherently aggressive and competitive instincts. We can explain this and other problems by reference to aspects of our mental functioning that have developed to assist us process information and make decisions in ways that are generally rapid and efficient. Often, we take account of evidence in ways that leads us to reasonable conclusions (cf. Fiske and Taylor 1991, p. 136). However, the cognitive mechanisms we use to do so can also lead to problems in some situations, and it is an ethical requirement on us to understand them and deal with them in ways that avoid harm or injustice. The general point is shown very clearly in group dynamics.

One implication already discussed is to caution us against cynicism. Another is to assist us in recognising obligations we have to others because of our shared limitations. There are many contexts where the limitations we have as decision-makers are given some explicit recognition. National political systems and others often have some institutional safeguards built in to guard against inappropriate forms of influence over people's decisions, whether tied to group allegiance or otherwise. Electors have to be given due notice, for example, and there are often restrictions on forms of advertising or canvassing for votes. In other contexts also decision-makers are protected against inappropriate forms of influence, for example by being afforded 'cooling-off' periods. Sometimes, there may be ethical limitations on what is appropriate, that go beyond explicit legal restrictions (see e.g. Treitel 1995, pp. 287–8). A contract signed by someone who was unwary or overwrought might be legally binding, but the ethics of enforcing it may be questionable. It is not new to suggest that we have obligations to heed one another's limitations. In organisational politics, awareness of the factors that may bias people's perceptions and decisions can assist us in understanding what our ethical obligations are towards others who are engaged in the process.

INFLUENCE, POWER AND LEGITIMACY

So far, the emphasis in our discussion has been on factors that impact on our cognitions and thereby on our decisions, but there are some factors which seem to affect decisions more directly. One example is the mechanism of 'reciprocity' mentioned in Chapter 1. Cialdini's use of the '*click,* and *whirr*' imagery brings out the point that our responses to some forms of influence are almost automatic, machine-like. There is the same connotation to the term 'trigger principles' which Cialdini uses to explain people's influence over one another. Examples of trigger principles include: reciprocity, where people reciprocate favours; scarcity, where people influence others' choice by giving them an impression about the scarcity of a resource; authority, where one allows oneself to be perceived as an authority on a particular matter; and others (Cialdini 1987, p. 161).

It seems clear that these sorts of triggers can influence us without our consciously deliberating about what to do, and we can use the triggers on one another. Here we find some ethical issues about modes of influence in organisational politics. In assessing ethical requirements on the use of 'trigger principles', Cialdini contrasts two sorts of case. The first he refers to as ones where people 'smuggle' influence triggers into a situation, whereas the second are more legitimate cases where we act as 'detectives' to discern triggers of influence that already exist in the situation. Thus, we might smuggle in the influence of reciprocity by contriving a situation where we allow others to believe that we are responsible for some benefit they have achieved, or we may acceptably use the trigger of authority if we show them expertise we genuinely have. He suggests that 'it is acceptable to use the trigger if it resides naturally in the existing setting; it is objectionable, however, to import and use the trigger if it is not an inherent part of the setting' (1987, p. 160). By using 'natural' triggers, he suggests, it may be possible for us to be both ethical and effective. This suggestion of Cialdini's will be considered again when we come to discuss some related ethical issues in more detail in Chapter 8.

Another psychological mechanism which is reminiscent of those discussed by Cialdini in its '*click*, and *whirr*' operation is our tendency to conformity with others in social situations. Sherif carried out an experiment which in its own way had findings as striking as the experiment on reciprocity described by Cialdini:

> Sherif ... led individuals to a totally dark room and turned on a tiny bulb. This procedure creates the illusion that the stationary light is actually moving ... Sherif exposed people to a number of trials, each time asking subjects to indicate when the light began to move, when it stopped and how far it moved. Individuals were strongly influenced by the opinions of those around them. Indeed, Sherif was able to dramatically increase or decrease individuals' estimates of movement if he paid confederates to offer particularly large or small estimates. What was most impressive was that once people changed their estimates in response to group influence, they maintained similar estimates on subsequent judgments, even when they no longer were accompanied by group members. From this it would seem that people had truly changed their private perceptions about the amount of light movement they were seeing, and were not simply going along with the group in order to avoid conflict. (Baron, Kerr and Miller 1992, pp. 11–12, citing Sherif 1936)

Other experiments have confirmed and extended the result. For example, it has become clear that as judgements by members of any particular group tend towards uniformity, their overall judgement will come to a different final outcome than that of other groups. Other experiments by Asch demonstrated substantial conformity effects in people's expressed judgements even when that was at odds with their own perception (Baron, Kerr and Miller 1992, p. 64). Thus, conformity is to some extent a matter of expression, to some extent a matter of perception. Overall, 'conformity effects have been reported across such a wide range of judgements and subject groups that it represents one of the most substantiated and fundamental phenomena in social psychology' (Baron, Kerr and Miller 1992, p. 65).

Results about group conformity have been used in discussions of the phenomenon of 'groupthink', where 'leadership style, group cohesion and crisis combine to suppress dissent within groups to such a degree that group members end up supporting policies (norms) that are extraordinarily ill-considered' (Baron, Kerr and Miller 1992, p. 71). The process may occur in a step-by-step fashion, and a combination of factors may operate including 'pressures on dissenters to conform to the consensus view', but also 'an illusion of unanimity and correctness' (Brown 1988, p. 158). Such effects can help explain the documented cases of the victimisation and intimidation of whistleblowers who have attempted to bring corrupt organisational practices out into the open (see Glazer and Glazer 1989, and Provis, McKay and Tomaino 1998). Rothschild and Miethe comment that in many cases the responses appear to an observer to be 'out of proportion', and even to go to 'extraordinary lengths' (Rothschild and Miethe 1994, pp. 265, 261). From the outside, it often seems that the organisation would have been more rational to admit shortcomings and try to bring the matter to an end. Repeatedly, accounts note how whistleblowers have been startled by the antagonism they have met. In such cases, it seems clear that often the pressures which make for conformity of opinions within groups are strong enough to persuade group members that their perceptions are veridical and that dissenters must be perceiving things wrongly.[13]

Such conformity effects and the other mechanisms by which people are influenced raise a series of questions about how we can respect people's autonomy, and show consideration for them as responsible decision-makers. If people's decisions are so susceptible to such influence, is it perhaps best simply to treat them as objects to be manipulated? If we wish to treat them as autonomous and responsible, how in practice can we do so?

Such questions are entwined with the nature of power in organisations, which are often based on mechanisms of influence and people's tendency to conformity with other group members. This emerges to some extent from the early and often-cited account of power in organisations given by French and Raven (1960). They suggested classifying power in terms of different bases it can have. Considering a situation where O may have power over P, they suggested (pp. 612–13) that five bases for such power may be:

(1) reward power, based on P's perception that O has the ability to mediate rewards for P;

(2) coercive power, based on P's perception that O has the ability to mediate punishments for P;

(3) legitimate power, based on P's perception that O has a legitimate right to prescribe behaviour for P;

(4) referent power, based on P's identification with O;

(5) expert power, based on P's perception that O has some special knowledge or expertise.

Clearly, some conceptual puzzles arise if we analyse this taxonomy too closely. P might identify with O because of O's expertise. It is hard to draw a line between reward power and coercive power, since withholding a reward may amount to a punishment, and vice versa. French and Raven did not suggest that the taxonomy was complete or final. However, there are clear ethical issues that arise from it. One textbook on organisational behaviour that uses it as the basis for discussion of power puts to students the question whether reward power may perhaps always be preferable to coercive power, for example (Robbins et al. 1994, p. 528). Whatever the relationship may be between power and influence, a similar set of questions arises about the sorts of power that French and Raven identify as arise about the forms of influence discussed by Cialdini. When and how is it ethically acceptable to exercise power? Are there some forms of influence that somehow maintain respect for others as responsible agents, to be contrasted with forms of coercion and manipulation?

Especially important for our purposes, and tied to pressures for group conformity, there are questions about the notion of 'legitimate' power. French and Raven note that it is more complex than the other forms they identify (1960, p. 615). Although their initial characterisation of it refers clearly to P's 'perception', their discussion sometimes implies that what is at issue are norms and standards that create a basis for real legitimacy rather than just a perception. To the extent that we remain centred on people's perceptions, there will always remain questions about the extent to which the power that results from these perceptions really is legitimate. For example, French and Raven note that such perceptions may be founded on people's acceptance of certain cultural values or of a given social structure. If so, there may be questions about the real acceptability of those values or that social structure (see e.g. Lukes 1974, and below, Chapter 4).

Habermas notes that 'if belief in legitimacy is conceived as an empirical phenomenon without an immanent relation to truth, the grounds upon which it is explicitly based have only psychological significance' (1976, p. 97, commenting on 'Max Weber's ambiguous conception of "rational authority"'). In later chapters, I accept that the idea of legitimacy can be of more than purely psychological significance, but it may still be true that people's perceptions of legitimacy are a potent psychological force in their own right. It is certainly true that perceived legitimacy is a clear basis for the exercise of power. Ridgeway comments that the idea of legitimacy 'is notoriously difficult to define', but takes as a working definition that 'something becomes legitimate when it becomes normative in the group and therefore subject to collective sanction when violated' (Ridgeway 1993, p. 112). Various studies have shown the importance of norms in group behaviour, 'shared patterns of perceiving and thinking, shared kinds of communication, interaction and appearance, common attitudes and beliefs, and shared ways of doing whatever the group does' (Argyle 1983, p. 168).

The instinctive pressures on us to conform with other group members, along lines demonstrated by Sherif and Asch, can be supplemented by explicit sanctions when norms have become established. Then, 'legitimacy' is closely associated with 'reward power' and 'coercive power'. Coercive power usually depends on being able to mobilise support from others, and such collective support usually goes along with conformity to norms and perceptions of legitimacy. We should not ever underestimate the importance of people's perceptions of legitimate authority. Stanley Milgram's experiments are by now well known (see e.g. Milgram 1974). Normal subjects showed unforeseen and disconcerting willingness to inflict pain and harm on others when they believed that they were being instructed to do so by someone whom they perceived to have legitimate authority.

There is a clear implication that we must not assume that because a course of action is sanctioned by legitimate authority within an organisation it is necessarily ethical. But there is also an implication that we must be aware of the force that perceptions of legitimate authority may have on members of an organisation. Whether or not such perceptions are sound, they are a real part of the situation, and cannot be ignored.

Explicit and formal agreement on what is accepted and legitimate is often supplemented by varieties of subtle and complex non-verbal communication which function to enhance, maintain or discourage different patterns of behaviour. The general mechanisms are all-pervasive in social interaction, in organisations and elsewhere. For example, they include processes of turn-taking interactions between people that confirm their understanding and expectations of what is appropriate behaviour (see Marková, Graumann and Foppa 1995). One approach to the study of people's understandings and expectations in their interactions has been labelled 'positioning theory', and has given some special attention to 'the moral positions of the participants and the rights and duties they have to say certain things' (Harré and van Langenhove 1999, p. 6). Positioning theory is 'the study of local moral orders as ever-shifting patterns of mutual and contestable rights and obligations of speaking and acting' (p. 1). The theory may be conceived as developing some ideas implicit in the understanding of social episodes as often conforming to established 'scripts'. In particular, for example, it notes that one individual may speak or behave in a way that creates some pressure on another to act in a complementary way, in conformity with some script. We may imagine a woman gracefully smiling her thanks as a gentleman opens a door for her, or a clerk explaining his absence in response to a manager's admonition.

People can resist the pressure on them to conform to the requirements of a script, as the woman may do when the door is opened for her, whether with a smile and comment like 'Age before beauty' or an acerbic 'I'm strong enough to do that myself', or more explicitly drawing attention to her rejection of the traditional script. But successfully rejecting the pressure for conformity in such a case may depend on the fact that objections and alternatives have been publicly articulated and discussed. The argument that the script functions to maintain images and roles for women that are oppressive allows the woman's rejection of the pressure to be understood.[14] Whether her refusal to respond as expected is straightforwardly accepted or not, it is not likely nowadays to draw the same response as the clerk probably will if he ignores the manager's comment on his absence. For him, there is no well-articulated alternative, and if he rejects the pressure to respond appropriately then he faces possible accusations of deviance and ultimately banishment from the organisation.

In general, norms of behaviour within an organisation as elsewhere are sustained at least to a significant extent by the reciprocal turn-taking that confirms the corresponding scripts. Positioning theory notes that individuals' use of such norms and scripts to exert influence over others can involve manoeuvring to obtain a favoured position for oneself, and such moves by participants can sometimes be a significant part of organisational politics, as we shall note further in subsequent discussion.[15] Participants' adroitness at identifying alternative possible scripts or contriving situations that circumscribe others' positions can be an important aspect of organisational politics.

One way of construing French and Raven's 'legitimate power' is merely as increased opportunity to 'position' others in ways one wishes to. However, we need not assume that collective acceptance of authority or power necessarily creates real legitimacy: cases like the Milgram experiments show that acceptance does not necessarily create genuine moral legitimacy.

On the other hand, we should also note that what is openly accepted as 'legitimate' is not the only basis for group conformity and social power. We can well imagine circumstances in which forms of discrimination or malpractice are common and endorsed tacitly but not openly. The idea that communication takes place through a number of 'channels' is a familiar one, as is the fact that 'back-channel' communication can confirm or disconfirm the message being sent on the main channel (see e.g. Argyle 1988, p. 111, Wallbott 1995 and Provis 1996b, pp. 480–83). The idea is summed up in the idea that 'a nod and a wink' can convey messages that are not explicitly articulated or even at odds with what is said openly. While the point is often made with respect to face-to-face communication amongst individuals, the same point can be generalised more widely, and so it has been noted that managing organisational culture requires 'consistent cues' to be given to organisational members (Brown 1995, p. 131). The difference between what is open and what is covert or tacit can play a significant part in organisational politics. Organisational politics can often involve covert communication, alliances and support for certain course of action. Such activity raises significant ethical issues. On the other hand, so does an organisational climate where deliberate maintenance of a regime of 'consistent cues' amounts to a technique of control (see e.g. O'Reilly 1991). Willmott has argued forcefully that people's autonomy cannot be realised in 'a monoculture that rigorously suppresses critical reflection' (1993, p. 531).

We shall touch further on a number of these points in later discussion. At present, though, we should note that pressures toward conformity are endemic in organisations, and often associated with perceptions of legitimacy. We cannot merely set aside our susceptibility to such pressures as a moral failing, but neither need we assume that they leave no room for ethical decision-making. Like cognitive heuristics and other factors in our psychology that lead us to decisions that are not always sound, pressures to conformity can be approached critically and reflectively, in an attempt to be realistic about what is practicable for people in organisations as responsible agents.

SUMMARY

The preceding discussion has drawn attention to some of the mechanisms that it is important to bear in mind in thinking about organisational politics and ethical issues that arise in it. These mechanisms include:

(a) schemas and scripts that guide our cognitions and our patterns of behaviour;

(b) priming effects and self-fulfilling prophecies;

(c) differing perceptions of one's own group and its members, compared to others;

(d) influence factors like reciprocity, scarcity and authority;

(e) tendencies for individuals to conform to group norms.

These mechanisms are all ones that can be recognised in organisational politics.

We have already noted some relevant ethical implications, as our discussion has proceeded. People's actions in organisational politics will be affected by their experience and by the consequent variety and depth of their cognitive schemas. Some people will have greater skill at the process and appreciation of possibilities, both possibilities for their own action and possible explanations of actions by others. Sometimes, the schemas that guide perception may also be scripts that guide action. Where people share a script about a particular situation, it leads not only their expectations about what they and others will do, but their beliefs about what is appropriate; what they ought to do.

These expectations and beliefs can be reinforced by priming effects. They can also be reinforced by self-fulfilling prophecies. These can take various forms. Kelley and Stahelski's experiment on 'cooperators' and 'competitors' is a vivid example where people's general understanding about what other people are like is confirmed by their own behaviour. At simpler levels, we can expect that normative beliefs about what is appropriate behaviour can be reinforced by seeing that is how others act.

Beliefs about what people will and ought to do will often go along with beliefs about how to deal with members of one's own group, or with outsiders, whether the group be a department, a clique, or something else: it seems clear that we tend to identify with groups that may have even a slight and transitory existence. This group identification can be associated with biased perceptions of fairness and desert. Although in some circumstances we do have reciprocal obligations to other members of our own group, it may be a problem to decide what are genuine ethical obligations and to what extent our perceptions about fairness or obligation are the result of in-group bias.

Reciprocity is a source of real obligation, but also can be used as a means of deliberate influence. There are other mechanisms discussed by Cialdini that tend to operate in a *'click*, and *whirr'* fashion, such as the use of authority. Such mechanisms are not uncommon in organisational politics, and often ethical questions will arise about their use. In particular, there will be some questions about the extent to which actions in organisational politics ought to respect and enhance people's autonomy. This question arises in the context of various means of exerting influence or exercising power, and in the context of pressures toward group conformity and in regard to the scope of legitimate power. The issue of 'legitimacy' is a central issue in discussing the ethical issues of organisational politics. It raises the question whether some appropriate organisational or institutional authority can legitimate political actions that might otherwise be unethical. But it also will lead us to consider the ethical status of perceptions of legitimacy, which often are the *de facto* basis for the exercise of power.

NOTES

1. See Mill (1952), Book III, chaps. VIII–X, where he articulates what have come to be known as 'Mill's Methods'; cf. Fiske and Taylor (1991) chap. 2.

2. For some early discussions of 'schemas' and 'scripts' using those terms, see Neisser (1976) and Schank and Abelson (1977).

3. E.g. Fiske, Kinder and Larter (1983), although this and other such studies primarily address citizens' understanding of public politics in nation-states.

4. I have argued this in more detail in Provis (2000b). The point arises further in Chapters 8 and 10 below.

5. To help us do so may perhaps be the function of some traditional questions or mental reminders that function as heuristic devices, questions like 'What would I have done in their shoes?', or thoughts like 'There but for the grace of God go I.'

6. In Werhane (1999), Patricia Werhane considers in detail how scripts and other 'mental models' affect ethical decision-making; in particular, she discusses the extent to which we can accept that there is an objective point of view transcending such models, but here we can take it that there is a fairly straightforward way in which such models can distort our views in many cases, by leading us to conclusions we would reject on fuller examination.

7. 'The maxim of translation ... that assertions startlingly false on the face of them are likely to turn on hidden differences of language': Quine (1960), p. 59.

8. See *An Enquiry Concerning the Principles of Morals,* in Hume (1902), Sect. V, Part II, and also e.g. Harman (1977), chap. 12.

9. See e.g. Deal and Kennedy (1988), Anthony (1994) and Brown (1995). An example of work that draws on ideas about managing corporate culture in regard to corporate ethics is Aguilar (1994). See also Treviño and Nelson (1995), chap. 9.

10. For examples, including use of the term in pattern recognition research by Artificial Intelligence theorists like Marvin Minsky, as well as Erving Goffman's idea of 'frames', see Neisser (1976), pp. 57–9.

11. See e.g. Kahneman (1992), Tversky and Kahneman (1981), Tversky and Kahneman (1986) and Kahneman, Knetsch and Thaler (1991). A detailed example is presented in Chapter 9.

12. On this and what follows, see Baron, Kerr and Miller (1992), pp. 135–44 and Brown (1988), chap. 8.

13. Another sort of case where problematic behaviour was sustained by 'social proof' can be seen in Pfeffer's account of fraud by OPM Leasing: Pfeffer (1992), pp. 210–11.

14. For further discussion of the example, see below, Chapter 10, p. 208.

15. See in particular Chapters 10 and 11 below. That scripts can be a basis for social influence is clearly noted by Goffman: see e.g. Goffman (1971), p. 13.

PART TWO

Dilemmas, Loyalties and Authority

3. Ethics, Prudence and Politics

In the previous chapter we have considered a number of mechanisms that play a role in the dynamics of organisational politics, and which will assist us in considering some ethical issues. Before that, we considered general issues about the nature of organisational politics. There, we gave some examples, but we also noted the difficulties associated with giving either a single comprehensive definition of organisational politics, or a comprehensive set of examples. In this chapter, we shall try to show how some ethical issues can arise in a specific case, and use this as a basis for some of our subsequent discussion. The issues will not exhaust the ethical dilemmas that can arise in organisational politics, but they include several rather different kinds of issues that are recurrent and important.

We shall see how there may be conflicting pressures on an individual in organisational politics. Some of these are tensions between ethics and self-interest, which are no novelty in any part of human life. However, there are also possible conflicts between principled commitments and loyalty to friends, and questions about ethical requirements in weighing evidence. The details of these issues we put aside until subsequent chapters, and focus rather on the question whether the political obligations we may have in organisations should actually be distinguished from our moral and ethical obligations. This is the problem of 'dirty hands', as it arises in organisational politics. I shall suggest that the dirty hands problem merely reflects the fact that in organisational politics as elsewhere we may be subject to conflicting ethical demands, and that there may not be any straightforward, routine way to deal with such conflicts.

TRICIA: DAMNED, OR NOT?

In a textbook on organisational behaviour we find an example given the title 'Damned If You Do; Damned If You Don't' (Robbins et al. 1994, pp. 556–7). We shall not give all the fine detail of the case, but the essentials are as follows.

Tricia Gibson has been in her current position for some time, but has been short-listed for a senior position with another firm. She wants the other job very much. The only person in her current organisation who knows that she is being considered for the other job is Simon, another manager and a friend of hers who is her only referee from her present organisation. He has promised to maintain confidentiality about the other job, since her current employer would look with disfavour on the fact that she was considering a position elsewhere.

Tricia has now been approached by Jennifer, a junior employee, who is upset and has told Tricia that Simon has been sexually harassing her since soon after her commencement at the firm several months ago. The harassment has grown progressively worse, until now he has threatened Jennifer that if she does not sleep with him then he will give her an adverse appraisal report as her period of probationary employment comes to an end. 'Jennifer said she had come to Tricia because she did not know what to do or whom to turn to. "I came to you, Tricia, because you are a friend of Simon's and the highest ranking woman here. Will you help me?"' (Robbins et al. 1994, p. 557).

The textbook follows the example with some questions or points for students to discuss. One of these is 'Analyse Tricia's situation in an ethical sense. What is the *ethically* right thing for her to do? Is it also the *politically* right thing to do?'

It is hard to know what to make of this. On the surface, it seems like an invitation for students to emulate Machiavelli in separating interests from ethics, an invitation first to consider ethical demands, perhaps, but then to meet those demands only if they are consistent with political interest.

If that is the implication, then the response seems to be straightforward. *Prima facie*, there is an ethical requirement on Tricia to take the matter up on Jennifer's behalf, but if she does so then she does something politically unwise, since Simon can then provide an adverse reference to the other firm and also let it be known within their current firm that she is seeking a position elsewhere, harming her current situation as well as her prospects at the other company. The issue then is a not uncommon one, where ethical demands on us are contrary to our self-interest; where the ethics and prudence conflict. But this is no news. There is nothing unique or especially interesting about this particular conflict between ethics and prudence. It serves only to demonstrate that similar ethical dilemmas arise in organisational politics as elsewhere. What is the line between what is obligatory and what is beyond the call of duty? How much risk to myself am I morally obliged to incur in order to save someone who is drowning? And so on.[1]

The first issue that this case raises for further discussion is therefore whether in organisational politics there is anything special about conflicts between ethics and prudence.

However, it is possible that the textbook's question whether the ethically right thing to do is also the politically right thing to do may not be raising a question about conflicts between ethics and prudence. It may, rather, be suggesting that 'ethics' and 'politics' are different spheres of activity, and that different kinds of criteria are to be used to make ethical and political evaluations. To that extent, the implication may be that ethical considerations can be put aside in this political context. This raises the dirty hands problem mentioned in Chapter 1: whether doing the right thing politically may require us to disregard the morally right thing.

Suppose, for example, that Tricia has a strong commitment to the rights of women in the workplace. It might be contended that in this case the politically right thing for Tricia to do would be highlight Jennifer's allegations and make it clear that the sort of behaviour alleged is completely unacceptable. How ought she balance such a commitment against other ethical considerations? How much should it influence her that any allegations need to be well-evidenced, for example? Alternatively, we might imagine a manager in this sort of situation thinking primarily of the organisation and its reputation, regardless of the rights of the individuals involved. Again, that might be conceived as a political approach to the issue.

Thus, this is the second question for consideration. Is it possible to make a distinction between ethical and political considerations in a way that construes them as distinct spheres of evaluation? A garden might be good to look at, but no good as a source of food, or vice versa. Might actions in organisational politics be like that: good in one way, but bad in another, without there necessarily being any way to come to an overall evaluation?

The issues identified so far, to do with conflicts between self-interest, ethics and politics, will occupy us for most of the remainder of this chapter. However, before we proceed to examine them in more detail, let us briefly identify some others that arise in this case, to be examined subsequently.

EVIDENCE AND LOYALTY

We have suggested that asking what is the politically right thing to do, as distinct from the ethically right thing to do, may be drawing attention to conflicts between ethics and prudence, or issues about dirty hands. However, it may alternatively be an invitation to consider options, from a political point of view.

For example, it may be that Tricia has some other friend, inside or outside the organisation, who can raise the issue of Simon's behaviour with more senior managers in the organisation, without Tricia's involvement becoming known. There might be some way that Tricia can arrange some transfer for Jennifer until after the resolution of her own application for the other job. It would be an unacceptable *deus ex machina* just to assume that some such option is available. But the point may be that commonly in organisational politics such options are available although they may require some political skill to identify and take advantage of. To do so requires clear vision of causal relationships and linkages, and the ability to think of different possibilities. To that extent, the situation is that same as that of negotiators, where experience creates a wider variety of schemas, so that they have more chance of thinking of new options.[2]

However, the importance of considering possibilities arises not only in thinking of options. Tricia also needs to consider whether the facts are really as they are presenting themselves to her. It seems from what Jennifer says that Tricia's picture of Simon is awry, even though she has known him for some time, considers him her friend, and trusts him sufficiently to have confided in him about her application for the new job and cited him as her referee. How is she to weigh the evidence? She can call on her other knowledge of Simon, on her knowledge of Jennifer and on what she knows generally of people and their relationships. She knows, as we do, that long-time acquaintances and friends can sometimes have an unsuspected side to their character. But she knows, also, that people can be confused in their communications, both in impressions they give and in impressions they receive. Might this be happening in Jennifer's case? Tricia has not known Jennifer as long as she has known Simon, and does not know how reliable she is.

These points about belief and evidence are not incidental to the case. Often, points about belief and evidence provide difficult and fundamental complications for ethical issues in organisational politics. Often, in these cases, there is an ethical dimension to weighing evidence and drawing conclusions on which to base decision and action. The problem is not like that of a scientist to come to a conclusion after all necessary investigation and experimentation, with the opportunity to delay a conclusion until all necessary evidence is acquired. It is more like a court of law which has to come to a conclusion on the basis of limited evidence and take account of the costs of an incorrect decision as well as the benefits of a correct one.

Tricia's situation is like that of many real-world decision-makers who have to use limited evidence to come to a conclusion that will have a range of good and bad possible outcomes. When constructing a bridge, an engineer does not have all relevant evidence about support, loads and the like, or about all the possible costs and benefits. However, there are some factors about Tricia's situation that are less generally common, although they are very common in organisational politics. In particular, should her weighing of the evidence be affected by the personal relationships she has with Simon and Jennifer?

We have already noted that reciprocity can be a source of influence but also a source of real obligations. Such obligations can sometimes be labelled 'loyalty', loyalty to individuals, groups, or whole organisations. It seems at least to be arguable that where people have developed personal relationships over an extended period, they may have obligations to trust one another. It seems consequently that Tricia may have an obligation to Simon not to give credence to allegations about him without quite strong evidence.

This, then is another issue raised by Tricia's case: what ethical requirements are there on Tricia in her coming to conclusions? In particular, should considerations of loyalty come in to play?

Contrary to suggestions that Tricia may have loyalty-based obligations to Simon, Tricia may on the other hand have obligations to Jennifer because of Jennifer's vulnerability and the fact that she has approached Tricia for help. Jennifer's comment that 'I came to you, Tricia, because you are a friend of Simon's and the highest ranking woman here', suggests two other sources of obligation also. Tricia's friendship with Simon may create some obligation, because it puts Tricia in a position to influence Simon. Another is that Tricia's seniority or experience in the organisation may create some obligation. Her experience may do so if it has imparted to her some understanding and skill in organisational matters (as a doctor may have obligations to an injured person that an ordinary passer-by does not have). Her seniority may do so if her position creates expectations and obligations about 'leadership', for example.

Further still, there are questions that arise because Tricia is in a difficult situation partly through her organisation's attitude towards her applying for a position elsewhere. Other things being equal, this seems to be an unreasonable attitude by the organisation, yet it is one source of Tricia's difficulty. If the organisation's attitude was more reasonable, then she would not have had to keep her application so strictly secret, Simon would probably not be the only referee she might call on from within the organisation, and approaching him about Jennifer's allegations would not be so much of a hazard. Can Tricia use the fact that her organisation has unreasonably placed her in a difficult situation to excuse herself from blame if she does not act?

Whatever the answer may be to that last question, this and the other complexities taken together do serve to bring out one very important point about the ethics of organisational politics: there often is enormous scope for self-deception. If Tricia is disposed to focus on her own interests, and put aside Jennifer's distress with a few soothing words, then there are a number of ways that she can rationalise doing so. She can emphasise to herself the obligations of friendship she has toward Simon, she can question the substance of Jennifer's account, she can transpose blame to the organisation that has placed her in this situation, she can suppose that she will seek out options, and allow time to elapse as she does so. Equally, if Tricia had some disposition toward being a martyr or appearing a hero, she could discount any possible obligations of friendship to Simon and accept Jennifer's allegations without question.

There may be some other issues that might be identified in this example, but the discussion so far has brought out a number of major ones. Let us now turn to consider in more detail the first two we identified. Some of the others we shall address later.

ETHICS AND SELF-INTEREST

The first issue was the conflict between ethics and self-interest. So far as our discussion is concerned, we have no specific interest in the conflicts between ethics and self-interest, unless they have some specific dimension that is especially salient in organisational politics. We are not interested in the general issue, since that has been dealt with so much. The only thing that could make the issue of special interest here is the tendency in some sorts of organisations to foster or maintain self-interested behaviour. As noted in the previous chapter, we need not believe that all human behaviour is self-interested, but it is possible that 'priming' effects and imitation may affect people's expectations and how they act.

In fact, there is evidence that organisational politics does raise issues about self-interested behaviour in a special way. Consider the following passage from *Moral Mazes*. Jackall is commenting on the fate that befell a manager called White who took a principled stand in regard to the health of employees who were threatened with hearing loss from their work with loom and spinning equipment in Weft Corporation:

> One might say that White suffered from a peculiar kind of disability for his particular occupation, that is, an unwillingness, perhaps an actual inability, to see the hearing issue in more pragmatic terms. But, one might ask, why should his moral stance make other managers uncomfortable? Managers are, after all, men and women with exactly the same kind of moral sensibilities that White possesses although they may express them in different arenas of their lives. Here the political vagaries typical of corporations provide the clue to the riddle. Without clear authoritative sanctions, moral viewpoints threaten others within an organization by making claims on them that might impede their ability to read the drift of social situations. As a result, independent morally evaluative judgements get subordinated to the social intricacies of the bureaucratic workplace. (p. 105)

Jackall is making two related suggestions, I think. In terms we have used, one is that organisational legitimacy has an important impact on individuals' behaviour and their willingness to engage in principled actions. Principled behaviour is inhibited without 'clear authoritative sanctions'. But there is a second suggestion also, that somehow an ethical approach may interfere with people's understanding and perception, their 'ability to read the drift' of organisational dynamics. How can that be?

The apparent answer is that if moral principles are accepted then in cases where they are inconsistent with directives or rules that have organisational authority, members of an organisation can find it difficult to predict others' behaviour because they are uncertain how the others will weigh the contrary factors.

A simple response to that would be to say that moral and ethical principles necessarily have overriding authority, so that we may shape our expectations and predictions on the basis that people's conduct will be ethical. With that, however, there are two problems.

One problem is that as a matter of fact our behaviour often departs from what is ethical, and we have the phrase 'unrealistic expectations' ready to hand to refer to assumptions that we actually always will do what is ethical. We cannot anticipate that people always will act in accordance with ethical demands when they conflict with organisational requirements, since organisational requirements often are backed by sanctions and pressures that can be contravened only with a degree of self-sacrifice that cannot be expected on a regular basis.

The other problem is that there may be ambiguity and contestation about what really is ethical. We do not have to assume that ethical matters are inherently subjective to accept that often there is room for argument about what is ethical, and so even if we expect people to act conscientiously in the face of conflicting pressures, that will not necessarily lead to a set of stable expectations about what will happen in the organisation.

The overall implication is that organisational dynamics can inhibit ethical behaviour and sustain self-interested behaviour because the latter is more comprehensible to others. There will still be 'social intricacies', but they will be easier to diagnose and respond to.

Another associated factor that has the same effect is identifiable in a different passage from *Moral Mazes*. Here, Jackall comments on the fate of Brady, an executive who discovered major financial irregularities in his company and sought to have them investigated.

> Finally, the managers I interviewed feel that Brady's biggest error was in insisting on acting according to a moral code, his professional ethos, that had simply no relevance to his organizational situation ... Moreover, by insisting on his own personal moral purity, his feeling that if he did not expose things he himself would be drawn into a web of corruption, he was, they feel, being disingenuous; no one reaches his level of a hierarchy without being tainted. Even more to the point, Brady called others' organizational morality, their acceptance of the moral ethos of bureaucracy, into question, made them uncomfortable, and eroded the fundamental trust and understanding that make cooperative managerial work possible. (p. 110)[3]

Our earlier brief discussion of 'positioning theory' noted that people can attempt by what they do to manoeuvre others into positions where their actions are constrained by available scripts and norms. When someone acts in a way that is ostensibly and avowedly ethical, that can push others to acknowledge that their own behaviour falls short of ethical requirements. That can not only make them feel uncomfortable, but can also put them at a political disadvantage in other respects. Claims about ethical commitment can be used as a political tactic, and even when they are not being so used there may be suspicion that they are. This combination makes us wary of noticeably ethical behaviour to such an extent that we have pejorative terms like 'moralistic' to use in attacking it.

Are there any implications? One stands out. We have already noted that the conflict between ethics and self-interest is no novelty, but in organisations the tension is maintained partly by these social dynamics. The need for predictability and the possible use of moral principle as a political tactic cause ethics to be viewed askance. Therefore it may often be counterproductive for us to flaunt ethical action. This point again is not a new one, in itself. In Matthew's Gospel, Jesus enjoins his listeners to 'beware of practising your piety before men in order to be seen by them' (Matthew 6:1),[4] and Kipling's *If*—— recommends that we 'don't look too good, nor talk too wise'. Such advice undoubtedly has merit beyond ethics and organisational politics, but one general point behind it may well be that an audience will discount our sincerity and the worth of an action if they perceive it to be done to improve our image, reputation, or political position. To that extent, the action may be counterproductive in the sense that it is unlikely to elicit cooperation and may elicit opposition.

How can we act in an ethical way without flaunting the fact? Sometimes it will be possible to act in an ethical way covertly or discreetly, but sometimes there will be difficulties. Whistleblowers and characters like White and Brady whom Jackall depicts in *Moral Mazes*, sometimes find themselves 'backed into a corner', where they can do nothing but pursue a course of high principle whatever others may think and however their actions may be construed. Glazer and Glazer noted in their interviews with many whistleblowers and their associates that

> Whistleblowers, we discovered, are conservative people devoted to their work and their organizations. Those we studied had built their careers – whether as professionals, managers, or workers – by conforming to the requirements of bureaucratic life. (1989, p. 5)

Many who eventually become whistleblowers embark initially on a straightforward, unobtrusive course, only to find gradually that they have no recourse other than open, public action.

To the extent that social processes in organisations inhibit ethical action, we might ask if there is some implication that we ought to try to change organisations so as to make explicitly ethical behaviour more common and more easily accepted. It is plausible to believe that many modern commercial organisations foster an atmosphere in which pursuit of self-interest is both endorsed and encouraged. So far as the goals of organisations are stated to be success at the expense of other competing organisations, a climate may be created that encourages similar behaviour by individuals within the organisations. It is difficult to say to what extent that is avoidable or manageable.

What is at least possible is to draw attention to the fact that ethical behaviour can be maintained without being paraded unnecessarily. There is still then one important empirical point, to what extent ethical behaviour ought to be visible in order to provide some model and encouragement for others. While we may note the Biblical advice to 'beware of practising your piety before men', we may set beside it the injunction not to hide our light under a bushel (Matthew 5:15). Here, perhaps, we come to one of the many places where ethical issues of organisational politics interact with the skills required by an effective participant. We shall have more to say about impression management, but here we may note that while skills of impression management can often be self-serving, they need not be, and the same ability to cast oneself in a favourable light may also be used to disarm suspicion about the motives behind an ethical action. It may thereby be possible to make ethical behaviour visible without seeking or seeming to seek special favour for it.

Unfortunately, that is not necessarily of much help to Tricia. Although it is true that social dynamics can give a special twist to the conflict between self-interest and ethical obligation in organisational politics, Tricia's case seems more straightforward. She has to make a decision about what to do in a situation where if she decides that helping Jennifer is the right thing to do, then in all likelihood the adverse outcomes she will suffer are not just having her motives misconstrued but failure to obtain the other job she longs for and simultaneously erosion of her current position as word is passed that she has been looking elsewhere. What can she do?

Clearly, those are substantial considerations of self-interest, but suppose that she is prepared to put them aside, in order to do the right thing. What is that? So far, we have been assuming that Tricia's main concern is to balance concerns of self-interest, or prudence, against ethical considerations. We came to that issue by noting the contrast between the question 'What is it ethically right for Tricia to do?', and the question 'What is it politically right to do?' So far, we have been interpreting the latter as the question how she may reasonably have regard for her own self-interest when ethical demands pull her in a different direction. But we noted earlier that there is another issue that may be raised by the contrast between considerations of ethical and political rightness. This is the question whether politics and ethics may be different evaluative spheres.

ORGANISATIONAL POLITICS AND DIRTY HANDS

The possibility we envisaged above was that Tricia might have a general commitment to women's political and social emancipation, and a particular commitment to stamping out sexual harassment. This is one way we can imagine the question what is politically right presenting itself to her as a different question from what is ethically right. As the dirty hands problem, it might be put by considering whether it could be appropriate to set aside any considerations of friendship or loyalty to Simon, perhaps even to set aside a certain amount of doubt about his innocence.

However, the dirty hands problem might arise in a slightly different way. If Tricia were a committed company employee, she might consider that the welfare of the company and its stakeholders were paramount, and that these ought to take precedence over the substance of Jennifer's allegations. Tricia might, that is to say, consider the problem as a purely political one about 'what would be best for the company'.[5] It seems plausible to believe that this could be a stance taken by managers in many modern corporations, but is equally plausible as a scenario in the mediaeval church or a modern department of state.

In broad terms, it is possible that parties in organisational politics might subordinate questions about what is ethically right to questions about what is politically right, where the latter are grounded either in a commitment to some political cause, or in a commitment to the organisation for its own sake. Either of those commitments might ground obligations reasonably termed 'political' obligations.

Although we have envisaged the first possibility in terms of Tricia's commitment to women's emancipation, it is easy to imagine other such cases. For example, take C.P. Snow's classic novel of organisational politics, *The Masters*. The narrator, Lewis Eliot, is prominent in the party seeking to have Jago elected as Master of their Cambridge college. It is the 1930s, and Eliot is on the political left, deeply opposed to the fascism of Germany and Italy, but believes that Jago will be the best Master, despite the fact that he is far to the right. Another of Jago's supporters has been Eustace Pilbrow, an older fellow of the college and similar in his politics to Eliot. Pilbrow has just returned from a visit to the Continent, and is speaking to Eliot late at night, in the latter's rooms:

> 'All our friends are in danger. Everything you and I believe in is going. ... Our people are just sitting by and watching. And dining in the best houses. Bloody fools. Snobs. Snobbery will make this country commit suicide. These bloody snobs can't see who their enemies are. Or who are their friends. When a country is blinding itself to that, it's in a bad way.'
>
> He told me of some of his doings. He had somehow managed to visit friends just out of a concentration camp. He was a very brave old man. He was also an acute one, underneath the champagne-like gaiety.
>
> 'I came to tell you,' he said suddenly. 'That's why I was glad to see your light. I wanted to tell you before anyone else. I can't vote for Jago. I can't vote for someone who won't throw his weight in on our side. It's your side as well as mine. That's why I came to tell you first. ...' (Snow 1972c, chap. 33)

The case is similar to the one we envisage for Tricia, at least so far as it involves some overriding commitment of political principle determining Pilbrow's choice. It would not be hard to go back to other times of widespread conflict over matters of principle, to find cases where people have allowed such general commitments some overriding force: the anti-communist period of the 1950s, the Vietnam war, and many others.

It is equally easy to imagine other examples of the second sort of case, where we envisage Tricia thinking first and foremost of the welfare of the organisation. Consider Frank Serpico's exposure of corruption in the New York police force (Glazer and Glazer 1989, pp. 53–8). Although some of his opponents were themselves corrupt, others may well have believed that his statements would harm the force. Politically, they may have thought, it was inappropriate to come out in public. Better to take things slowly, aiming for quiet, piecemeal reform within the force. Similarly, perhaps, opponents of Joe Wilson in the case recounted by Jackall are described as emphasising 'expediency', and emphasising what was 'practical' (Jackall 1988, p. 117; see above, Chapter 1, pp. 15–16). In both cases, we can see members of the organisation who believe that official organisational goals will be compromised by too delicate a regard for truth and principle.

In these latter whistleblowing examples, it may well be that the sort of moral compromise being made by loyal organisational members is between the goals and welfare of the organisation, as opposed to abstract moral principles like regard for truth, or concern with corruption or risk to public safety. There are other issues that arise more clearly in Tricia's situation. As we have stated Tricia's case, there are for her two possible sources of obligation that are especially notable. One is her friendship with Simon and the claims of loyalty it makes on her. We might refer to that as a 'personal' obligation. The other is Jennifer's vulnerability and appeal for help. We might refer to that as an 'ethical' obligation. To some extent, Jennifer's appeal is phrased in terms of Tricia's institutional position – 'the highest ranking woman here' – but clearly it calls on factors beyond the institutional position: Jennifer 'did not know what to do or whom to turn to', and came to Tricia partly also 'because you are a friend of Simon's'. One way or another, we can accept that Jennifer's appeal grounds an obligation that might be called an ethical obligation, in distinction from her personal obligation to Simon. Those two obligations pull in opposite directions, but they both differ from the other calls on Tricia that we have identified as 'political' obligations.

One of those other political obligations is Tricia's possible commitment to the rights of women (there might be other sorts of general commitments that would have similar implications in cases of alleged sexual harassment, but we may consider that one for the purposes of our discussion). As a source of political obligation we may refer to this as commitment to an ideal. It is in that respect like Pilbrow's liberal or anti-fascist commitment, like a commitment for or against communism, Christian knights' commitment to liberation of the Holy Land, or a commitment against apartheid.

The second sort of political obligation we have noted is Tricia's possible commitment to the organisation. We imagine that when Jennifer comes to her, Tricia's first thought is, 'How will this affect the company?', and 'What should I do so far as the company is concerned?' This source of political obligation we may refer to as commitment to an institution, society or organisation. It may be conceived as essentially similar to patriotism, where patriotism engenders an attitude of 'my country, right or wrong'.

Often, the two sorts of political obligation might pull in opposite directions. A citizen of South Africa might have felt loyalty to country at the same time as opposition to apartheid. Many Americans remained fiercely loyal to the USA at the same time as they bitterly opposed the Vietnam war. There are also cases where the two sorts of obligation coincide. At times in the history of the Soviet Union, its citizens might have felt loyalty to their country that was hard to separate from their commitment to communism. Similarly, obligations based on face-to-face relationships may also run in the same direction as these other sources of obligations. Those same citizens of the early Soviet Union might have helped friends out of their sense of loyalty to one another, as well as to advance the interests of their country and of communism. In those cases, there is no major problem. The difficulty arises when these sources of obligation pull in different directions.

We might refer to these various putative sources of obligation as 'personal obligation', 'ethical obligation', 'commitment to an ideal' and *Realpolitik*, respectively. If we accept the dictionary definition of *Realpolitik* as 'politics based on realities and material needs, rather than on morals or ideals',[6] it seems reasonable to use the term to refer to the fourth possible source of obligation we have identified. At the same time, it distinguishes ideals from morals and to that extent suggests that it is reasonable to use 'commitment to an ideal' to refer to the third possible source of obligation.

Is that taxonomy useful? It would provide some general basis for the idea that we can usefully distinguish the question 'What is the ethically right thing to do?' from the question 'What is the politically right thing to do?'

We should note in passing that we are not at present concerned with the fact that people may dissimulate or dissemble to others and even deceive themselves about their motives. It is quite possible that someone might ostensibly act out of idealism while in fact be moved by personal animus or loyalty or that someone might pretend to be keeping a promise to a friend while actually having in mind the long-term good of the organisation. Such things are the very stuff of organisational politics, but just at present we are concerned only with conflicts of obligation. How our motives affect the ethical character of our actions and how to evaluate various acts of deception or concealment about our intentions and motives are important issues, but at present we are not concerned with them: only with the possible types and sources of obligation that may be associated with various different sorts of motivation. Is it useful to distinguish obligations in the categories we have identified?

In fact, it emerges quickly that such a taxonomy is fragile. Criticisms are sometimes made of *Realpolitik* because its exponents are attuned to consequences rather than to matters of immediate obligation,[7] perhaps putting aside considerations of 'morals or ideals', in the words of the dictionary. However, that is an oversimplification, at least in some cases. David Thomson mentions Bismarck and Cavour in particular as exponents of *Realpolitik* (1966, pp. 295, 319–20). But it does not seem that they were without ideals: 'both men, it can be agreed, cherished certain aims, and both had minimum programmes, which they devoted all their energies to completing' (p. 320). Trevelyan's depiction of Cavour includes the following:

> Any fool, he said, could govern by martial law. According to him, it was the business of a statesman to govern by Parliament, not indeed obeying every behest of ignorant partisans and corrupt interests, but persuading the country and the Chamber to take the right course, by weight of the authority due to wisdom, knowledge and experience. This ideal, seldom realised in any country, was the actual method by which Cavour governed Piedmont in the fifties. (1909, p. 27)

There can be differences amongst historians about individuals' actions and motives, but it still seems true that *Realpolitik* does not necessarily involve renunciation of idealistic aims. It may involve 'realism', as opposed to quixotry, in that it eschews gestures or actions that do not contribute in a clear and identifiable way to the achievement of those aims. It may essentially be appreciation of the complexities of political life and understanding the limitations conventional morality has in dealing with them. Equally important for us, it may also involve willingness to subordinate some ideals or principles to others.

In short, a problem about dirty hands in politics does not rely on assuming that people with dirty hands are without ideals, far less that they have motives that are base or reprehensible. In our case, the problem will arise for Tricia if she forsakes personal loyalty to Simon for the sake of her commitment to women's rights in organisations or forsakes any obligation she has to assist Jennifer in favour of larger organisational goals.

However, the problem arises not because there is a conflict between calls of ethics and demands of politics. Stocker has argued that an action that involves dirty hands in the relevant sense is one that is 'a violation and a betrayal of a person, value, or principle', where this is a sacrifice made for some moral or ethical demand that has a more pressing call on us (1990, p. 18). As he points out, such problems are not unique to politics. What may be true is that they arise with special salience in politics because political action is so often at the intersection of competing demands. Hampshire identifies this as 'Machiavelli's Problem'. The problem, he says is simple:

justice is the opposite of aggression, conquest, domination, violence and deceit. Yet all these denials of justice are indispensable means to secure the survival of any city or state under any foreseeable conditions of political life. (1989, p. 162)

The terms we could use in the case of organisational politics might not be so extreme as 'aggression', 'conquest', and the like. Our references might be to 'forcefulness' and 'takeovers', perhaps, and these do not have such pronounced overtones. But the idea is still familiar. Survival of the organisation, and its achievement of its goals, sometimes require approaches and actions that run counter to commitments we have to persons, values, or principles. There are not separate and independent spheres of evaluation, but quite direct clashes between different considerations.

The fact that such different considerations may clash with one another could impel us to seek a common currency in which to relate them. Focussing on consequences can be one way to try to do so. For example, Tricia might be enjoined to consider harm done to Simon from credence given to a false allegation against the service done to the many women faced with genuine harassment. Or she might balance the harm done to the company share price if the affair becomes known, against the harm done to Jennifer by hushing the matter up and arranging her transfer to another section. This consequentialist approach is given its clearest form in classical utilitarianism, the approach to ethical decision-making which contends that an action is right if and only if it conduces to the greatest happiness of the greatest number.

Utilitarianism is attractive just because it promises a way to balance competing considerations against one another using a common scale. However, there are major and well-known difficulties with utilitarianism and with other forms of consequentialism (see e.g. Hodgson 1967, Smart and Williams 1973, Sen and Williams 1982 and Scheffler 1988). In Tricia's case, for example, it is hard to say just what harm is done to Simon from credence given to a false allegation. Is it confined to loss of income if he loses his job because of it? Does it include harm to his reputation? What of his feeling of betrayal by a friend? Does that count at all? Does it count for less if she believes she is doing the right thing? How could it actually be possible to evaluate in quantitative terms any benefit to women more generally? The benefit might be real and important, but the question is how it could be put in a balance to allow a worthwhile utilitarian judgement. Utilitarianism and other forms of consequentialism purport to give a way out of ethical dilemmas, by allowing some reasoned weighing of alternatives. However, when put in concrete terms, they only seem to restate the problems. It is no easier to resolve problems of dirty hands by weighing consequences than by directly confronting the conflicting moral and ethical demands that organisational life can make on us.

Chapter 6 will take us back to some more specific questions about loyalty. In general, however, it seems as though we can say this. In organisational politics, as in politics generally and not only in politics, there will be occasions where we are subject to conflicting demands and obligations. However, there is no obvious reason to say that in cases like Tricia's there are conflicts between ethical and political obligations, as though these are two separate species of demand and obligation. We can divide obligations into different types in all kinds of different ways: demands of loyalty, of ideals, of principle, or however we wish, but we do not thereby solve the problem that we sometimes are caught in a web of conflicting demands that are all real and pressing and call for us to make decisions. We do not have to assume that the conflicts are always between one kind of obligation and another. Sometimes conflicts can occur between different obligations of the same type, as when we have conflicting obligations to two different friends. Neither can we assume that obligations of one type always take precedence over obligations of another type: that loyalty always trumps ideals, or vice versa. Nor can political obligations be identified and consistently overcome the demands of ethics, or the other way round.

As we proceed, it will emerge that this sort of point is a recurring one. There are many occasions in organisational life and politics where there are no straightforward rules for 'how to do it right'. Again and again, it is possible to say what kinds of considerations are relevant, but not how to weigh them in a routine, automatic way. It has sometimes been suggested that 'if you can't measure it, then you can't manage it', and it can certainly be harder to manage things you cannot measure compared with things that you can. However, the fact that some things are not susceptible of measurement in any straightforward way cannot be taken to show that they are not important, or that we should not do what we can to 'manage' them in one way or another. Examples abound, from love and trust to some forms of sporting prowess or the taste of good wine. Ethical participation in organisations and their politics may not be possible without making some hard choices that defy measurement-based decision processes (see Provis 2001). 'Hard', that is, in the sense of difficult: not hard, necessarily, in the sense of ruthless, unfeeling or dispassionate. Sometimes, the right choice may involve overriding friendship and personal loyalty, but it is not possible to say that obligations based on factors like those never should prevail. The choices will be hard just because factors like those and others will always have to be taken seriously, and they will always have to be taken seriously because sometimes they ought to prevail.

Thus, it may be that in Tricia's case she ought to be moved by Jennifer's youth and vulnerability, whatever harm it may do the organisation to champion Jennifer's cause. We, unfortunately, cannot say. We do not know enough about the facts. Added detail to the description of the example could be enough to justify a decision either way. Some of the possibilities we shall consider further below.

We cannot say that one sort of consideration necessarily trumps another sort of consideration. But we cannot say, either, that there are two different questions, 'What is ethically correct?', and 'What is politically correct?', if the implication is that there are two sorts of considerations that cannot be weighed against one another. One sort of error may be to believe that for any case where we are torn in different directions we can weigh consequences in a common scale and thereby routinise our decision. But another sort of error may be to think that there are two different sorts of considerations that cannot be compared with one another at all, that political considerations are quite distinct from ethical considerations and that we perhaps choose to be swayed just by one rather than the other.

We could choose, perhaps, to rate some ideals above all else, or to be guided only by organisational expediency, or always to consider our friends before any abstract principles or institutions. But it is difficult to know what to make of someone who does. If they do so just because it is impossible to compare the different sorts of considerations, that is problematic. Because we cannot routinise our decisions by finding some uniform common scale to weigh things up, that does not mean that we must put aside all considerations that will not weigh in the scale we choose. Sweet and salt are different sorts of taste, but we can still decide whether some dish of food is preferable to another, even though each includes a degree of salt and sweet in its makeup. How we could routinise the decision is hard to say, but we make such choices all the time. The title given by the textbook to Tricia's case was 'Damned If You Do; Damned If You Don't'. It recalls Coady's description of a moral problem where 'you are damned if you do and damned if you don't, but one route can still make more moral sense than the other' (1990, p. 272).

SUMMARY

The case study of Tricia's situation raises a number of issues, and we shall continue to refer to it. We can put aside the issue of how she ought to balance matters of self-interest against what is ethical, because it is an old issue, and our concern here is primarily to deal with questions about what actually is ethical. It is true that the conflict between obligation and self-interest can have a special twist in organisations because of the forces that inhibit us from avowedly ethical behaviour, but while that is a significant point in itself, it does not help us with Tricia's case.

The textbook's suggestion that what is ethically right may not be politically right took us on to the issue of 'dirty hands'. However, it is not clear that a taxonomy which distinguishes different sorts of obligations, like 'ethical' and 'political' obligations, is very useful. It might well be that what is politically required can be in conflict with what is conventionally or traditionally accepted as ethical behaviour, but that may just demonstrate the limitations of conventional precepts or the additional complexities of political action. A dirty hands problem just seems to reflect the fact that moral choices are sometimes hard choices, and that the rules of thumb we often use are limited in their scope and application. It would be comforting to have some rules that could take away the difficulties, such as a focus on the consequences of different alternatives, but there are well-known difficulties with that approach.

We might nevertheless consider whether there are any other rules that might be relied on, and one suggestion about how we might try to routinise such decisions is worth some special attention. This is the suggestion that Tricia can work out how she ought to act by considering the requirements of her role in the organisation. Questions about the relationship between organisational roles and responsibilities arise particularly out of issues to do with the nature of legitimate authority in organisations, and so we shall now move to take up that general issue, beginning with the question how Tricia's responsibilities may be connected with her organisational role.

NOTES

1. For general discussion of such issues, see e.g. Baier (1958) and Rachels (1995), chap. 6.
2. See above, Chapter 2, p. 34. Examples of how politics generally may utilise skills of identifying novel possibilities can be found in Riker (1986). The importance for ethical action of envisaging a wider range of options is part of the theme of Werhane (1999).
3. See also Jackall (1988) p. 97, discussing a similar point with the comment 'Managers feel that sermons have a somewhat hollow ring in back rooms'.
4. This and other biblical quotations from the RSV.
5. For the purpose of developing these points, we may ignore the fact that the original description of Tricia's situation makes it seem unlikely that she would take either of the possible stances depicted as a 'dirty hands' scenario.
6. *The Australian Concise Oxford Dictionary* (based on *The Concise Oxford Dictionary of Current English*, seventh edition).
7. Cf. the discussion of Sartre's play *Dirty Hands* by Walzer (1973), p. 161.

4. Authority and Norms in Organisations

Tricia seems to be caught in a web of conflicting obligations. Even if we put aside the demands of prudence and self-interest, she may be torn between her commitment to the cause of women's rights, her loyalty to Simon, Jennifer's vulnerability and appeal for help, and her dedication to the organisation and its goals.

In the last chapter, we noted that this sort of situation supports the idea that political action necessarily gives rise to dirty hands, a duty to do something that nevertheless involves setting aside some other obligation or commitment. I suggested that we may not be able to routinise our decisions in these sorts of situations. Often they involve balancing considerations that cannot be measured in any straightforward way. In particular, they cannot be disposed of simply by weighing consequences of different courses of action.

In saying that often the issues cannot be determined by weighing consequences, I do not mean that consequences ought not be taken into account. There will be many decisions in organisations and in organisational politics where consequences will be paramount in deciding what it is ethical to do. If we work in a hospital, then the fact that something is necessary in order to save a patient's life may easily outweigh other competing considerations. If we work in a computer firm, it might be crucial that some course of action would allow easy public access to sensitive confidential records.

Often, the activities of an organisation will be directed toward achieving benefits or preventing harms which are important for the community, and the effect of decisions within the organisation will therefore be important to the welfare of community members. It will often be important to take these sorts of consequences into account when deciding on one's duty. Actions taken by Lord Beaverbrook to maximise production of aircraft for the Battle of Britain may have been contrary to many ethical requirements that would ordinarily have prevailed, but those actions may have been justified by the benefits achieved and the harms averted (see e.g. Deighton 1977, pp. 14, 180–82). To say that consequences do not finally determine issues is not to say that they are irrelevant. It is to point out that ethical decision-making is not straightforward or reducible to routine calculation. Even though Beaverbrook's actions may have been justified, that is because the situation was unusual, and consequences were comparatively more important than other considerations. Because that can happen sometimes, it is possible for managers to deceive themselves about other cases and to ignore ethical constraints for the sake of organisational outcomes. It is tempting to do so, just because of the difficulties of making ethical decisions which require more than routine quantitative comparisons. Ethical decision-making often can be difficult because it requires reflection that goes beyond routine.

It may nevertheless be suggested that there is one way that such decisions can be made more straightforward. It may be suggested that at least in many cases what one ought to do will be defined by one's role, and that examining the requirements of one's role will clarify both one's duties and one's rights. It is to this suggestion that we now turn; it will lead us on to the idea of 'legitimacy' in organisations.

ROLES AS A SOURCE OF AUTHORITY

It is not controversial that one's role may define duties and rights that one has. A fisheries inspector has a right and a duty to view my fishing licence, where others do not, because that is part of a fisheries inspector's role. It may be said that is a legal right and legal duty, not a moral or ethical right or duty. But the point is clear enough in many cases of ethical rights and duties also. In accepting a role as a child's guardian, I assume moral rights and duties as well as legal ones. Medical practitioners have ethical as well as legal privileges and obligations by virtue of their role.

People's roles can give rise to both legal and moral rights and duties. This is true whether the roles are clearly defined legal roles or less well-defined customary roles. 'Medical practitioner' and 'fisheries inspector' are quite formally defined roles, at least in modern western societies. 'Child's guardian' can also be quite formally defined, but also could be given an informal sense. 'Gardener' or 'teacher' could be more or less formally defined. Many roles will have significant legal rights or responsibilities associated with them even though they do not seem to be so formally defined as a role like 'medical practitioner': examples might perhaps be 'vendor' or 'shopkeeper' or 'householder'. At the same time, they will have moral or ethical duties and rights associated with them as well. Often, the ethical and legal responsibilities will overlap: as a householder, I have both a legal and moral responsibility to ensure that blocked drains in my house do not cause effluent to invade a neighbour's property. Sometimes, they diverge: as a vendor I may have legal duties that go beyond what ethics would require, or I may have ethical duties to buyers that go beyond what the law requires (see e.g. Treitel, 1995, pp. 287–8).

Roles give rise to duties and rights, whether the roles are more or less formally defined. It is hard to see what might be meant by a social 'role' that did not have some duties or rights associated with it. It is therefore natural for someone to suggest that a person in Tricia's situation might determine their obligations by reference to roles they have. This can be one way of approaching the dirty hands problem. The advice Machiavelli gives his readers about the virtues of a Prince seem often to revolve around the Prince's role, to the effect that whatever may be virtuous or obligatory for people in general, the Prince's role imposes duties that run contrary to those common virtues or obligations. To discern what a Prince ought to do, Machiavelli seem to turn to the question, 'Well, what is the role of a Prince?' The answer to that question then seems to give the answer to any question about the Prince's duties and rights.

In Tricia's case, we alluded to the possibility that asking what is the politically right thing to do, as opposed to the ethically right thing, might be an invitation to consider options. One possibility we noted was that Tricia might have some other friend, inside or outside the organisation, who can raise the issues of Simon's behaviour with more senior managers in the organisation. But perhaps the first possibility to be considered, which on the view we are presently considering may be the only proper one to consider, is what her official organisational role requires.

In one view, for Tricia to go beyond her official organisational role transgresses what is legitimate, because it is the formal lines of authority that define what is legitimate within the organisation, and that defines the boundary of her organisational rights and duties. In this view, to accept anything else would be an invitation for prying do-gooders to upset smooth organisational functioning by raising issues that are none of their business. That is undoubtedly how it would be regarded in some parts of the organisations Robert Jackall reports on in *Moral Mazes*.

We can see some point to this view. Moralism, meddlesomeness and pecksniffery can certainly go beyond what is ethically required or ethically permissible. Organisations need some boundaries drawn around people's activities and responsibilities, to allow predictability and comprehensibility, and to allow things to be done in a reasonable time.

However, that is different from saying that we should ignore things we know about, when they are significant, and when we can reasonably expect our action to make an ethically significant difference. It seems difficult to contend that Tricia's responsibilities are completely defined by her organisational role. If she comes across a collapsing visitor to the organisation, and she knows first aid, then she may have an ethical duty to render assistance, whatever her organisational role.

All right, the response may be, but there are some important distinctions to be made here. One is a distinction between cases where the rights and duties associated with Tricia's official role are silent on what she ought to do, contrasted with cases where the organisational rules that define her role have something relevant to say. It is one thing for a member of an organisation to render first aid to a visitor or passer-by. Organisational rules are silent about this just because it is clear what ought to be done, and people's responsibilities are just as they are in any other circumstances. Official roles do not affect such obligations and responsibilities unless they make some specific exception to them. But Tricia's case is not like that, it may be said. Jennifer's complaint is just the sort of issue that does fall within the purview of defined organisational roles and responsibilities.

As far as it goes, this response seems reasonable. Organisations are different from the wider political society that surrounds them in that they have a circumscribed sphere of operation: they make products, or deliver services, of a specific type, and that is their proper sphere. Within that sphere, it may be argued that their role prescriptions for members of the organisation, directed to achieving those organisational functions, ought to take precedence over personal inclination.

However, there is one clear difficulty with this line of argument: often, it is not clear whether something comes within the sphere of organisational role prescriptions or not. A bookkeeper or finance manager may have a relatively well defined organisational role, but other roles may be more vaguely defined ('handyman', 'project officer', 'deputy manager', and many others). Some roles may not be official ones at all: 'raffle organiser', 'car pool coordinator' and others. Often, it will be contestable what the official prescriptions of a role actually are, and Tricia's case may be one example.

Official role prescriptions are tied to organisational authority. What organisational roles require is determined by official authority in the organisation; at the same time, what is determined by official organisational authority is also a matter of what is done by individuals or groups who have prescribed organisational roles. The duties of a bookkeeper are determined by the job description or contract that has been approved by one or more managers who have duly delegated authority to give such approval. Whether they have that authority is determined by their own contracts or job descriptions, and so on.

Here, there is to some extent a classic chicken–egg problem: which comes first, the roles or the authority? The problem also occurs in nation-states, and has been considered by political theorists and philosophers of law. Is the law determined by individuals in roles of legislators or judges? If so, how do those individuals come by their authority?

AUTHORITY, CIVIL SOCIETY AND ORGANISATIONS

The question has been problematic for philosophers of law, because of the repeated circularities that seem to be involved. A country's constitution may determine who has authority as judges and legislators, but who is to interpret the constitution? A government may appoint judges, but who is to determine that the appointments are valid? Elections can choose governments to make laws, but who makes the laws that determine who can vote in the election? Such issues have attracted much discussion and some classic treatments (see e.g. Peters 1958, Hart 1961 and Dworkin 1977).

The question what constitutes official authority in organisations may seem a little more straightforward than in national politics, because official or legitimate authority in organisations seems to a significant extent derivative from authority in the surrounding community. The issue of authority is recurringly difficult for legal and political theorists because of the difficulty there is in defining a source of authority for state or legal power outside of the state or the law itself, with the resulting constant tendency to circularity. In the case of organisations, the situation is potentially a little easier because we can see a source for authority in organisations from whatever surrounding legal framework there may be.

Thus, for example, the Companies Act (or whatever it may be called) can define what is required for a company to be constituted and for authority to inhere in the Board and the Chief Executive (whatever terms may actually be used). Other laws about trusts and associations and employment can define relationships amongst individuals, and between groups of individuals and other organisations like banks and county councils and the like. Eventually, by looking at the law of the land and the documents that record agreements amongst people which have some legal status, we can arrive at some conclusions about official authority within organisations. Jones is the President of the Board, on whose behalf she hired Smith to act as Chief Executive, with authority defined in his contract, and so on. If it is accepted that the law of the land reflects morally legitimate authority in the surrounding community, then it is plausible to argue that it transmits its own moral legitimacy onward to rules and determinations within the organisation, so far as they conform to that surrounding community law.

That is an orthodox view about the way organisations derive any moral authority they have. We noted Aristotle's comment about the priority of the state, and Rousseau said that 'the social order is a sacred right which serves for the basis of all others' (1947, p. 6). The approach subsumes questions to do with authority in organisations under wider questions about general political authority. Organisational roles may then be a major source of rights and duties, because they are established through authority that derives its legitimacy from the same source as the law of the land.

Unfortunately, there is often vagueness or ambiguity within organisations about what is officially sanctioned, what an individual's authority actually is, and what a role actually prescribes. Often, this is a key aspect of moves in organisational politics. Consider Antony Jay's example:

> Suppose he is a new chief executive. At once you want to know how far he will restrict your freedom in practice. You have an important project which will cost more than the £100,000 you are allowed to authorize, but only a little more. You know it is unlikely to be authorized for this year if you put it up. So you cost it at £98,000 and 'discover' later that it cost £110,000. What you are doing, in hippopotamus terms, is defecating on territory he has enclosed within his defecatory ring. (The colloquial term for this is very similar in its idiom.) Only just over

the edge, but over it. His reaction will soon tell you if you can try it on again. (1967, chap. 5)

But the case is not quite so clear as Jay implies. The allowed authorisation might be for projects reasonably projected to cost no more than £100,000. If so, the issue comes down to what a 'reasonable projection' is. Or it may simply be unclear whether the allowed authorisation is for projects which will actually cost no more than £100,000, or for projects reasonably projected to cost no more than £100,000 (the written authorisation may say 'projects that will cost no more than £100,000'). In that case, we have a situation which embodies a kind of vagueness that is very common in organisations. It can also be found in the law of the land, and then it is normally left to courts and judges to determine what the most reasonable interpretation is. Indeed, there are rules of procedure that determine to whom such issues must be referred, and how. In organisations, it might be provided that such issues are to be referred to a more senior manager for determination, but that is uncommon. It is more likely for there to be some argument and perhaps some other form of contestation. If the new chief executive challenges the expenditure, then you may respond with your alternative interpretation of your authorisation. You may decide that to do so is unwise, because you believe that to do so will harm the relationship between the two of you, and imperil other things you value. You will to some extent be guided by what is at stake and what your estimate is of the other's likely response. You may take account of the other powers that the chief executive undoubtedly has, such as power to evaluate your overall performance, as well as your estimate of his or her disposition. But often you will have scope to take those considerations into account, because what is authorised is defined with an element of vagueness. Often, there will be use of terms like 'adequate', or 'appropriate', or 'reasonable'. Sometimes, there will be scope for argument in terms of overall organisational goals and policy. Sometimes, even if there is logical room for argument, the chief executive will not accept it. The eventual outcome in many cases is the 'looking up and looking around' that Jackall describes vividly as a frequent occurrence in managerial life, where, because things are vaguely defined, managers pay close attention to one others' expectations and intentions, to avoid blame for a wrong decision (1988, chap. 4).

Thus, a senior manager might contend that dealing with Jennifer's plight is outside Tricia's responsibilities. Tricia might respond by alluding to some of Jennifer's reasons for coming to her, in particular the fact that she is 'the highest ranking woman here'. The question then becomes whether that sort of consideration ought to be given official organisational heed, and the issue is probably vague enough not to determine the outcome, which will be decided instead by other considerations like regard for Jennifer, loyalty other managers may feel for Simon, or concerns about the image of the organisation if it does or does not take action over this issue.

This sort of problem is a general one. The rules and processes that establish and maintain organisations as recognised legal entities will not prescribe all the detail about what is allowed or required within them, but will leave open a variety of things to be determined within the organisation in any way that is reasonable or proper, but that introduces categories of evaluation of a general ethical type. One reason why official roles do not suffice to resolve issues about apparently conflicting obligations is therefore that role descriptions often will be vague just where conflicting obligations seem to arise. Where a role description says 'take appropriate steps' to do so-and-so, and some other requirement points toward not doing so-and-so, role definitions alone will not be enough to tell us what to do. We began by considering whether role-defined obligations and responsibilities may suffice to overcome the problem of dirty hands in organisational politics, cases where it seems that some duty one has necessarily involves setting aside some other binding moral or ethical commitment. In many cases, we shall not be able to rely on defined roles to resolve these or other cases of ethical conflict, because of the vagueness often inherent in organisational role definitions.

VAGUENESS, AMBIGUITY AND CONFLICTING RULES

What is more, difficulties will arise not only from the vagueness of official roles, which carries over into vagueness about what legitimate organisational authority prescribes in a particular situation, but also from ambiguity of official roles. While vagueness and ambiguity are often run together as sources of unclarity, it is useful for us to note the difference between them.

In simple terms, the idea of 'baldness' is vague: whether someone is bald is a matter of degree, and there is no clear dividing line between someone who is bald and someone who is not. Hence the well-known sorites paradox, where it is proved that no one is bald, since a person with a full head of hair is not bald and a person with one less hair than a person who is not bald cannot be bald either. Ambiguity is different: here, things are well defined, but with two clear alternative interpretations. Thus, for example, 'note' can refer to a musical sound or a brief written message, and 'grass' can refer either to any plant of the family *Gramineae* or specifically to the plant *cannabis sativa*. Hence the fallacy of equivocation, where a term is given one clear meaning in the premiss of an argument and another in the conclusion.

The sort of importance this can have in organisations is brought out in the following example Charles Handy draws from an article by N. Dornbusch. It refers to socialisation of cadets in a Coast Guard Academy:

> The cadet is subject to two sets of rules; the 'regulations' and the 'traditions'. One function of the regulations is to punish violations of the traditions. This is done by labelling any offence against the traditions as a breach of the regulations. The

traditions are norms enforced by peers, or by student superiors, rather than by instructors. Although described as 'unwritten rules' they are presented to new cadets in writing in the orientation manual. When there is a conflict between the regulations and traditions, the traditions win. For example, when a swab [i.e. a new cadet] violates the regulations by carrying out the orders of an upperclassman, and receives demerits, the upperclassman continues to excuse him from other official rule violations until his demerit account has been balanced. (Handy 1985, p. 144)

In this Academy, there is ambiguity about the behaviour required of a new cadet. There are two sets of rules or norms that prescribe different and incompatible pieces of behaviour in various situations. The rules are not vague: they do not leave it unclear what to do. The trouble is that different rules clearly prescribe different things.

While that is a particularly striking example, there are many other documented cases of such ambiguity of organisational norms or standards. On the factory floor, 'rate-busting' is a well-known term which refers to actions by workers who contravene unwritten norms about productivity and output, in favour of officially sanctioned organisational standards and goals. On the other hand, a 'work to rule' is a form of industrial action where some organisational goals are disrupted by workers' too close adherence to officially sanctioned rules and standards whose violation is normally encouraged to some extent in the interests of efficient production. In either case, the conflict is between two norms which are both clear, but which point in opposite directions.

The case cited by Handy is noteworthy because of the fact that there is some documentation of the 'traditions'. In many cases, conflicting demands of ambiguous roles are embodied on the one hand in documented norms or standards but on the other in social rules that are unwritten. Alternatively, the conflicts may be derivative, in that some rule provides for specific behaviour, while another more general rule enjoins obedience to some authority which makes demands that are inconsistent with the more specific rule. This kind of problem is recounted in a number of whistleblowing cases. For example, there is Dobie Hatley's case, where she was instructed by her boss to contravene regulations about keeping records of construction details at nuclear facilities:

> My boss called me in and told me that we had to get the books to match. If we did it right, it probably would have taken a year. So what were we going to do? We had to pass the audit and the only way to do that was to rewrite the documentation. We destroyed the records and wrote new ones to match what we needed. That's falsification of documentation. (Glazer and Glazer 1989, p. 128)

Dobie Hatley was subject to two conflicting demands: instructions from her superior, and more specific role requirements. Turning to role demands does not solve the ethical problem of how to act in such a case.

Of course, such problems arise also in the law of the land. There are possible legal conflicts and problems about interpreting statutes which have to be dealt with by courts. To some extent, there are established principles about how to do that, and analogous principles might be brought to bear in situations like Dobie Hatley's: for example, that instructions from a superior are not binding if they contravene specific legal requirements. However, there will be many cases where there is no straightforward way to resolve such a conflict, so that an individual is caught in a 'double bind'.[1] In some cases, a supervisor's instruction will run counter to some internal organisational documents that prescribe the appropriate process, and the individual will be bemused about which has greater authority. Or the individual will be subject to conflicting instructions from different people, like an immediate supervisor and the company accountant.

In recent years a certain amount of attention has been given to cases of this kind which arise in multinational corporations. Suppose that a company originated and has a head office in the US, but now has a division in Country X, that division being registered as a company in Country X in its own right. Various legal arrangements can be imagined, but in general there will be a problem about norms and roles that are legitimated by Country X law, and norms and roles that are legitimated from the US head office. In many cases there will be no inconsistency, but sometimes there will be conflict, and then for workers in Country X there could be real questions about what they ought to do. A case which has become the subject of discussion and comment in recent years is that of bribery, where local law may permit processes that would be illegal in the US and are contrary to head office policy. Sometimes, there may be conflicts between formal legal requirements. More often, there will be conflict between what is prohibited by one legal code but legal and informally encouraged in the other country: for example, where one prohibits bribery, but the other encourages gift exchange. The more formal cases may be dealt with as 'conflicts of law'; the others may be less tractable.

Although they have attracted more recent publicity, in principle the cross-national cases do not raise any issues that may not arise for organisations within a single nation-state. What is required or allowed by the law of the land can leave organisational members with substantial ethical conflicts to resolve, conflicts that will not be finally resolved by the law of the land. In broad terms, this should not surprise us. The issues to which organisational authority has to be applied are too diverse and fine-grained, and organisational processes too complex, to expect that the authority of the surrounding nation-state can suffice to establish all moral authority in organisations.

NORMS AND LEGITIMACY

If 'official' role requirements often do not provide a way out for us when we confront ethical dilemmas like Tricia's, because of difficulties in saying what is 'officially' required, we may ask whether a solution will emerge if we put aside the question what is officially prescribed, and simply consider role prescriptions of any sort, whether official or otherwise.

Often, role prescriptions are based on accepted social norms. In Chapter 2, we noted that perceptions of legitimacy go along with group norms and conformity pressures as a major source of influence on people's behaviour in organisations. Whether or not some norms in an organisation can be identified as official organisational requirements, we may ask how far organisation members can rely on the norms that surround them to determine what they ought to do. It seems clear that local norms are at least an important source of the authority people accept. The significance of group norms within organisations is well known (see e.g. Miner 1992, pp. 181–3, Spector 2000, pp. 275–6 and Jay 1972, pp. 162–3). Where there is vagueness about the normative demands within organisations, that often results in the emergence of norms that resolve unclarity. In Chapter 2, we noted Sherif's study about group conformity. Cartwright and Zander commented that this classic study 'demonstrated that, in a situation where the individual is unable to tell whether his answer is right or wrong, he is almost completely dependent upon the group for selecting a response' (1960, p. 167). They suggest that when a group like a committee determines an answer to a previously open question, thereafter 'this shared agreement has a greater reality for each member than his previously private beliefs' (p. 170). Where some standard emerges about how to deal with a recurrent issue or situation, the agreement constitutes a norm for the group, where

> a norm is a scale of values which defines a range of acceptable (and unacceptable) attitudes and behaviours for members of a social unit. Norms specify, more or less precisely, certain rules for how group members should behave and thus are the basis for mutual expectations amongst the group members. (Brown 1988, p. 42)

Norms function at least in part to 'bring order and predictability to a person's environment' (Brown 1988, p. 44). They can range from norms that result from explicit agreement like the committee example given by Cartwright and Zander, to the tacit rules that govern non-verbal aspects of interpersonal exchange (e.g. Wallbott 1995).

The ambiguity and vagueness we have discussed often may be found together, in particular because there may be vagueness about how to respond to some ambiguous demand. When Forsyth writes that 'a group facing an ambiguous problem or situation lacks internal consensus, but members soon structure their experiences until they conform to a standard accepted by the group' (1990, p. 161), the point applies with equal or greater force to situations where requirements are vague, as well as ambiguous. Norms may deal with situations where requirements would otherwise be unclear. Where, as often happens, the law of the land results in no clear, unequivocal specification of role requirements in an organisation, is it possible that legitimate requirements are instead defined by whatever the local organisational norms may be?

In our discussion of legitimate power in Chapter 2, we noted French and Raven's point that people's perceptions of legitimacy within an organisation may be founded on their acceptance of certain cultural values or norms: they wrote that 'we may think of legitimacy as a valence in a region which is induced by some internalized norm or value' (1960, p. 616). Setting aside the technical context, the question that we alluded to earlier is the extent to which acceptance of a norm automatically constitutes some line of action as 'legitimate'.

The point is difficult. To begin with, it has often been noted in the philosophy of law that not all regularities of behaviour necessarily constitute norms. As Hart says, 'mere convergence in behaviour between members of a social group may exist (all may regularly drink tea at breakfast or go weekly to the cinema) and yet there may be no rule *requiring* it' (1961, p. 9). How may we distinguish rules or norms from mere regularities of behaviour? One possible cue is the use of terms like 'must', 'should' and 'ought to' in the case of rules or norms, as opposed to mere regularities of behaviour. That is to say, in some sense or other a rule or norm has prescriptive force that a mere regularity does not have. But the implication is that in some sense or other, whatever a rule or norm prescribes actually is obligatory for a member of the group to whom the norm applies. If I am a cricketer, I ought to accept the umpire's ruling on a dismissal. If you are lawyer, you ought to keep confidential anything told to you by a client. In order to characterise something as a norm it seems that we have to accept that in some sense or other the behaviour that it refers to is obligatory, rather than just what people usually do.

However, if we say that what is legitimate within an organisation is what people in it accept as legitimate, we preclude questions about whether something really is legitimate even if people accept it as such. The implication is that if the guards at Auschwitz all accepted the legitimacy of the organisational rules, then we have to say that those rules really were legitimate. Such a conclusion is problematic not only in extreme cases like that, but in many cases where we want to be able to evaluate organisational norms against some more basic standards. We suggested earlier that perceptions of legitimacy may not be correct perceptions, considering cases like Milgram's experiments, and here there are questions that go to the very heart of the notion of 'legitimacy' in organisations.

There seem to be three classes of case where people hold actions of a certain sort to be legitimate. One is where such actions comply with some general moral rule or principle, such as 'Do not harm others without good reason', or 'Respect others' rights to make their own decisions in matters that concern only themselves', or the like. A second is where the actions conform to some accepted social rule or group norm that does not have any independent support from a general moral principle. Examples of such rules or norms include ones to do with bodily adornment or hairstyle,[2] or conventions like which side of the road to drive on, and many others. The fact that from afar they may seem questionable or banal need not lessen the weight and import they can have for those they affect. A third is where actions emerge from agreements or understandings individuals have given to one another: for example where you have given me permission to use your office, perhaps.

Of these, I suggest, it seems fairly clear how the first and the third are cases of genuine legitimacy, but less clear how the second is.[3] It seems apparent that accepted social rules or norms have on many occasions been misguided, or that changing them has created no moral problem. Norms that have prescribed long hair or short hair, that have precluded certain groups from voting, or proscribed certain sorts of sexual activity – the list can be extended indefinitely. The point is easy to make about norms within national or community cultures, but equally so about norms within organisations.

As far as organisations are concerned, another way to see this point is to note that in many cases, the culture within an organisation is not uniform or homogeneous, and there will be an issue about the extent to which a sub-culture does actually establish certain behaviour as legitimate. We know that there may be sub-cultures in organisations with norms that run counter to one another and to official organisational norms (Van Maanen and Barley 1985). The previously mentioned factory floor case of rate-busting is an example of a sub-cultural norm that runs counter to official organisational norms. The fact that such norms are not written or explicit does not count at all against their genuineness as norms: 'group norms, if written down, become the formal rules of the group, but in most instances norms are adopted implicitly' (Forsyth 1990, p. 160). Clearly, though, if the different norms run counter to one another, there can be a problem saying that all the conflicting behaviour they prescribe is legitimate.

THE SIGNIFICANCE OF GROUP SIZE

One way or another, either because on occasion some organisational norms contradict what we would generally accept to be reasonable ethical imperatives, or because norms of sub-cultures are inconsistent amongst themselves, it seems clear that they cannot provide a general source of legitimate authority to resolve ethical dilemmas.

However, the fact that often in organisations there are sub-cultures or sub-groups where different norms are accepted than the official norms or the norms that prevail in the rest of the organisation, also draws our attention to the fact that often our organisations are quite large. That fact itself can affect how far norms of behaviour generate demands on us that are morally binding. The point that there is significant difference between smaller and larger groups is made against theorists like Hobbes, Locke and Rousseau, who tried to work out answers to questions about the state and civil society by imagining a 'state of nature', typically amongst small numbers of people. Some arguments against state of nature theorists suggest that there are logically significant differences between smaller and larger groups of people. The classic statement is Hume's:

> Two neighbours may agree to drain a meadow, which they possess in common; because 'tis easy for them to know each others mind; and each must perceive, that the immediate consequence of his failing in his part, is the abandoning of the whole project. But 'tis very difficult, and indeed impossible, that a thousand persons shou'd agree in any such action; it being difficult for them to concert so complicated a design, and still more difficult for them to execute it; while each seeks a pretext to free himself of the trouble and expence, and wou'd lay the whole burden on others (1897, p. 538).[4]

We may have reservations about parts of what Hume says, for example about the 'impossibility' of agreement amongst a large number, or about the inevitability of each seeking to avoid the costs involved. However, there still may be differences between small and large groups in what cooperation requires amongst their members.

Studies about effect of group size have tended to focus on process dynamics rather than ethical implications, but they still have implications for ethics. One approach to groups has been embodied in assumptions about the rational self-interest of members, with attempts to model processes on that assumption. Mancur Olson's work is perhaps the best-known example. One of his important conclusions was that there are significant differences amongst small and large groups. In larger groups, he argues, there are greater possibilities for 'free-riding', where individuals may obtain the benefits of group membership without contributing to the group's efforts, so that in this case, 'no collective good can be obtained without some group agreement, coordination, or organization' (1965, p. 46). As we noted earlier, there are some questions about assuming that individuals are predominantly self-interested. However, some of the difficulties that result from group size do not depend on great assumptions of self-interest. Driving on one side of the road rather than another is an example. All of us may want to avoid collisions, but that makes it no easier to work out which side of the road to drive on, unless we have some idea what others will do.[5]

In that kind of situation, we can achieve a mutually satisfactory outcome (all drive on the left, say), provided that we can convey information to one another about our expectations and intent. In small groups, this may be possible because we can tell one another about things by using simple interpersonal communication. In Laslett's words, a face-to-face society is capable 'of proceeding by means of conversation between its members, permitting mutual response in terms of the whole personalities of those who compose it' (1956, p. 160). But this is not possible for larger groups. A process of face-to-face communication is not there enough to explain people's mutual expectations. In many groups, as Brown suggests, it is 'norms' which support mutual expectations amongst group members, even though in a small face-to-face community, norms may be secondary to explicitly or implicitly conveyed indications about one's expectations or intentions.

There is then still a question about the source of such norms, and the extent to which they ground moral obligation. Members of a group might accept them as legitimate, but it is not clear to what extent people's acceptance of them as legitimate creates genuine moral obligation to conform to them, as would be necessary for the prescriptions of accepted norms to have real moral force. If they were statements of conventions or rules that emerged from people's agreements or undertakings, it is clear how they might ground obligation, but if they have some other origin it needs to be explained whence they can derive any moral force.

We shall return to this point in Chapter 10, but here we may anticipate our later discussion by noting that sometimes norms are associated with expectations which lead to obligations because others' expectations are a fact of life and to act contrary to them may do the others harm. Thus, for example, I have an obligation to drive on the side of the road prescribed by our community not so much because my conformity to the norm sustains others' expectations as because given those expectations it is likely to harm others if I do otherwise.

However, even in such cases, if there is room for communication amongst the members of the group to override their norm-induced expectations, then what they are ethically required to do may also be modified. Behaviour which in the wider community might give offence, and be a bad thing to do for that reason, might be understood differently within a family, for example. In that case, the family members need not be construed as forgiving bad behaviour; rather, if people in the family have different expectations of one another, then there may be no offence and no reason to look askance at the behaviour. It might be bad to offend others, even one's own family members, but the same behaviour may not offend them as would offend others.

This suggests that it is the expectations and intentions that we convey to one another by what we do that are the more direct source of moral praise and blameworthiness, compared with norms that in many cases may create or sustain those expectations.[6] Where norms exist, we ought not pretend otherwise, any more than we ought to ignore other realities of our situation when we are making decisions. But that does not mean that we have to accept them as having any intrinsic moral force, beyond the extent to which they shape

our and others' expectations. The ground for saying so is that if we are in a
position to change the expectations that norms sustain, then we seem morally
free to do so, unless the norm is simultaneously an expression of some
general moral principle, such as a norm against killing, or the like. The mere
fact that there is some group norm does not in itself seem to sustain any
moral obligation.

To that extent, group norms are essentially a secondary basis for legitimacy: secondary, that is, to such considerations as whether they reflect
general moral principles or have effects on people's expectations. In smaller
groups, communication amongst members will very often sustain agreements
or undertakings amongst individuals that create obligations in a fairly clear
way. This is especially important in the context of organisational politics,
because a great deal of organisational politics takes place in smaller groups
and communities, where there is more scope for expectations and intentions
to be affected by direct communication. Laslett drew attention to the
significant wider implications this point has, because a good deal of the
politics of larger groups is actually carried on through mechanisms that
involve groups only of this smaller, 'face-to-face' character. He mentioned
not only the family but 'the directive groups of voluntary bodies, of industrial
enterprises, of nation states and of international organizations' as examples,
together with 'the central and local committees of political parties, of soviets,
and of the whole class of parliamentary and representative bodies', arguing
then that

> It seems to be the case that any given sample of individuals capable of acting
> collectively has only one procedure open to it. It must discover from within itself,
> or have discovered for it, a group of a critical size which can act, and act
> continuously, as a face to face society ... (1956, p. 160)

The idea is a crucial one for us because it reminds us that a great deal of
organisational politics is the politics of face-to-face groups within larger
organisations. The group may be a factory workgroup, an executive committee, the staff of a particular school, or a board of directors, or any of many
other sorts of groups.

To whatever extent that is finally true, and to whatever extent the process
has been affected by modern electronic communication within groups that
form 'virtual communities', it at least seems to be true that many large
organisations devolve decision-making to groups who interact often if not
always face-to-face, and that explains some of the things that Jackall describes so vividly in some large modern corporations. It is for this reason that
so much of 'organisational politics' is often conceived of as 'closed politics'
in C.P. Snow's sense.[7] It is why in management groups Jackall's 'looking up
and looking around' is so fundamental: established norms often take a back
seat compared to specific interpersonal relationships and expectations.

On the other hand, the members of small groups within organisations will still be subject to the constraints of official authority in the wider organisation: as Jackall notes, 'business cannot be conducted without formal authorization by appropriate authorities' (1988, p. 39). The requirement for such formal authorisation is often a fact of organisational life. The question remains to what extent such formal authority creates genuine moral obligations. So far as we have yet seen here, organisational norms do not in themselves seem to be a source of genuine moral authority. Such norms may be significant in affecting what others expect of us, and that may create derivative obligations on us, but we need to look elsewhere if we wish to find a general source of legitimacy for organisational demands.

SUMMARY

Our discussion began by considering Tricia's situation, and how she might resolve pressures of apparently conflicting obligations. We considered the possibility that she might appeal to the obligations of her official organisational role to clarify what she ought to do. But what her role obliges her to do is a matter of how it is defined by official organisational authority. While we might have been attracted to the idea that organisational role descriptions gain their official authority from the law of the surrounding community, and that this might have made Tricia's obligations clear, that idea does not ultimately provide us with a resolution of the issue. There are too many cases where matters are left vague, unclear or indeterminate. It may be that requirements on individuals in organisations sometimes are made clear by the terms of the surrounding legal environment, but there will be very many occasions when they are not.

Instead of relying on prescriptions from outside the organisation, we might look to internal organisational norms. Such norms function to some extent to clarify requirements on organisational members. The difficulty with this is that while we may for the sake of argument assume that prescriptions of the external legal environment satisfy whatever requirements they have to in order to be regarded as legitimate, it would beg too many questions to make that assumption about internal organisational norms. We know too well that norms of groups can vary in the extent to which they create obligations that we regard as ethically binding. In small groups, agreements and communication can generate obligations, and more generally we may need to take account of others' expectations, but even where these give rise to some obligations that we have, those obligations emerge from those expectations others have, not directly from organisational norms.

In particular, recourse to internal organisational norms would not provide us with a generally convincing way to resolve any conflict that Tricia may feel between obligations that are created by organisational rules and norms, and obligations that are created by personal relationships, whether her longstanding friendship with Simon or the expectations that Jennifer has of her. We return, in effect, to the issue raised by E.M. Forster's hope that he would fulfil an obligation to a friend over an obligation to his country. There is nothing we have been able to discover thus far that would ground any general obligations to comply with official organisational requirements or the demands of organisational roles. In the next chapter, we consider some possibilities that may arise out of analogy with reasons that have been given why citizens have obligations to comply with the authority of a nation-state.

NOTES

1. The idea of a 'double bind' has been used in discussion of conditions that may induce mental illness: see e.g. Laing (1969), chap. 9.

2. Hampshire (1982) takes hair style as 'a clear example of a norm or ideal which is essentially diverse and non-converging' (p. 146).

3. It may be argued that general moral rules or principles are only instances of more widespread norms than the second category of social rules or group norms, but I shall take it here that there is a distinction to be made.

4. Hume's *Treatise*, Book III, Part II, section vi; Hardin comments that 'Common sense does not generalize to a hard rule, however, and Hume's "impossible" is surely an exaggeration' (1982, p. 40).

5. Technically, solving coordination problems as well as resolving prisoners' dilemmas is made more difficult by increasing group size.

6. Since this passage was drafted, Garrett Cullity has drawn my attention to Thomas Scanlon's argument that duties like the duty to keep promises derive not from social practices so much as from what we owe to others when we have led them to form expectations about our future conduct: see Scanlon (1998), chap. 7.

7. C.P. Snow seems to have given that phrase currency in his Lectures *Science and Government* (1961), where his primary emphasis is the contrast with 'open', or public, politics (see pp. 30, 36). In his subsequent *Postscript* (1962), he expressed concern about the way decisions were made in the episodes of closed politics he described, but those concerns are especially oriented toward cases where decisions with wide public implications are made without the general public being informed, not necessarily about closed politics as such (see *Postscript* pp. 3–6). Its 'closed' nature may incidentally explain why 'organisational politics' is sometimes used as a synonym for 'office politics'. It is possible with care to distinguish different meanings for the three terms 'closed politics', 'organisational politics' and 'office politics', but there many instances of each which are instances also of the others.

5. Legitimacy, Consent and Fairness

So far as we have yet seen, individuals confronted with situations like Tricia's where there is some apparent conflict of obligations, cannot necessarily turn to their official role requirements for help. If we genuinely wish to confront the issue Forster raises, how to weigh obligations to friends against obligations to countries or organisations, we need to look more carefully at the issue of organisational authority and specifically at the strength of the obligations it may create. The question is essentially the same question as what creates legitimacy for the political and legal requirements of a nation-state, to an extent that makes it morally obligatory on citizens to comply with them.

In mediaeval times, the sorts of answers that might have been given had to do with divine sanction or the authority of tradition. The phrase 'the Divine Right of Kings' reflects the idea that citizens were required to accept monarchical authority as ordained by God, and the idea of people having their own proper individual stations equally reflects the idea that traditional arrangements have their own weight and authority (see e.g. Benn and Peters 1959, pp. 301–18).[1] However, neither divine nor traditional authority nowadays provide a widely accepted basis for accepting political authority, and we may assume that they would not provide a widely accepted legitimation for organisational authority, either.[2]

An approach to justifying political authority in nation-states which is a more likely candidate as the basis for legitimate organisational authority is the view that individuals have obligations to comply with legal requirements of their community because they reap benefits from community membership that they can legitimately claim only if they do what is required of them in exchange. Another, closely related but not quite the same, is that individuals are subject to state authority because of some agreement that they have entered into, handing to a sovereign their authority over themselves in order to maintain their lives through membership of a community. This, in effect, was Hobbes' view, espoused subsequently in different forms by successors like Locke and Rousseau.[3]

The two views are closely related, and tend to become intertwined. To the first contention, that individuals are obliged to accept requirements of the nation-state because of the benefits they obtain from it, it may be responded that no obligation is created unless the individuals choose to obtain them and have a reasonable opportunity to renounce them. That then pushes the interlocutor to the second position, that individuals have in fact entered into some 'social contract' with one another to incur obligations in exchange for benefits.

Another way of presenting this view is to say that people have obligations to comply with legitimate authority because they have given their consent to it, in much the same way that I have an obligation to honour the terms of a contract with another person because they embody my agreement and consent. Benn and Peters make the point that 'the theory of consent is, among other things, a way of claiming that political obligation should be viewed as a moral obligation' (1959, p. 318). The consent theory of political obligation can be construed as an attempt to reduce political to moral obligation by explaining it in terms of obligations we may have to other individuals, rather than an obligation to an abstract, impersonal nation-state.

If we give our consent to another, we are doing rather the same sort of thing as making a promise to them, and have rather the same sorts of obligations as a result. In the terms of our earlier suggestion that there seem to be three classes of case where people hold actions to be legitimate, we may construe this account as grounding legitimacy and obligation not in general moral rules or in group norms, but in agreements or understandings that individuals have given one another. If we join together with several others, we can still give one another our mutual consent for a particular arrangement, and have clear and straightforward mutual obligations as a result. We may set up a tennis club, with a bank account, rental of a court and agreement about how and when to use it. If one of us contravenes the agreement, then the others can bring us to book by reference to our explicit prior agreement. Obligations we have in that sort of group arrangement are discernibly the same sorts of obligations as we have to one another as individuals. It is in that way that explaining political obligations in a nation-state on a similar basis can be an attempt to show how political obligation is a form of ethical or moral obligation.

That approach has often been criticised because of the lack of real similarity between a nation-state and a tennis club. However, such criticism can still admit that some group arrangements do give rise to moral obligations in just that way: Benn and Peters note that often voluntary associations do originate like this (1959, p. 319). From the point of view of organisational politics, that is of major importance, because it means that members of some organisations do have obligations because they have expressly consented to a particular set of arrangements. Consider Tricia's situation once more. Let us suppose that she is the Secretary of the tennis club when Jennifer, a recently joined member still undergoing a period of probation, comes to Tricia with a complaint that Simon, a longstanding member and friend of Tricia's has been harassing her.

In this situation, Tricia's choice still might not be perfectly straightforward, but it seems a little clearer what she might do. She may have some feelings of loyalty toward Simon, but sympathy also to Jennifer. There will be an issue about the facts of the case, and what Tricia ought to accept in that regard, but assuming for the moment that that can be dealt with, Tricia can balance obligations she may feel to Simon and to Jennifer not only against one another, but also against obligations she may have to the tennis club, by bearing in mind any undertakings she has given to the other members about her role. She can take account of any general ethical or moral demands, but she may also consider what she has agreed to about her position of Secretary, and what other members can reasonably expect of her. She may have undertaken to seek amicable resolution of conflicts amongst members. She might feel that this issue was a matter that went beyond the sorts of things that anyone envisaged when she gave that undertaking, but that is something that can be considered in fairly concrete terms. She can to a significant extent work out the requirements of her role by reference to the explicit undertakings she gave when she accepted the position and the mutual understandings that members of the club had at the time it was established.

That will not necessarily make her decision an automatic one, but it does mean that she is weighing discernibly similar sorts of considerations against one another. She can consider her undertakings, what she and others expect of one another as members of the club, Jennifer's allegations, and her friendship with Simon, all as competing human demands. She can consider particular past interactions, like club meetings, and whether things that she said or accepted there should influence how she acts here. Overall, in that type of situation, some of the obligations people have in organisational politics can be explained as a matter of explicit consent. There is none of the additional complexity which can result from the size and abstractness of a large corporation. The situation is like that of the face-to-face groups mentioned in the previous chapter.

There are then two questions. One is what limitations there are on people's consent even in cases like the tennis club. The second is to what extent such an account may somehow be generalised to larger and more abstract organisations. Without trying fully to separate those questions, we turn now to a number of issues in more detail. One of these is the nature of consent, and how far it is reasonable to construe people as having given consent to organisational arrangements. This raises issues about the difference between explicit and tacit consent, and about the extent to which people may need to have alternatives to a particular arrangement in order to be taken as consenting to it. Whether members' consent is morally required depends at least in part on the aims of the organisation and effects on external stakeholders. Nevertheless, there are problems when careless or unscrupulous parties in organisational politics contrive arrangements that have some appearance of consent but are actually only a counterfeit version of genuine consent.

Because of the various difficulties about justifying authority within organisations on the basis that people have given their consent to it, it will also be worthwhile to consider the other possibility we mentioned above, the suggestion that members of a group may have an obligation to comply with its requirements not necessarily because they have consented to it, but simply because of the benefits they gain from it.

Unfortunately, while the various sorts of grounds we consider as possible bases for legitimate authority in organisations all may be relevant factors in assessing what one's ethical obligations are in different situations, I shall argue that none of them gives a satisfactory general account that we can always call on.

CONSENT AND CONTEXT

In terms of general political theory, the sort of view we are considering has often been phrased by saying that obligations to comply with political authority rest on a 'social contract' amongst members of society. A similar view might be put about obligations to comply with organisational authority: that people have entered into some contractual arrangements to do so. So far as we are considering the view about general political authority, there is the clear and well-known response that there is no explicit contract. By and large, a similar response will also hold in organisations. Employment arrangements often try to obtain express consent from individuals to their organisational roles, using a contract entered into at the start of employment. In fact, though, the terms of such contract often are as vague as any other prescriptions on organisational members. They have implicit as well as explicit terms, to an extent that at least makes it doubtful to what extent an individual party gives such express consent to the terms of the contract as may create moral or ethical obligations. Certainly, such explicit contractual arrangements do not resolve all the ethical issues that confront individuals in organisations.

In effect, when attempts are made to ground people's obligations in agreements they have entered into, the question is: By what ascertainable links are individuals' obligations related to undertakings or commitments they have given? Locke gave an answer that revolved around the idea of 'tacit' consent:

> There is a common distinction of an express and a tacit consent, which will concern our present case. No body doubts but an express *consent,* of any man entering into any society, makes him a perfect member of that society, a subject of that government. The difficulty is, what ought to be looked upon as a *tacit consent,* and how far it binds, *i.e.* how far any one shall be looked on to have consented, and thereby submitted to any government, where he has made no expressions of it at all. And to this I say, that every man, that hath any possessions, or enjoyment, of any part of the dominions of any government, doth thereby give his *tacit consent,* and is as far forth obliged to obedience to the laws of that government, during such enjoyment, as any one under it; whether this his possession be of land, to him and

his heirs for ever, or a lodging only for a week; or whether it be barely travelling freely on the highway; and in effect, it reaches as far as the very being of any one within the territories of that government. (1980, pp. 63–4)

As a theory about legitimate authority and political obligation in a nation-state, this account has been trenchantly criticised (see Simmons 1979, pp. 83–100). The simplest point is that for the subject of a state to make the best of a bad thing, by accepting opportunities for survival, does not seem like consent in any meaningful sense, unless there is some straightforward opportunity to renounce the arrangement. At the time when Locke was writing, the turbulent civil unrest of the recent past makes it understandable that he should put a case that would promote stability and order as strongly as possible. However, if we were to put the analogous view as a basis for legitimate organisational authority it would amount to saying that inmates of Auschwitz had an obligation to accept their captors' authority because they accepted the meagre food they were offered.

Nevertheless, Locke's argument is a worthwhile starting point for discussion of organisational authority, because even if his account of tacit consent extends it far beyond what we might accept, nevertheless the basic structure of his argument can be considered without that wide definition. In particular, it may still be that we can start by considering consent as a possible basis for accepting obligations within an organisation, by focussing on the 'common distinction of an express and a tacit consent'.

In fact, of course, although Locke's use of the idea takes it far beyond what is plausible, tacit consent is not uncommon. Feinberg sums up the point: 'That one can consent to another's action without saying "I consent," or indeed without *saying* anything at all, is a perfectly coherent suggestion which finds a hundred corroborative examples in everyday experience' (1986, p. 183). An example given by Simmons applies in the present context:

> Chairman Jones stands at the close of the company's board meeting and announces, 'There will be a meeting of the board at which attendance will be mandatory next Tuesday at 8:00 rather than at our usual Thursday time. Any objections?' The board members remain silent. In remaining silent and inactive, they have all tacitly consented to the chairman's proposal to make a schedule change (assuming, of course, that none of the members is asleep, or failed to hear, etc.). As a result, they have given the chairman the right (which he does not normally have) to reschedule the meeting, and they have undertaken the obligation to attend at the new time. (1979, pp. 79–80)

As Simmons notes, the consent here given is not in any way weaker than consent given by some overt act: it is simply that in certain appropriate circumstances consent is expressed just as well by what is done or not done as by some explicit statement like 'I consent'.

The difficulty is not that tacit consent is less real or less significant than express consent. The difficulty is saying just what amounts to tacit consent.

Locke's far too wide suggestion is one example of how the issue arises, but organisations are full of others. Sometimes, the chairperson at a meeting will invite a formal indication of consent: 'All in favour, say "Aye"'. Then, agreement or consent will be overt and explicit. But sometimes, the request from the chair will be less formal: 'All o.k?'. A nod or a word will express consent, but consent will equally be given by saying nothing. Some present may give express, and others tacit, consent. There are many similar occasions in organisational life, where there is opportunity given to agree or disagree with a proposal, and contextual factors may equate silence to one or the other.

Difficulties arise in a number of ways, even in small-group situations like that. One way is where different parties interpret the contextual factors differently. The person in the chair of a meeting may take something to be agreed by consensus, where some present were waiting for a vote before making their position known. Or one manager circulates a proposal, expecting dissent from those against the proposal, whereas they anticipate a meeting to discuss it, and so say nothing until too late. Again, in some cases, one party will attempt to manoeuvre another into a position where silence will be able to be interpreted as consent, but there are costs to the alternative of open disavowal. Clearly, to some extent, what can be taken as consent will depend on a party's competence, sophistication, and so on.[4] These difficulties are magnified and extended when we go beyond small-group situations to the larger organisation. If we pursue Locke's idea that tacit consent may create genuine obligations to comply with organisational demands, can we give an account of things people in organisations tacitly consent to that legitimates organisational demands on them?

Pursuing an analogy with Locke's contention about wider political obligation would suggest that any sort of participation whatsoever in the activities of an organisation amounts to tacit consent to its demands and thereby gives them legitimacy. Then analogous replies are equally at hand as to Locke's argument. In particular, for example, one needs to have some alternative available in order to be construed as giving tacit consent to an arrangement. For acceptance of an arrangement to amount to consent, alternatives not only have to be conceivable possibilities, but reasonably practicable.

THE AVAILABILITY OF ALTERNATIVES

For citizens of nation-states, the most straightforward alternative they might have rather than accepting current arrangements would seem to be emigration, but often that option confronts clear difficulties (see Simmons 1979, pp. 97–100). The other alternative would be opportunities to modify the arrangement: for example, by voting for a different government. In the case of an organisation, there seem to be two analogous sorts of alternative that people have as reasonably practicable alternatives to participation in its current activities. One is the possibility of leaving the organisation; the other is changing the organisation's activities in a way that makes them acceptable.

Both of these kinds of alternatives can readily be imagined in concrete form. We can easily envisage cases where it is said to people: 'Well, if you don't like it, you can resign', or 'Well, if you didn't like it, why didn't you do something about it?' In each case, an implication may be that the person's failure to act amounts to consent to some arrangement, which to that extent is legitimate in any demands it makes. Tricia might be told that if she does not like the organisation's expectation of her, then she can find a job elsewhere. Or she might be reminded of the policy memo that was circulated several months previously about how to deal with matters of this nature, which – it is implied – she might have contested if she had concerns about the policy.

Clearly, if Tricia is told that she can find a job elsewhere, there are quite significant issues about what is reasonably practicable. Whether leaving the organisation is a reasonably practicable alternative depends on a whole range of things, such as the state of the labour market and people's financial and other commitments.

At one extreme, if George is a financial market analyst with plenty of alternative positions available in equally attractive firms, similar remuneration packages and no problems from having to move house, then it is hard to see why we may not take his continued participation in the organisation as consent to its arrangements. If this particular firm requires its analysts to wear relatively formal attire, then he consents to the requirement if he can go at minimal cost to another firm that does not. We can say that the firm's requirement on him in this respect is legitimated by his consent.

At the other extreme, if Jean is a single mother of three with a mortgage and no alternative work available without a long bus ride that would leave her children unsupervised in the evenings, and the firm requires her to do unpaid weekend overtime or to falsify company records in order to avoid tax, we may well wish to say that the requirement is not a legitimate one. Even if she complies with it, her lack of reasonably acceptable alternatives may mean that her compliance falls short of consent.

Unfortunately, there is no easy way to specify a criterion that will clearly distinguish cases where the availability of alternatives means that people's inaction amounts to tacit consent to an arrangement. We can see the sorts of things that are relevant. In particular, clearly, the costs are important, but so may be the arrangement in question. Having to wear a suit to work may be a matter of less moment than having to work unpaid weekend overtime, or falsifying company records. What is required in the job may affect what alternatives need to be on offer for inaction to amount to consent (Feinberg 1986, chaps. 23 and 24). Individuals who want to assess their own obligations will have to consider what their alternatives were when an arrangement was put in place, and its significance. Others can put it to them that they had other options; if they disagree that they were real or acceptable options, then there is room for discussion and consideration. But, as we noted earlier, there are many occasions in organisational life and politics where there are no rules that define our obligations in a simple, measurable way. Again and again, it is possible to say what kinds of considerations are relevant, but not how to weigh them in a routine, automatic fashion.

Essentially the same thing is true when we consider the possibility not of leaving the organisation but of contesting a policy or arrangement. Freeman and Medoff built on Hirschman's distinction between 'exit' and 'voice' to argue that it is a function of labour unions to provide employees with 'voice' as an alternative to leaving if they do not want to accept an organisation's policy. They suggest that this

> changes the employment relationship from a casual dating game, in which people look elsewhere at the first serious problem, to a more permanent 'marriage', in which they seek to resolve disputes through discussion and negotiation. (1984, p. 94)[5]

Indeed, the idea that unions have a place in organising consent from workers to the arrangements under which they labour has sometimes been used as a basis for criticising them (but cf. Burawoy 1979, pp. 110–13). In principle, at least, however, it seems possible that individuals may have some genuine opportunity to alter organisational arrangements and proposals through collective bargaining with their employer. If they do have genuine opportunity to change things, but refrain from doing so, then it will be arguable that they have tacitly given their consent to the arrangements and are to that extent obliged to comply with them.

While collective bargaining may give employees opportunities to alter things, it is not the only possibility, and for many managerial and professional employees there are clear opportunities to participate in organisational decision-making processes, where that participation will sometimes allow them to alter a policy or a proposal. For other employees also, participatory work arrangements may sometimes give them opportunities for input into decision-making on a range of matters that affect them. The general point is that sometimes there is and sometimes there is not genuine opportunity for people to alter policies and arrangements that affect them. If they have the opportunity, then it is possible that failure to exercise it amounts to consent.

There is the same range of questions here as about 'exit' possibilities. To what extent one's failure to attempt change amounts to consent depends at least partly on the costs of the attempt. Carnevale and Keenan note that there is some evidence for an 'organizational-punishment model of involvement in conflicts' (1992, p. 239). In one study,

> The personnel who were directly involved in workplace disputes, including both employees and managers, were more likely to receive punishments (poorer performance ratings) and less likely to receive rewards (raises and promotions)

than personnel not involved in conflicts. (Carnevale and Keenan 1992, p. 239, referring to Lewin 1987)

Accounts of whistleblowing are replete with examples of individuals who have been victimised for speaking out against organisational policies. If people know that opposition to a proposal will be held against them, then often it will not be clear what to say about their silence. In *Moral Mazes*, Jackall makes observations about the importance of consensus:

> The knowledgeable practitioners of corporate politics, whether patrons or leaders of cliques and networks, value nothing more highly than at least the appearance of unanimity of opinion among their clients and allies, especially during times of turmoil. (p. 53)

He refers to 'the vocabulary of team play', and quotes a manager who would include as part of the definition of 'a team player' that such a person 'agrees to the consensus on a decision even though he might see things differently'. We can envisage pressures on individuals to conform to group decisions, whether as union members in collective bargaining, or as part of a management team, and it is not always quite clear what to say then when an individual opposes the group position initially, but accepts it as the majority position becomes clear. Does that individual consent to the decision?

These kinds of questions are equally significant, and equally difficult, in the politics of the nation-state (see e.g. Wollheim 1962). In what circumstances is an individual morally bound by a decision of the majority? We may be inclined to say that at least if someone had opportunity to oppose it, but did nothing, then their inaction amounts to tacit consent. But what if they reasonably believed that their opposition would not affect the outcome? What kinds of processes can be taken to allow genuine involvement in decision-making?

We have noted that the size of a group can affect its dynamics, and that there may be greater possibilities for communication and participation in smaller groups than in larger groups. When we think of the advertising campaigns of US Presidential elections, or the complexities of voting in most western democracies, or the tortuous path for any policy to become law, we can see a wide difference from the face-to-face politics of a tennis club. The size of a group or organisation is at least a relevant factor in considering the extent to which participation can reasonably be taken to reflect an individual's genuine choices. Thus, Finley's (1983) picture of ancient Athens and de Tocqueville's (1961) account of an early nineteenth-century town show small-scale political arrangements that allowed effective participation by all citizens to an extent that implies that their failure to oppose a policy could reasonably have been taken as consent.[6] Recent political theory has moved toward increased emphasis on participative citizenship everywhere (see e.g. Phillips 1993, p. 76), but in relatively small communities like those of Athens or New England it is more straightforward to see how the ideal might be attained. We can well imagine organisational arrangements which involve issues being explained to people, with them all being given time to consider them, and to put and consider alternative points of view, all taking account of both the importance and complexity of the issues.

However, the differences due to group size could be overstated. We have commented on the quite surprising group conformity effects that were evidenced by the work of Sherif and Asch. Such processes even in small groups make it unclear to what extent individuals' conformity to group opinions can be considered a matter of rational decision-making. We normally accept that genuine consent requires our mental processes to be free from undue influence. Such influence may not be another's deliberate attempt to manipulate us. Feinberg refers to 'the moods, emotions, passions and pains whose demands on our attention can be so peremptory in their several ways that we are, while under their influence, utterly distracted from whatever business may be at hand' (1986, p. 321). It is problematic to what extent we can give genuine consent under such conditions: 'Careful deliberation is difficult at best under such circumstances, and expressions of consent may distort rather than represent the abiding desires of the normal self who will soon return'.

The fact that people can fall short of rational decision-making is central to much of our discussion. Later, we shall consider how it bears on the ethics of communication and influence. In the present context, however, we may note that the problem is again one of degree. Our reasoning and decision-making processes are never perfect. What influences create so great a shortfall from perfection as to mean that we do not give genuine consent to proposals before us? Two bottles of whisky may certainly do so, one glass of wine, not. Where is the line to be drawn? There may be no general answer to the question, but it is once again the sort of question that confronts us in many situations, not just in organisations (see e.g. Schumpeter 1954, p. 253). Despite the inherent imperfections in people's individual and collective reasoning and decision-making, we can imagine examples of effective participative citizenship, and many of us have encountered some. As with other such questions, the important thing may be an awareness of what factors are relevant, and a wariness of quick or simple answers.

ORGANISATIONAL GOALS AND ACCEPTED SCRIPTS

The general implication seems to be that the possibilities for genuine participation in organisations may sometimes allow a reasonable inference of people's consent if they do not oppose some particular policy or proposal. It is true that group dynamics contain substantial pressures making for conformity to majority opinion, but still on occasion we accept that effective participation in group processes and decisions is possible. When it is, then we seem reasonably able to take people's acceptance of decisions as consent. However, even in smaller organisations the fact of consent by organisation members cannot always be relied on to legitimise organisational policies and practices, or the decisions and actions that are bound up with those polices and practices.

So far, then, we still do not have any general presumption that organisational demands and official policies create genuine ethical obligations for organisational members. It is consistent with this to accept that organisational imperatives can be a significant factor in deciding what actions within organisations are ethical. Management texts at best are equivocal about the merits of employee participation in decision-making, broadly on grounds that question its effectiveness in furthering the goals of the organisation (e.g. Robbins and Barnwell 1994, p. 359). Many organisations have specific goals and responsibilities to stakeholders other than those who work in them. There can be tension between those goals and responsibilities, and establishing processes that allow deliberate participation by members. Responsibilities to stakeholders may be important. It may still be that a lack of participative mechanisms within an organisation entails that organisational members do not consent to policies and practices of the organisation. In that situation, it may be necessary to weigh the benefits to stakeholders against the violation of employees' autonomy. Often, those benefits might outweigh the violation: benefits from implementing disease prevention measures in a community may easily outweigh the violation of autonomy of employees of the public health department who were not adequately consulted about the department's implementation process. We noted earlier that consequences of actions are one factor to be considered in evaluating actions. But benefits to stakeholders will not always outweigh violation of the autonomy of organisation members. If they did, that would imply that slavery might be justified by benefits to others. Nor does it mean that lesser violations of autonomy can be ignored. If the public health department would not be significantly hindered in implementation by consulting employees and having them accept the suggested processes, then there may be an obligation for the department to do that.

Even if it is true in many cases that the interests of stakeholders will be enough to justify some course of action, there will be many other cases where the absence of consent by organisation members to some process or decision will be a matter of concern. This will especially be the case where people's decisions and actions are taken more with an eye to their own advancement or power than with a genuine concern for stakeholders.

Where organisational members do have opportunity for participation in the processes of groups where organisational politics is conducted, and where their inaction may reasonably be taken as consent to the arrangements that result, there is still a question how far that consent extends into the detail of the arrangement and its future ramifications. If members of a department accept its relocation to a new site a few suburbs away, does their consent embrace matters about the architecture of the new site? If a hospital gains acceptance of a new way to calculate resource allocations amongst wards, does that extend only to the general principle, or to details of the allocations? If design engineers work on a product, to what extent do they implicitly consent to its being made available to the public?

To some extent, clearly, the answer lies in the terms in which the arrangement is proposed and discussed. Sometimes, the discussion will embrace implications about details yet to be determined, as to whether they are to be further discussed. But sometimes the answer lies in the ideas of scripts and schemas that we noted earlier. Sometimes, acceptance of a certain arrangement implicitly extends to some further details or developments because they are part of a well-understood 'script'. In effect, people may give tacit consent to developments they expect as conforming to the standard script. Problems arise when there are departures from the script. Thus, Frank Camps, the senior design engineer who had worked on the Ford Pinto, expected that management would rectify the problems that created risks. When they did not, then so far as Camps was concerned, that was a departure from what might be legitimately expected.[7]

The phrase used to justify the company position might have been the same as Jackall uses in describing the views of other managers about Joe Wilson's case: 'Authority has the prerogative to resolve technical disputes'.[8] For management to resolve technical disputes may be an accepted script. However, matters where public safety is at risk plainly may raise questions about the applicability of the script. The likely situation when there are such differences of opinion is that organisational authority will prevail, which brings out the gap between what is accepted in organisations and what is accepted in wider politics in most contemporary Western countries. Glazer and Glazer refer to 'a clear definition that corporations are not organized democratically and have limited tolerance for dissent' (1989, p. 19). If so, however, that simply emphasises questions about the moral legitimacy of organisational demands (and raises questions about 'employee rights': see Velasquez 2002, pp. 465–84).

Even where there are appearances of consensual deliberation that elicit consent, there may be problems about the extent to which the consent is genuine. We have noted that if people do not have alternatives, then their inaction cannot be taken to signify consent or to legitimate a proposal or arrangement. However, we need to note that their inaction may not amount to consent even if they do have alternatives. We may say that if people have no alternatives then their inaction does not amount to consent, because consent obtained by force is no consent at all. But neither is consent obtained by deception or fraud, and unfortunately that is often a significant point in organisational politics.

COUNTERFEITING CONSENT

Readers of *The Hitchhiker's Guide to the Galaxy* will recall the Vogons' response to complaints from people on Earth about the proposal to demolish our planet in order to build a hyperspatial express route through our star system:

> 'There's no point in acting all surprised about it. All the planning charts and demolition orders have been on display in your local planning department in Alpha Centauri for fifty of your Earth years, so you've had plenty of time to lodge any formal complaint and it's far too late to start making a fuss about it now.' (Adams 1979, p. 31)

Alpha Centauri is a long way away, for people on Earth. But proposals may be almost as unlikely to attract scrutiny if they are buried in committee papers or long reports. It is often possible to present something to people in a way that they will not object to, because their attention has not been explicitly drawn to some aspects of the matter, or because they have insufficient resources in time or otherwise to examine everything about it. It is possible deliberately to distract people, or to highlight some aspects of a proposal rather than others. Contrivance of apparent consent from others, or behaviour that can subsequently be argued to evidence consent, is a ploy that can often be used in organisational politics. If we consider other sorts of occasions on which such ploys may be used, it seems quite clear that they are not ethically acceptable. Such tactics when used to elicit participation in a sale can void a contract or amount to fraud (McDonnell and Monroe 1952, pp. 177–9). So far as such tactics arise in organisational communication generally, we shall consider them further in Chapter 9. Here, the point is that they do not elicit genuine consent, but only its appearance.[9]

Sometimes, methods of eliciting consent that are accepted as illegal and unethical outside organisations are accepted within them. Pfeffer notes the following example:

> When the Cadillac division was deciding whether to launch the Allante, the price was set at $55,000. There was some question whether the projected volume and profits could be attained with that price: 'Originally, GM's internal staff projected sales of three thousand cars, with a $45,000 price tag. But at that volume and price, the project failed to generate a 15-percent ROI, so the division's answer was to raise both estimates to make the project work on paper.' This internal manipulation of numbers to support one's position is, of course, somewhat unseemly, and besides, one might get caught. (1992, p. 251, quoting Keller 1989, p. 216)

But such manipulation is not just 'unseemly': it is unethical. Used as a means to elicit consent to a proposal, it fails, just as lying about one's intentions fails to get genuine consent from another, and just as lying about the value of a property fails to get genuine consent to a sale. A good many examples of organisational politics amount to no more than that one, in ethical terms: they elicit some expression of agreement or consent without actually gaining consent that is meaningful in ethical terms.

The point is significant amongst other reasons because it brings out the importance of legitimacy in organisations. The idea is not only relevant to academic theory, but of practical importance in management. Pfeffer says that

> Power is most effectively employed when it is fairly unobtrusive. Using rational, or seemingly rational, processes of analysis helps to render the use of power and influence less obvious. Perhaps as important, decisions are perceived to be better and are accepted more readily to the extent that they are made following prescribed and legitimate procedures. (1992, p. 249)

This 'appearance of legitimacy,' he says, 'is crucial for attracting support and resources' (p. 250). And so, he notes, there often is emphasis on presentation of information to justify a decision in terms that those involved will accept as right and proper: 'decisions made either without information or simply by directive from above do not have the legitimacy or produce the same level of comfort as decisions that are made on the basis of information and analysis'.

Appropriate forms of deliberation can elicit agreement and support from those who are involved. We noted that group and organisational norms are closely tied to perceptions of legitimacy, and behaviour is closely tied to those norms. But legitimacy may be counterfeited. Whether or not there are other avenues that may legitimise organisational calls on individuals, it is difficult to see how arrangements can be legitimate if consent and compliance are elicited through deceptive manipulation of information.

There can be similar general concerns about Pfeffer's account of the use of consultants to further the particular ends of the members of organisations who hire them. As in the preceding example, an appearance of legitimate, well-grounded decision-making is important:

> Because of the need for the appearance, if not the reality, of rational decision processes, analysis and information are important as strategic weapons in battles involving power and influence. In these contests, the ability to mobilize powerful outside experts, with credibility and the aura of objectivity, is an effective strategy. (p. 254)

Pfeffer's words may remind us of Cialdini's comment that 'there is a lot of expert worship in our culture' (1987, p. 156). Unfortunately, as Pfeffer suggests, 'the nice thing about using consultants is that they can usually be relied on to further the decision you have in mind' (1992, p. 252). We may then recall also Cialdini's suggestions about how to be ethical at the same time as being effective in the use of influence. One option is to return to Cialdini's idea about 'trigger principles' and the idea that 'it is objectionable to import and use the trigger if it is not an inherent part of the setting'. Here, the implication would be that it may well be perfectly appropriate to use reports by expert consultants to bring about acquiescence to an organisational proposal, if those experts arrive at their conclusion in a detached, objective way, but not if they are unduly influenced in their recommendations by the wishes of the parties in the organisation who hire them.

Overall, we can say that if agreement and compliance are elicited by deception and fraud then they no more amount to genuine consent than they would in a court of law, and they no more create ethical obligations on people than they would create a legally binding contract. In fact, it seems plausible to suggest that so far as techniques of manipulation and deceit are used to elicit agreement and compliance, they have the opposite effect: they render problematic any arrangements they are used to sustain. Again, this raises questions about deceptive persuasion to which we must return below.

In regard to our present concerns, we are left still with the question what is necessary for an organisation's demands to be morally legitimate. Some things clearly are ethically unacceptable, but equally clearly some processes like the example from Simmons outlined above do genuinely elicit consent.

We have noted that an organisation's purposes may sometimes legitimate its demands, but that even then there can be questions about the legitimacy of pursuing them in a particular way. We have not considered all other possible grounds that may allow organisational arrangements to be considered legitimate to an extent that they are morally binding on employees, but so far we have reached this point: there are some occasions when individuals have opportunities to go elsewhere, and some occasions when they have opportunities to change things, to an extent that means they are morally bound to comply with organisational policies if they do not take the options available to them. We cannot spell out some clear, measurable criteria for discerning when people's situation is like that, but we can give an idea in broad terms of the sorts of things involved.

In some circumstances, then, people may have obligations because of organisational arrangements they have consented to, either expressly or tacitly. But organisational arrangements often do not have people's consent in any meaningful way. They just accept them, because the organisation insists on the arrangement, and the people need the work. Does their participation in the organisation ever mean that such an arrangement creates moral obligations on people to comply with its demands?

LEGITIMACY WITHOUT CONSENT?

At the outset of the chapter we noticed two approaches to justifying political authority in a nation-state. The first was to say that individuals have obligations to comply with the law of their community because of the benefits they receive from being members of it. The second was to say that in some fashion or other they consent to the requirements. It seemed as though the second approach was likely to have more force, but having seen the difficulties that arise for it as a general account, it is worthwhile to consider the first approach a little further.

Recent political theory has thrown forward one notable alternative to the sort of consent theory that was articulated by Locke and his successors. It is most fully and clearly shown in the work of John Rawls, and says, in effect, that legitimate political arrangements can create obligations on citizens not because they consent to them, but because the arrangements are part of an overall fair system. The principles are justified not because people do in fact consent to them, expressly or otherwise, but because they are principles to which rational people would agree if they did not know what their own specific personal advantages and disadvantages would be as they came to live their lives in a community governed by the principles (Rawls 1972, pp. 11–17 and 118–50).

Once more, it is beyond us to present in detail either Rawls's view or the many discussions of it that have appeared since its publication.[10] Once more, also, the view's main form addresses justice and legitimacy in civil society as a whole, and a first question is whether a similar approach can cast light on legitimacy in organisations. With this, there is some difficulty. Rawls himself notes that the principles he articulates 'may not work for the rules and practices of private associations or for those of less comprehensive social groups' (1972, p. 8). Although Rawls's basic conception is simple, as we have stated it, he uses it to yield more specific principles that seem as though they may have limited applicability to organisations. For example, a major principle of his theory is that 'social and economic inequalities are to be arranged so that they are both (a) reasonably expected to be to everyone's advantage, and (b) attached to positions and offices open to all' (1972, p. 60). The thrust of Rawls's position is to defend equality, in particular by seeking principles that people would accept before they knew what their own individual talents or disabilities might be. That major principle is then derived on the basis that people would accept some inequalities only if doing so made everyone better off. But in Rawls's approach, inequalities within an organisation might not need to make everyone in the organisation better off, so long as the organisation's internal arrangements conformed to an overall scheme which was to the advantage of everyone in the community.[11]

We have seen in Chapter 4 that there are difficulties in establishing the legitimacy of arrangements in organisations by assuming that legitimacy may derive from the legal and political institutions of the surrounding community. It is difficult to see how even legitimate social institutions could ensure detailed legitimacy for all of the internal arrangements of organisations within the community. The institutions of the surrounding community might be able to rule out certain general forms of illegitimacy, such as discrimination on grounds of race, gender, or the like, but there seems to be no possibility of an exhaustive list of all forms of illegitimacy that might be proscribed, and positive efforts to transmit legitimacy from surrounding institutions into the organisation seem to founder on the necessary vagueness of any positive prescriptions, which leave open matters of detail to be decided within the organisation. These arguments seem to apply even if the institutions of the surrounding community were to satisfy Rawls's requirements for justice and legitimacy.

Nevertheless, despite Rawls's note that his principles may not apply to internal rules of organisations, we might borrow his general approach and consider adapting it to legitimacy within organisations. Rawls's central idea is that of 'justice as fairness'. The detailed exposition in *A Theory of Justice* may be considered a way of working out this idea. Then we may consider whether the same broad idea could have application to organisations. We have accepted that in many cases organisational arrangements are not justified by people's consent to them, because it cannot reasonably be claimed that there is such consent, express or otherwise. It could still be that the arrangements are legitimate and individuals in the organisation obliged to conform with them because they are in some sense fair arrangements. Thus, for example, we might suggest that legitimate arrangements require people to be fairly rewarded or acknowledged for what they do, and that the requirements that are made of them take account of their abilities and their other commitments outside the organisation.

This is, in many respects, an appealing suggestion. In particular, it overcomes a difficulty of the consent theory of legitimacy that people might unreasonably withhold their consent. We noted in Chapter 2 that we tend to misperceive our own situations compared to others', and our difficulty about being objective and impartial in assessing our own entitlements could well mean that we would not assent to a set of arrangements because we believed that it was not fair to us, even though a detached external observer might believe that it was. It seems unreasonable to deny that arrangements are legitimate for lack of consent, when that consent is unreasonably withheld. It would overcome that difficulty to say that arrangements are legitimate if they are ones that people would reasonably consent to.

However, it is clear what problems there are with this approach. Difficult though it is to say in particular situations whether people have at least tacitly given their consent to some set of arrangements, we have some idea what sorts of things are relevant: whether they had some alternatives or an opportunity to oppose the arrangements, whether they were given reasonably detailed and accurate information about them, whether the details of implementation were as might reasonably have been expected, and the like. Room though there clearly is for differences of opinion in these sorts of matters, those differences may well be dwarfed by differences about what people might reasonably consent to. Consider remuneration, for example. How do we compare the reward that is deserved for effort with the reward that ought to be given for skill and talent? To attain a given result may cost one person great effort: another, who has more skill, may attain the same result for much less effort. Then should we pay just for the market value of the result? But market values within organisations are quite imponderable. The production department may achieve great results which cannot be sold because of errors in design or marketing. And so on.

Or go back to Tricia's situation. We started to consider the extent to which the demands of her role prescribe certain obligations for her. These are part of the organisational arrangements whose legitimacy we may be considering. Suppose there was a rule that any employee with a grievance must take it up in the first instance with her direct supervisor, or else with that person's supervisor. It could be said that people might reasonably consent to such an arrangement. But it might preclude Tricia from helping Jennifer. Then it might be said that cases of alleged sexual harassment need some special provisions. This, too, might be reasonable. But there is room for argument in such things, to an extent that means the idea of arrangements that people might reasonably give consent to does not assist us in determining what are legitimate demands, if we are trying to decide that in order to decide what people's obligations are in a particular situation. It may be true that legitimate arrangements are ones that it would be reasonable for people to consent to, but that truth does not assist us in working out our obligations: there will be just as much contestation over what people might reasonably consent to, and we may as well consider directly what people's obligations are. It is still true that fairness is an important ethical consideration. There will be many cases where we have to take account of what is fair to people, in deciding what to do. But there seems no good prospect that we can often determine what are overall fair arrangements within organisations, that we might reasonably expect people's consent to, and then refer to those as a basis for determining what could legitimately be required by official authority.

SUMMARY

In sum, then, we have been unable to find a clear general basis for legitimacy of organisational demands. We can see some factors that are relevant from time to time, such as the legitimate prescriptions of the surrounding community, the extent to which members of the organisation have given express or tacit consent to the demands, and the fact that some obligations may derive from benefits which members obtain from the organisation. However, neither separately nor together do these various factors give us a comprehensive account of organisational legitimacy.

We came to this discussion by way of an effort to discern what ethical obligations there are on people in organisational politics. The suggestion we have been considering is that legitimate authority in organisations may provide some clear guidance to people about their obligations. At the very least, however, it is clear that it cannot provide a general solution to problems of conflicting obligations within organisations. Prescriptions by the legitimate institutions of the surrounding community; consequences of the various alternatives; consent that some arrangements have won from organisational members; all may be relevant considerations. However, they will not provide any straightforward, routine way to address hard ethical choices in organisational politics. The requirements of organisational authority and one's organisational role will be things to take into account, but they will be vague enough and contestable enough to provide no final court of appeal.

It therefore seems that to ascertain what ethics requires of us in a particular situation, generally we shall have to look at a number of considerations. The sorts of factors we have considered will be included amongst them. However, in the next chapter I suggest that they will also importantly embrace obligations of interpersonal loyalty.

NOTES

1. The weight that might be attributed to traditional arrangements is seen in Charles Dickens, *The Chimes*:
   'O let us love our occupations,
   Bless the squire and his relations.
   Live upon our daily rations,
   And always know our proper stations'.
2. There are notable exceptions amongst nation-states, as in some modern Islamic countries, and there may also be special organisational cases like churches or other religious organisations, but we can put those aside here.
3. See Hobbes (1968), Part II, Chap. xvii, p. 227; Locke (1980), Chap. VIII, p. 52; Rousseau (1947), Book I, Chap. vi, p. 15.
4. For a comprehensive account of these and related issues about consent, see Feinberg (1986), chaps 22–26.
5. Hirschman first develops the distinction between exit and voice in Hirschman (1970): see also Chapter 6 below.
6. Finley notes elsewhere that the point about Athens is not affected by the fact that 'citizen' had a meaning that today would be considered highly restrictive in excluding slaves, women and others.
7. How organisational members' expectations may be formed and sustained about various sorts of organisational matters has been examined in literature about 'psychological contracts': see, for example, Donaldson and Dunfee (1994) and Rousseau (1995).
8. Glazer and Glazer (1989, p. 19) refer to Jackall (1988) in making this suggestion; for the case, see above, Chapter 1, pp. 15–16.
9. The title of this section, 'Counterfeiting Consent', is drawn from the title of chap. 22 of Feinberg (1986): 'Consent and its Counterfeits'.
10. One collection which draws together some notable discussions is Daniels (1989).
11. Cf. Rawls's comments on free trade: Rawls (1972), p. 99.

6. Individuals, Groups and Loyalties

We are still confronted by the question what ethics requires of Tricia. The various different sorts of considerations we have examined may all be relevant to what someone ought to do: what is prescribed by official authority, what she has agreed to, what others expect of her, and so on. However, we have so far touched only briefly on Tricia's friendship with Simon and the potential significance of interpersonal loyalties in organisational politics. There has been some hint of such things in the suggestion that some issues about obligations and legitimate requirements may be more straightforward when analysed in terms of specific mutual agreements and undertakings within small groups, than when they are considered by reference to abstract authority or general norms. However, we must now look more closely at some fundamental issues about how official organisational requirements interact with obligations that emerge from direct interpersonal relationships and interactions. Added to this is the related issue of how personal loyalties interact with general moral obligations.

OBLIGATIONS OF LOYALTY

The importance of people's actual expectations is a prominent theme of our discussion: the need to accept people's real understandings and expectations rather than idealised or assumed understandings and expectations. We have noted that although consent may create real obligations, consent cannot be assumed without genuine attention to the facts of the case. Our later discussion about communication and influence will also emphasise the importance of people's actual intentions, expectations and understandings. We ought not assume intentions or understandings or expectations that ideal or even typical agents might have in that situation, provided that we have reasonable opportunity to check what the reality is.

This approach is associated with the view that we have a general obligation to respect persons as autonomous decision-makers, who nevertheless have finite capacities with often predictable limitations. It attempts to integrate the fact that our special capacities and aspirations set us apart from other beings we know of, but that we still are part of a physical and biological order, with associated limitations on our cognition and decision-making.

106

In certain respects this approach may remind us of an approach which emphasises the importance of 'the historical self' in moral decision-making. That term is used by George Fletcher at the commencement of his book *Loyalty: An Essay on the Morality of Relationships,* to call attention to the fact that 'we all live in networks of personal and economic relationships – of friends and acquaintances, of families and nations, of corporations, universities, and religious communities' (1993, p. 3). Fletcher's emphasis is more especially on the social realities of our existence, and less on our psychological limitations, but it is once more an emphasis that we need to take account of those realities rather than assume an idealised human nature or an idealised human society.

In particular, as Fletcher notes, this emphasis runs counter both to Kantian and to utilitarian moral views. While Kant's ethical views are often seen at the opposite end of the theoretical spectrum from the utilitarianism of Bentham and his successors, nevertheless they share basic ideas of impersonality and detachment. For Kant, 'the good will' that lies at the heart of ethics must eschew any laws which are 'merely empirical' (Kant 1964, chap. II, p. 76). Duty is derived from universal reason, not from any accidents of an individual's own situation. For utilitarians, our duty is to achieve the greatest happiness for all; each person's happiness to count with equal weight (see e.g. Sidgwick 1907, pp. 382, 385–6). It has been a problem for utilitarians to account for the feelings of special obligation we have to members of our family and others to whom we stand in close personal relationships, since in their view we ought to be quite impartial in counting the worth of different people's happiness. Kant, Bentham and their successors have ways open to them to accept some special obligations that people have by virtue of their close personal relationships. For example, there may be obligations that stem from undertakings that we have given to those close to us, or we may have better opportunities for enhancing their happiness (e.g. Sidgwick 1907, pp. 257–9, 437). Nevertheless, their views pull in a different direction than a view which endows our relationships with some special ethical status.

For many in modern times, it seems that accepting the latter is tantamount to favouring ourselves over others, and that this is contrary to basic moral requirements (see e.g. Baier 1958, Falk 1965 and Rachels 1995, chap. 6). On the other hand, to emphasise the significance of our social relationships is contrary also to some dominant modern economic theory which unashamedly accepts self-interested behaviour. Around the same time as Kant and Bentham were writing, so was Adam Smith. He is widely credited as the founder of a tradition which accepts as right and proper those efforts we make to foster our own interest, on the basis that our efforts to promote our own interests will enhance the interests of all, so long as those efforts are embedded in social and economic arrangements which minimise the effect of traditional social ties. We may not wish to attribute to Adam Smith himself all the views that have been widely promulgated under the *laissez-faire* banner, but it does at least seem as though during the two hundred years since he wrote there has been a widespread acceptance that productive and efficient economic arrangements depend on participation in markets by separate and independent agents.[1]

In general, then, there has come to be a dominant emphasis on such virtues as neutrality, impartiality and detachment, which can be contrasted with an earlier emphasis on such virtues as fidelity, loyalty and devotion as the primary basis for social arrangements (see e.g. Bloch 1965). In various ways there has been a modern Western tendency to decry loyalty as a moral virtue. However, that tendency has not gone unquestioned. The uncritical acceptance and use of market mechanisms of the type associated with Adam Smith's name have been discussed by Albert Hirschman in *Exit, Voice and Loyalty*, where he contrasts the 'exit' mechanisms of economics with the 'voice' processes of politics (1970, pp. 15–20).[2] Voice mechanisms involve parties who have concerns about their treatment by another maintaining their relationship with the other, stating and explaining concerns, and seeking remedy, rather than just leaving the relationship for an alternative. To that extent, they can be said to display loyalty to the other, and such loyalty has some good effects, allowing the other time and opportunity to remedy shortcomings (Hirschman 1970, esp. pp. 79–80).

More broadly, loyalty could be the central focus for a set of ideas and approaches to social relationships which stand in contrast to a dominant view about the importance of impartiality and detachment in social and economic arrangements. In discussing our earlier example, we have already alluded to the possibility that Tricia might have loyalty-based obligations either to her friend Simon or to her organisation. For us, the implication is that loyalty might be an important general source of obligation in organisational politics.

However, there is room to consider carefully how loyalty might work. In Hirschman's view it is important that exit remains a background possibility: 'the chances for voice to function effectively as a recuperation mechanism are appreciably strengthened if voice is backed up by the *threat of exit*' (1970, p. 82). This view, that it is important for the possibility of exit to remain in the background, is associated with the possibility that things will improve. Consider the situation for a member of an organisation, who is struggling with processes in the organisation that are somehow problematic:

> As a rule, then, loyalty holds exit at bay and activates voice. It is true that, in the face of discontent with the way things are going in an organisation, an individual member can remain loyal without being influential himself, but hardly without the expectation that *someone* will act or *something* will happen to improve matters. That paradigm of loyalty, 'our country, right or wrong,' surely makes no sense whatever if it were expected that 'our' country were to continue forever to do nothing but wrong. (1970, p. 78)

If we accept that view of loyalty, there may be no fundamental conflict between demands of loyalty and demands of Kantian or utilitarian morality. A Kantian or a utilitarian might reach a view about what their obligations will be if present trends continue, but suspend action until more certain of the future. Each could in one way or another justify postponement of exit behaviour to allow things to be repaired, to allow good and virtuous behaviour to recommence. Is that all that loyalty means?

At least in some cases, loyalty seems to require more than that. If we think about some of our closest personal relationships, it may be argued that sometimes in these it is appropriate to be *unconditionally* loyal. A parent's loyalty to a child may include a hope that they will try to return to virtue, but it need not be tied to that hope. The loyalty of a spouse may be 'for better or worse', in many senses.

Here, admittedly, we enter an area of controversy and complexity. In some views, we ought not remain loyal to a person, a group, or a cause that is quite devoid of virtue. Proper loyalty, in this view, is conceived along the lines suggested by Hirschman, where proper loyalties grow out of some virtue in their objects, and at best only delay abandonment of objects which lose their virtue. The general difficulty about loyalty is reflected in Ewin's comment that to a significant extent loyalty seems to require 'a setting aside of good judgement' (1992, pp. 411, 415). Considering the sort of approach that is suggested by Hirschman's formulation,

> I might stick with the group through the hard times, and I might do so because its past record suggests that good times will come again. But if that is why I do it, then I am simply a wise investor – loyalty would be called on to explain why I stick with the group despite the fact that all I see ahead is persecution and further hard times. (Ewin 1992, p. 412)

If apparently loyal behaviour really just reflects different assessment of risk, it is simply 'wise investment': not some basic commitment to the object of loyalty.

'Unconditional' loyalty may seem problematic, but we need not imagine loyalty to be unconditional in order to find some tension with many orthodox accounts of rationality and morality. Loyalty may just go beyond what is reasonably justified on the evidence. If I do, then in being loyal, I 'set aside good judgement'. While it may seem problematic that we should ever set aside good judgement, a moment's reflection is enough to remind us of many cases where we would think that virtue may not revolve around good judgement: all kinds of love and spontaneous affection and commitment to an ideal may draw approval, whether or not they emerge from considered judgement. What matters seems often to be the object of love or affection, or the nature of the ideal. Then Ewin may well be correct in suggesting that whether loyalty is a good thing depends on what it is to (1992, p. 418; 1993, p. 41). Loyalty to the Nazi party may not be a good thing, but loyalty to an errant child may be. We have alluded to individuals, groups and causes as possible objects of loyalty, and it may be that the sort of thing that is an object of loyalty will affect whether the loyalty is a good thing or not. For our purposes, in organisational politics, there are perhaps two particular cases that need consideration. The first is loyalty to other specific individuals in the organisation, while the second is loyalty to the organisation itself.

LOYALTY TO INDIVIDUALS

We can imagine various cases where loyalty to individuals may be important in ethical discussion, notably including loyalty to close family members, but perhaps the case most relevant to us in the context of organisational politics is the loyalty involved in friendship. Many writers from Aristotle onwards have discussed friendship, and it has become a case particularly considered in criticisms of Kantian and utilitarian ethics (see e.g. Cooper 2001, p. 582).

It seems clear that friendship is an important good for human beings. It is hard to conceive how we might all live our lives in a completely friendless way. Certainly, friendship seems to come in degrees and sorts, as implicit in phrases like 'old friend', 'good friend', 'best friend' or 'intimate friend'. In each case, the additional term seems to add to our understanding of the particular relationship being referred to, and to tell us more about the sort of commitment and loyalty that it might justify. People may well differ in their capacities for one or another sort of friendship, and different sorts of friendships may have different merits. But they seem to have certain important characteristics in common. One is that they further our knowledge and understanding of ourselves and of the world in general. Clearly, we care for our friends, but that is not all: 'the caring within a friendship is built up on a basis of knowledge, trust and intimacy' (Blum 1980, p. 69). Friendships allow us to engage with others in greater or lesser degrees of intimacy that go beyond the requirements and scripts of ordinary social intercourse – beneath the activities of 'impression management' – to explore our feelings and inclinations and understandings to an extent that would not be possible otherwise. However, they do so only by virtue of another characteristic they have, the fact that they involve some commitment to the particular individuals who are our friends, which goes beyond the sort of general commitment we have to other people. It is because that sort of commitment seems to involve special rights and duties that are not fully accounted for by Kantian or utilitarian ethics that friendship has proved such an important case in assessing those views.

Certainly, our friendships may be intermingled and overlap with relationships that have other characteristics as well that are sources of duties and rights. I may have made a promise to a friend that creates an obligation for me and a right for her in a way that is broadly similar to the way promises generally create rights and obligations. The fact of friendship itself may create expectations that friends have of one another, which they need to take account of in shaping their actions, as they might need to take account of others' expectations (Sidgwick 1907, p. 258). An act of consideration for a friend may give him more happiness than a similar act would for another, so that utilitarians who try to achieve the greatest happiness overall would prefer the act for a friend to that for another. And so on. But it does not seem as though the reasons that friendship give me for acting are reducible in any straightforward way to such considerations. There is at least a plausible case for saying that the obligations of friendship are special, because of the way they have particular others as their focus.³ If you are my friend, and need help, then it is natural at least to suggest that some degree of obligation for me to provide that help is built into the fact of friendship, implicit in the statement of friendship, aside from expectations or consequences.

It is therefore not surprising that discussions of friendship address some of the general questions about loyalty. In particular, for example, there is a question about the extent to which true friendship revolves around friends' virtues. Aristotle says that 'the perfect form of friendship is that between the good, and those who resemble each other in virtue' (1934, VIII, iii, p. 461). While it seems clear that there can be important and valuable friendships where neither of the friends is perfectly virtuous (otherwise, perhaps, there would be far fewer important and valuable friendships), there is the same question as with loyalty in general to what extent one ought to maintain a commitment to a friend whose behaviour falls short of virtue.

An example of that sort of question about friendship arose in our earlier discussion. Tricia and Simon are friends, but Jennifer comes to Tricia with allegations of sexual harassment by Simon. To what extent ought Tricia be moved by her friendship with Simon, given the suspicions that are raised by Jennifer's allegations?

A number of writers on business ethics have noted that friendship is an important part of life in organisations. Solomon comments that 'obvious as we might find the importance of friendship, it is a truth that too easily escapes our attention in the day-to-day workings of business and in the more abstract worries of ethics' (1994, p. 463). From accepting the importance of friendship it seems a natural extension to accept also that friendship generates obligations. Velasquez refers to an 'ethic of care', which accepts that 'we have an obligation to exercise special care toward those particular persons with whom we have valuable close relationships' (2002, p. 125). However, he notes that 'the demands of caring are sometimes in the conflict with the demands of justice' (p. 127), and Solomon comments more generally that 'the role of friendship in the good life, like the role of friendship in business life, is complex and interconnected with a great many other concerns and responsibilities' (1994, p. 465). Solomon gives the case where a meeting is scheduled unexpectedly, in conflict with plans for lunch with a friend. How do we weigh priorities and obligations? In such a case we can imagine a variety of factors at play: the purpose and importance of the meeting, and of the lunch; the extent to which it will put out one's friend to cancel the engagement; and so on. We may reasonably weigh in the balance the disappointment we ourselves would feel, but may also feel caught to some extent in a conflict of obligations.[4]

Tricia's case brings out this point more strongly, because of the seriousness of what is at issue. She herself has some substantial interests at stake, but even they do not seem so important as the concerns that Jennifer has, if what the latter says is accurate. The difficulty is at least in part that we do not have clear assurance of how accurate it is. It is just at that point that Tricia's friendship with Simon seems as though it may need to be given some weight. In general terms, it seems plausible to suggest that her friendship ought to make her slower to accept the allegations than she might be otherwise. It does seem to be part of friendship that we have some faith in our friends, other things being equal. Because we know about the complexities of human motivation, the ambiguity and vagueness around interpretations of people's behaviour, and the like, it seems as though we have some obligation to give friends the benefit of some doubt in such situations.[5]

On the other hand, it may be contended that in a situation like Tricia's, duties of neutrality and impartiality come to the fore. While arguing succinctly for acceptance that demands of friendship often create obligations of a different type from Kantian or utilitarian morality, and noting that often the obligations associated with friendship run counter to impartiality, Blum suggests that 'institutional-role contexts are ones in which impartiality is demanded of us' (1980, p. 49). Thus, for example, judges in courts of law have an obligation to be impartial, an obligation that revolves around their institutional role. If a judge has a special connection with a party to proceedings, then there is an obligation on the judge to step aside, and similarly, Blum suggests, with a number of other roles, such as a captain of a ship, a doctor or a nurse (p. 47).[6] We can think of many others. In each case it seems to be an explicit role requirement to act impartially or else to step aside. May that be true of someone in a position like Tricia's?

Here, we can accept Blum's general suggestion that impartiality is a requirement of a significant number of institutional roles, but still feel that it may not be a requirement on Tricia. For it is at least arguable that she is not, in the context of this issue, bound by any specific role requirements. As we noted in Chapter 4, organisational role requirements are often vague and ill-defined. Some requirements may be clear, but it is not at all clear to what extent there is a general duty of impartiality for people in a position like Tricia's. There may well be organisational roles like that of personnel manager or staff counsellor where there is such an institutionally defined role requirement, but it is less plausible to suggest that it is inherent in all organisational roles.

To some extent, it will be necessary here as it is elsewhere for someone in Tricia's situation to take account of the actual expectations of people around her, with some special emphasis on any expectations she has some responsibility for having fostered or maintained. Nevertheless, that does not seem to lead to any general obligation of impartiality. For her and for most people in organisations there is no clear general requirement of impartiality. There may be duties of impartiality in certain respects, as a clerk in a public utility may have an obligation to treat all consumers equally or a company secretary may have a duty not to favour some people more than others with detailed information about a company's plans, but their duties of impartiality then extend just to those others of a specified class: consumers or potential investors, for example, not necessarily to other members of their own organisation.

The reason for this is straightforward. We cannot live worthwhile human lives as members of organisations apart from such goods as friendship, and such goods place special demands on us. We can circumscribe certain defined areas of activity with requirements of detachment and impartiality, but not everything we do. Judges may be and must be impartial with parties who appear in court, but not with everyone with whom they come in contact. Organisations will vary in their formality and the amount of time that people spend carrying out activities *qua* organisational members, but work organisations and many others involve a great deal of people's time and effort. To require detachment and impartiality of everything that people do *qua* organisational members would stunt our lives by depriving us of important goods in these demanding activities. (This is part and parcel of the fact that informal structures and arrangements are of fundamental importance in understanding organisational life, of the fact that organisational politics is an inevitable part of that life, and that it can be a constructive part of that life.)

If that is correct, it suggests that in organisations the demands of friendship can sometimes run counter to requirements of impartiality and neutrality. Where matters involve our friends, in situations like Tricia's, we may be called on to suspend judgement to an extent not required of us in other cases. We do not have to imagine only cases where some misconduct is alleged. In the next chapter we shall consider a wider range of issues that revolve around evaluation of evidence and drawing conclusions, but here we may note that such issues are common in organisational politics, embracing not only claims about what people have done or not done, but also matters where policy positions have to be decided on. For example, in other situations we may have to consider giving friends the benefit of the doubt not when they have had accusations made against them, but in cases where they have taken a position on a policy issue. Where there are contentious issues being discussed and debated, and a friend has taken a clear position on them, our friendship may at least in some cases justify us accepting their position as our own. We may do so in some cases because we are once more giving them the benefit of the doubt, in this case believing that they must have considered the issue with due care and information, before coming to their position. In other cases, we may simply accept that our interests are bound up together, and that we ought to rise or fall together. The general point is that one way or another, in various cases, friendship can make a difference, and can properly lead us away from impartiality and detachment.

This account accepts that friendship does indeed warrant the sort of loyalty that involves to some extent 'a setting aside of good judgement'. We have noted that friendship comes in different degrees and sorts, and that alone implies that friendship does not normally justify all setting aside of good judgement. If friendships vary in degrees and sorts, then so it seems will the extent to which one ought to set aside good judgement for a particular friend. However, it does seem as though in many cases we ought to set it aside to some extent. That does not mean that in a position like Tricia's we would be justified in flying in the face of the evidence. It seems reasonable to suggest that if we had clear evidence that a friend had acted viciously or that the friend's position on an issue was a vicious one, there might still be things that our friendship would require of us, but not that we maintain the clearly false or bad position. How far we ought to maintain it as opposing evidence accumulates may vary with the strength and nature of the friendship, but it does not seem plausible to suggest that we ought to maintain it indefinitely in any circumstances.

Nevertheless, that we ought to maintain it to some extent seems implicit in the importance and nature of personal relationships in human life. To be someone's friend seems to give them a special place in one's view of things. Other people are an important source of our opinions and views, to be set next to our own experiences and reasoning (Coady 1973). Because friendship tends to involve going beneath the courtesies, simulations and impression management that are a usual part of social life, friends can give us information and understanding that is often worthy of special weight. Admittedly, we must not take that point too far. We may well have friends whose opinions and statements we know to be unreliable on many issues, and we discount them accordingly. Other things being equal, though, it seems reasonable to give some special weight to a friend's view or account of things. At the same time, we have some special obligations to give support to friends in situations where their interests are at risk, and in some cases the two things will go together.

In summary, interpersonal relationships are an important part of organisational life, and in general such relationships will properly include friendships of varying kinds and degrees of intimacy. Any such friendship can involve obligations which are specific to the relationship, even though their force and content will be affected by the nature of the friendship. Implicit in that point is the fact that such obligations may conflict with other general obligations. Tricia certainly has an obligation to Jennifer, and there are some tensions amongst that obligation, her friendship-based obligation, and other obligations as well. There is no general rule we can turn to that will tell us that one sort of obligation always overrides another. Their relative salience and weight will depend upon a host of details, including the nature and history of the friendship as well as details of the other issues. The context of E.M. Forster's expression of hope that he would betray his country rather than his friend is his comment that 'I believe in personal relationships', and the point that personal relationships are not based on contract: 'that is the main difference between the world of personal relationships and the world of business relationships', he says (1965, p. 76). But in organisations, the worlds of personal relationships and business relationships overlap and intermingle, and it is a challenge to balance their conflicting demands.

In particular, for example, the ethical requirements of the situation may be affected by the extent to which people's friendships are known to others. It is possible that Tricia's decision ought to take into account the extent to which Jennifer knows of Tricia's friendship with Simon. As the case is stated, that friendship is not only known to Jennifer, but part of Jennifer's reason for approaching Tricia. That may imply an expectation that Tricia could speak with Simon about the matter. If Jennifer did not know of the friendship, there may be a requirement on Tricia to let Jennifer know about the friendship, as part of a discussion about what best to do. These requirements are implicit in the requirement that we take genuine account of others' actual beliefs and expectations in such a situation. It may be that a prime obligation in many such situations is to clarify people's expectations, perceptions and beliefs before proceeding further.

As we consider such factors, we also need to bear in mind that in organisational politics people may sometimes contrive friendships with others as a means of enhancing their influence or advancing their interests. We noted that friendships vary in their kind and depth, and Solomon points out that Aristotle's category of 'useful' friendship is common in business organisations. He also observes that 'useful friendship' is not necessarily to be condemned, pointing to mentor relationships as a good and worthwhile type of useful friendship (Solomon 1994, p. 467). We can imagine various useful friendships, ranging from such mentor relationships to explicit political alliances. Here, again, it may be important to consider to what extent there may be some obligation to be open about such friendships, but in principle they do not seem to pose any unique ethical difficulties.

The sorts of contrived friendships that may be of more concern are those which result from one person engaging in some form of ingratiation, giving the other person a false impression of sincere regard, in order to gain some favoured treatment. This is just the sort of behaviour which has been analysed in other contexts as one person 'using' another (see e.g. Blum 1973, Wilson 1978). The situation can be difficult to evaluate, for various reasons, including the fact that people's motives may not even be transparent to themselves, let alone to others, and that it may be hard to gauge to what extent the other is really deceived. Certainly, we know that people's motives and intentions can be mixed or not fully worked out in these kinds of situations. It seems plausible to suggest at least that cold-blooded, conscious deception of another in order to obtain favour is unethical, for the same sorts of reasons as other deception is unethical. There seems to be at least some obligation on us to heed the other's expectations and understanding of the relationship, and not to seek or accept favourable treatment that we can see to be based on any false impression the other has. *A fortiori*, there seems to be some obligation on us not to contrive to give the other any such false impression. However, to say more will require the more detailed discussion of honesty and impression management attempted in subsequent chapters.

Overall, the implication is that friendships and other personal relationships may create obligations that are real and have to be weighed against other more general moral obligations. Heeding the demands of friendship is not necessarily irrational or unrestrained behaviour that runs counter to the demands of ethics, but it may be acceding to one sort of obligation over another. This is not to say that actions which emerge from a friendship never can be self-interested or immoral. Plainly they can. If two friends counterfeit documents in order to advance their own careers, their doing so is as unethical as it would be for either of them to so alone. Friends acting together can be guilty of the same sorts of sins and crimes as they might be individually, from avarice to murder, and of others besides, such as collusion or conspiracy to commit such crimes. It is only to say that personal relationships like friendship can give rise to genuine moral obligations, to be set beside others when deciding what one ought to do, all things considered.

LOYALTY TO THE ORGANISATION

However, even if relationships individuals have with one another can ground obligations of loyalty, there is still a question whether other relationships can do so. Fletcher's and some other discussions of loyalty focus to a significant extent on the moral status of individuals' loyalty to their country, and in the context of organisational politics, similar issues arise about individuals' loyalty to particular organisations.

It seems to be widely accepted that loyalty to one's country might generate some genuine ethical obligations. Opponents of E.M. Forster might weigh such obligations more heavily than obligations of friendship. The tension that his comment highlights is between two putative loyalty-based obligations, and either or both of those might conflict with universal moral obligations. Indeed Tricia's situation, as we have discussed it, could be an example of such a three-way conflict, amongst her obligations to Simon, her obligations to the organisation, and the general moral obligations she has toward anyone like Jennifer who is vulnerable and distressed.

However, the argument we have put to the effect that there are characteristics of friendship and other such personal relationships that ground some important obligations does not obviously carry through regarding commitments to organisations, countries, or the like. Central to that argument is the mutual intimacy of one sort or another that such relationships characteristically involve. It is hard to see how this can have a counterpart in a relationship between an individual and an institutionalised group like an organisation or a nation. There does not seem to be scope either for the intimacy or the mutuality of friendship. It is not clear even how to conceive of mutual intimacy in this case, let alone to argue that it can exist.

That in itself does not show that there can be no obligations of loyalty between individuals and institutions like organisations or nations. It only suggests that the argument given in the case of friendship and other similar personal relationships does not carry through to relationships that may exist between individuals and institutions. However, it is hard to see what different argument could fill the gap.

On the other hand, it may be that even though the argument which applies in the case of individuals does not apply to rather abstract institutional entities like nations and organisations, nevertheless it can be extended beyond two-person friendship to relationships amongst groups of individuals. It is not hard to envisage three-way ties amongst people which involve the same kinds of mutual intimacies as a two-person friendship, and similar ties even among members of some slightly larger groups. A family, a workgroup, a committee and other such groups can sometimes involve the same sorts of mutual intimacy that a two-person friendship can.

In general, it is reasonable to believe that there can be 'common-bond' groups which do not rely for their existence on a shared group identity, so much as on bonds amongst members (Prentice, Miller and Lightdale 1994). However, it is implausible to suggest that all groups require shared affective bonds amongst members. One way or another, it seems that as group numbers increase then the degree of intimacy amongst members must tend to decrease. It seems reasonable to believe that in groups of greater size there can still be mutual commitment, but not the same intimacy as is possible for two-person friendships. The sort of detailed exchange and mutual response involved in that intimacy does not seem possible within groups of much larger size.

We noticed in Chapter 2 that group membership can have major effects on people's decision-making and cognitions, and this is true both of larger and smaller groups. Brown notes evidence for a 'switching' process that might take us in a relatively discontinuous way from seeing ourselves as individuals to instead focussing on our social identity (1988, p. 6, and pp. 226–8). It may need close study of a particular episode to see whether participants orient towards one another primarily on the basis of individual or group characteristics: 'most social situations will contain elements of both interpersonal and group behaviours' (Brown 1988, p. 8). Within organisations, we might expect group memberships to be relatively vague and ill-defined, and interpersonal interactions to have more salience. However, there seems no question that group membership can often be significant. Brown quotes a factory shop steward:

> I went into the army. I had no visions of any regiment to go in or different kind of preference for tank or artillery. But once I was in the artillery, to me that was the finest regiment. Even now it is and I've left the army twenty years ... I think it's the same as when you come into a factory. You get an allegiance to a department and you breed that. And you say, 'fair enough I'm a Development worker', and you hate to think of going into Production ... Once someone gets in a department you've got that allegiance to it. (1988, p. 21)

There can be no doubt that the effect of group membership on people's cognitions and decisions does in fact amount to loyalty to the group, even where the group is an abstract entity, and only in part made up from interpersonal bonds amongst members.

The fact that people do in fact display loyalty to groups and organisations seems unquestionable, but it is still not clear to what extent that sort of loyalty is associated with any genuine ethical obligation. We noted in Chapter 2 that in 'minimal group' studies, group members tend to favour one another, even when their group is essentially a fiction. If we seek some general understanding about the extent to which group affiliations sustain obligations, it seems plausible to believe that some contrary principles of fairness may come into play. One relevant principle of fairness may be that goods and benefits ought to be distributed in ways that are related to people's needs and deserts. That principle suggests that apart from considerations of friendship, which may justify some degree of partiality, and commitments we have given to other members of our group, which are tantamount to promises, we ought not favour some individuals over others simply because the former are members of the same group as we are. We know from social identity theory that we do in fact tend to act in that way, but even as we acknowledge that we do so, we may feel that there are ethical concerns about the fact. It may well be that if I have a longstanding personal relationship with another individual, an old friend, a spouse, or the like, then there may be some special considerations that come into play. But if the only thing people have in common is that they follow the same football team, or have skin of the same colour, then we may ask whether that can justify them preferring one another in the distribution of goods and resources.

This is not to say that people's membership of larger groups may not ground obligations of any sort. Most importantly, it is clear that group membership may ground obligations of a type that we have noted, obligations that emerge from people's reciprocal expectations. This point will occupy us further in Chapter 10. Here, we may note that when people know one another to be members of the same group, they may have interlocking mutual expectations that ground obligations to one another in much the same way that obligations can emerge from conventions such as the convention about which side of the road to drive on. If you and I are members of the same organisation, then despite the fact that we have no close personal relationship, we may have mutual expectations of one another that ground some obligations, depending on the detail of the situation. With some sorts of groups, such obligations will be especially salient because of the nature of the group. Membership of the same political party would be one example. In that case, however, the extent of our mutual expectations may be strongly associated with the voluntariness of membership of the group, tied to the fact that it possesses strong group norms about what is appropriate in some areas of behaviour (such as voting, canvassing, espousal of public positions, and the like). Here, my obligations are tied to such facts as that the group norms and commitments are well-defined and membership of the organisation is quite voluntary. To the extent that group commitments become less well defined or membership less of a free choice, so do membership-based obligations seem to become less.

Thus, we may accept that group membership can bring with it some obligations, but they are not obligations of loyalty to the group analogous to obligations of loyalty one may have to friends and family. By and large, they are obligations to other individuals: not to the group or organisation as such.

SUMMARY

If we are correct so far, then Tricia's situation does involve her in some conflicting obligations, even though she may not have some separate obligation of loyalty to her organisation which is like the obligations of loyalty that people may have to their friends. She still has her general moral obligations towards anyone who is vulnerable and distressed, and her position in the organisation may generate expectations from others that result in some obligations for her. That people can be subject to such complex opposing demands seems clear. Examples can be found in fiction, history and biography from *Antigone* onward.

If the argument here has been sound, loyalty which is based on friendship and such interpersonal relationships may create distinct but by no means overriding obligations. On the other hand, I have suggested, our memberships of groups and organisations do not create distinct obligations apart from our general obligations and our commitments to specific individuals. But there can be difficult interplay between commitments to specific persons, general moral obligations, commitments of principle and memberships of parties.

For example, we have just suggested that, other things being equal, principles of fairness might reasonably counsel us against giving preference to

members of our own group. But in organisational politics, there is one especially notable way in which this issue arises. A great deal of organisational
life revolves around communication and the exchange of information. It was
suggested earlier in the chapter that how one evaluates an accusation against
a friend might reasonably be affected to some extent by the friendship. But
there are many other ethical issues about communication processes in organisations. Suppose that we do accept that there is some such principle that we
ought not favour members of our own group over others, does that apply to
information and communication as much as to distribution of goods and
resources? The implication would potentially be difficult, given the extent to
which organisational politics may involve briefing allies and colleagues about
matters, in meetings or conversations that exclude others. This is a question
to which we shall ultimately return. Before doing so, however, we must
address a series of other issues that arise about communication and exchange
of information within organisations.

NOTES

1. For discussion of Adam Smith's actual views, see Werhane (1991) and (2000).
2. For some discussion built on a similar distinction, between the 'market' and the 'forum', see
    Elster (1986).
3. Although the issues are complex. There are questions to be considered about the way in
    which acting out of friendship is different from acting to achieve some end (see Stocker
    1981), and about the extent to which utilitarians can admit 'agent-relative' reasons and
    consequences into their calculations (see Pettit 1988).
4. Cocking and Kennett (2000) argue that demands of friendship often run counter to moral
    obligations, but it is consistent with this that at least in many cases what is at issue is a
    conflict between friendship and other moral demands.
5. For Aristotle's comment on the extent to which friendship is 'proof against calumny', see
    Aristotle (1934), VIII, iv, p. 467.
6. For some discussion about the case of nurses, see Provis and Stack (2004).

PART THREE

Communication, Expectations and Obligations

7. Ethics and Judgement

We came to consider the nature of legitimate authority in organisations by considering the situation Tricia found herself in when she was approached by Jennifer, a junior employee distressed and telling Tricia of sexual harassment by Simon, a friend of Tricia's. Tricia is pulled in different directions, partly by considerations of prudence or self-interest in the face of obligations she feels, but also by conflicting obligations. We have noted that her obligations might have different sources. One may be Jennifer's vulnerability and need for help, another her loyalty to Simon, others to do with commitments of principle to women's rights or a moral obligation to comply with legitimate organisational demands. How to weigh such obligations against one another is not straightforward. To push the difficulty aside by reference to organisational authority is not a general option, since we have seen that it is difficult to give a clear account of legitimacy in organisations that establishes any obligations created by official organisational authority beyond those general moral obligations that we have as persons. So what ought Tricia do?

For Tricia and for all of us, constantly, in organisational politics, one of our most recurrent difficulties is to come to conclusions on the basis of ambiguous, shifting and conflicting pieces of evidence, in circumstances where some people may be trying to mislead us, others have an erroneous or half-correct view they put to us, and some of the facts about others' intentions and expectations are not yet even fully determinate. Because it is such a fundamental and all-pervasive issue, we explore in this chapter some questions about drawing conclusions in organisational politics, issues about coming to beliefs and points of view within the political process.

ETHICS AND EVIDENCE

The first thing Tricia must do is weigh the evidence. This, undoubtedly, is a skill of organisational politics. It is endemic to life in organisations to be confronted with situations that are unclear, vague and ambiguous. What were Smith's motives in the comments he made at yesterday's meeting? What are Lee's intentions in regard to the departmental restructuring she has ordered? Did Brown support Green in the conversation he had with White about the new computer system? If we show opposition to Sasha's report on the new manufacturing process, will she interpret it as criticism of her? Will it lead her to oppose the new marketing initiative in retaliation? Will new legislation affect production costs for this organisation more than for others? These are sorts of questions that constantly recur. Is there any more we can say about the ethics of belief in such cases?

Some of the issues that we have to deal with in organisations revolve around technical, engineering or scientific questions. In many respects these can be approached in a detached and objective way, to predict possible outcomes and estimate probabilities. But the dynamics of organisations can still lead to difficulty. The *Challenger* space shuttle disaster of 1986 has become a well-known example, where engineers had warned that there was a danger with a seal in the booster rocket in the cold weather that was forecast for the launch. Decision-makers overrode the engineers' qualms and recommendations, because 'previous successful launches had lulled them into believing that the defects were not as serious as their engineers believed' (Glazer and Glazer 1989, p. 10).[1] Other such cases may have to do with consumer safety, employee health and well-being, the impact on local residents of environmental pollution, and the like. Some whistleblowing cases show how such issues can figure in organisational politics.

In some such cases, it seems clear that managers or other decision-makers accept their advisers' estimates about potential outcomes, but deliberately ignore them in making their decisions.[2] We do not need to say much about ethics in that sort of case, where there is a plain moral defect. In other cases, however, as suggested by that quotation about the *Challenger* disaster, their beliefs and expectations about outcomes are genuine but in error. Issues arise both about the experts' estimates and about the conclusions that decision-makers come to on the basis of the experts' advice.

The experts themselves can give some estimates of possibilities and probabilities, but in doing so they have to bear in mind what is relevant from the point of view of the people they are advising (see Graham 1975, p. 51). We can often evaluate their estimates to some extent by referring to accepted intellectual virtues such as detachment and regard for the weight of the evidence. There will be room for error, but the same room as always. However, there will be scope for some other considerations as well. Consider the situation of the scientists who were at work on early atom bomb projects. In the advice they gave, to what extent should they have weighed the uses to which the weapons could be put? More generally, how much should any technical expert weigh the likely effects of technical advice, given reasonable understanding of organisational mechanisms? The scientists had clear official obligations, but for many of them those official obligations were far from the final word. They had to consider how those obligations weighed against others.[3] Here, it might be said, we have an atypical case because of the magnitude of the issues. For the scientists, at least, there were matters to consider like the harm the weapons could do, their possible effects on the war then taking place and the impact on other countries like the Soviet Union. However, the principle seems to be the same. If the magnitude of the issues is relevant, then the experts have to weigh the magnitude of the issues in coming to a conclusion.

What of decision-makers who depend on the experts' advice? *Challenger* officials were both evaluating their engineers' advice and weighing it against other considerations when they went ahead with the launch. Here, the question is whether they did anything ethically wrong. There seems to be no doubt about the wrongness of subsequent victimisation and efforts to cover up. But if we can put that aside, was there a moral error in the decision to go ahead? In some sense, there certainly was an error, but at that point could the decision-makers be accused of an ethical short-coming?

It would be easy to say that, yes, they were clearly wrong because they put things like expediency and reputation ahead of concerns about safety and welfare. But it would require a close examination of the records to be sure of that. We cannot say that risks to safety always take priority over other things: some risks are so small as to be negligible, and as soon as we have admitted that, then we have to admit that some weighing is required. A term like 'negligible' has no clear or well-defined meaning in this context without reference to the actual sorts of risks and costs that are being considered.

Unfortunately, the experiments we noted above by Sherif and Asch, which demonstrated conformity effects even on very basic perceptual judgements, together with subsequent accounts of 'groupthink', have emphasised the sorts of social mechanisms in organisations that can distort decision-makers' judgements and analysis of risk. We do not have to assume that their judgement is distorted by self-interest, far less that they come to an accurate understanding of the facts and then disregard it. In organisations there are substantial social pressures at work which influence people's judgements and estimates of risk.

In that case, we need to be circumspect about attributions of moral blame. We can say that decision-makers ought to be conscientious and so far as possible make judgements and decisions that are detached from considerations of personal interest or commitment, and that they ought to give matters the weight they deserve. However, in many cases errors can still occur. To assume that there is always some ethical shortcoming when they do, would over-simplify the realities of organisational life and devalue the currency of evaluation and blame. To the extent that we are involved in establishing organisational processes and structures, we can try to put in place mechanisms that allow good decisions to be made,[4] but we also need to be aware of the problems.

Such problems occur even with regard to technical issues. However, the problem for Tricia is even more difficult than it would be if Jennifer had come to her to report some technical problem about organisational processes or products. Like very many cases in organisational politics, Tricia's decision requires judgement about quite complex matters of organisational dynamics. There are elements of confidentiality, personal involvement and personal relationships, and there are also just complexities that arise from the social nature of organisational life.

There are some long-held views to be found in the literature to the effect that there are fundamental differences between natural sciences and social sciences (see e.g. Ryan 1973), and there can be some suggestions built on this that the sort of judgement that we have to exercise in organisational politics – and which Tricia has to exercise in the present case – is fundamentally different from technical judgements based on natural science. Here, we need only accept that at least to some extent there are differences because in understanding events within organisations we are very often trying to come to judgements that have an evaluative element: we are at least to some extent assessing other people's decisions and actions as right or wrong, praiseworthy or blameworthy, worthy of support or deserving opposition. At least to some extent, in doing that, we need to understand how things seem from their point of view, what information they have based their decisions on, what their expectations and intentions are, and the like.

Here, we come to a key point for our subsequent discussion. Often, it is difficult to be sure of others' motives and intentions. The point is especially vivid in a case of alleged sexual harassment. Our summary of the case glossed some detail of Jennifer's allegations, but the words of our summary, that Simon 'has threatened Jennifer that if she does not sleep with him then he will give her an adverse appraisal report as her period of probationary employment comes to an end' imply a clear and unequivocal statement from Simon. There are such cases of sexual harassment, but many cases revolve around ambiguous and disavowable statements or actions (see e.g. Gadlin 1991). A *double entendre* may be deliberate, and offensive, but its author may disclaim it as unintentional. On the other hand, one party may interpret another's statements or actions in a different way than intended. It may be difficult to confirm or disconfirm the interpretation without causing offence or hurt.

Sexual harassment cases are a salient example of the difficulty we may have in understanding others' motives and intentions, but the same general sort of difficulty occurs in many other situations. Despite the difficulty, however, the evaluative element often involved in judgements about people's expectations and intentions makes such judgements very important. In the next section we shall focus just on this evaluative element, examining some implications of the fact that judgements may evaluate people's actions as right or wrong, blameless or culpable. Then, in the following section, we shall start to focus more especially on the significance of ambiguity.

DUE PROCESS AND INDIVIDUAL RESPONSIBILITY

Assume, then, that Jennifer is alleging some unambiguous demands and threats. In such cases, it seems important to consider matters about evidence and burden of proof. We can see fairly clearly some sorts of things that need to be taken into account, from analogy with a court of law. Jennifer's allegations would need to be reasonably precise in regard to time and place and exactly what was said and done. It would need to be considered whether there is any other evidence to confirm what Jennifer says, either by way of witnesses or otherwise. These are the sorts of considerations that might come most readily to mind. Such factors would be relevant in other cases where there are allegations of blameworthy behaviour.

Tricia can examine some of these sorts of things without major difficulty. But then we come to a point where the court analogy creates a difficulty. In cases where an accusation is made against someone, court process would require that person to be given clear details of the accusation, and an adequate opportunity to respond. Simon ought to have opportunity to hear the allegations and respond to them. This seems clearly different from technical matters. It seems to derive from requirements of fairness and respect for persons.

In organisations, however, it is not always clear how best to provide for this. How should it happen in the case confronting Tricia? One problem is that despite Tricia's seniority, a factor which partly explains why it is her whom Jennifer has approached, Tricia does not have official organisational responsibility for investigating the matter. There may be various courses open to her, but most obviously she could either approach Simon unofficially, or refer the matter to Simon's superiors.[5]

Here, temptation lies open for Tricia. She could approach Simon about the allegations quietly, in confidence, as a friend. She could avoid imputations of guilt, and offer to help, assuaging her conscience by making arrangements that will satisfy Jennifer also. Or she could quietly approach some senior manager about the issue and pass both Jennifer and the issue on to someone who has official responsibility for it, arranging for her own name to be kept out of it. Described thus, either course might be questionable. On the other hand, described differently, either course of action might be defensible on ethical grounds. She might go to Simon because she believes that she needs to keep faith with Jennifer, and that handing the matter over to someone else would leave room for the issue to be pushed aside. She might hand the matter to another manager because she believes that it needs to be addressed carefully and impartially.

The very fact that either course of action might be defended on ethical grounds reflects the fact that role requirements and considerations of organisational legitimacy do not pre-empt considerations of ethics. It seems as though there certainly may be some cases where the ethical thing for Tricia to do would be to approach Simon directly: not to pass the matter on in some formal organisational way. She cannot avoid the ethical requirement to consider the different options, using her knowledge of the organisation and particular managers in it, and her knowledge of Simon. One general ethical point about organisational politics we can reiterate here, which has continuing relevance in various parts of our discussion: we cannot mechanically, on purely formal grounds, set aside as irrelevant any knowledge we have that bears on an issue. Milgram's subjects could call on their own understanding of pain and its significance, not simply defer to the experimenter. We cannot say 'Well, that is not my job', when an ethical issue arises. This is a kind of thing where in particular cases equally conscientious judges might reach different conclusions on the same evidence, and we have to be careful not to encourage undue zeal just as much as to condone apathy, but the general point is that there is a need here for considered judgement, not for mechanical application of formal rules.

That said, however, we are still back with Tricia's dilemma. Ought she approach Simõn, or go to a senior manager? Given the information we have available, either course might show moral cowardice, but Tricia might also act ethically in either way, and there may be other options. If it were a real case, there might be detail we do not know that would make one choice rather than the other ethically preferable. In principle, we can see the sorts of factors that are relevant. They include the gravity of the issue, the extent to which there are clear, well-established organisational guidelines about processes in such matters, the consequences the different choices might have for Jennifer, and other factors. In Chapter 6 we have already noted that in some circumstances the fact of Tricia's friendship with Simon may be relevant.

In the present context, the emphasis is on the relevance of the sorts of considerations that figure in 'due process' in a forensic encounter. At least in some respects they go beyond what is relevant and required in making technical judgements. Because organisations do not provide the same well-structured environment as a court of law, we cannot finally say what Tricia ought to do, but only note a variety of things that may be relevant, depending on details of the case. They revolve around the fact that when we are making judgements not about inanimate objects but about persons, the judgements are likely to entail praise or blame, so that considerations of fairness and respect are relevant. Analogy with a court would suggest that people ought to be given opportunity to be heard, and that seems to be a reasonable general requirement where clear-cut accusations are at issue. However, it may be affected by such factors as the gravity of the issue compared with the cost of making a suitable arrangement. The ultimate point is only that there is at least one major difference between judgements which may attribute blame to others, and judgements in technical matters: in the former, because the judgements are about persons, there may be requirements of fairness and respect on the process of forming the judgements.

ETHICS AND AMBIGUITY

Thus, if we assume some well-defined facts in the case, we can point to some sorts of quasi-forensic considerations that are likely to be relevant when we are coming to conclusions or making a decision. They will still be relevant in other cases like the cases of sexual harassment which revolve around ambiguous and disavowable statements or actions. However, such cases where there is ambiguity in others' intentions or motives or expectations involve further considerations. Cases of such ambiguity are thrown into sharp relief in harassment cases, but occur in many other situations: they are endemic to organisational politics. Let us therefore now put aside Tricia's case and consider some general issues.

It is clear that ambiguity is important in organisational politics. Fairholm notes that 'using ambiguity' is a power tactic, characterised as 'keeping communications unclear and subject to multiple meanings' (1993, p. 41) and suggests that 'keeping the situation ambiguous allows us to maintain a central position in the communications systems and flexibility in negotiation and decision making', noting that 'in effect, it keeps open a choice that would be closed off were the problem, situation, or language made more explicit' (p. 69). While that is useful as a start in thinking about ambiguity in organisational politics, cases of sexual harassment show that it is not the whole story. In such cases but also in many others, ambiguous or otherwise disavowable communications and actions can be used to avoid blame and possibly to channel blame elsewhere. It is not surprising that survey respondents may give diverse and inconclusive responses to a question about the ethics of using ambiguity as a power tactic (see Fairholm 1993, p. 76), considering the range of possible ways in which it can be used, the situations in which it can be used and purposes for which it can be used.

We can imagine a number of ways in which ambiguity may be deliberate when people communicate. The idea of a message being 'disavowable' is one key one here. It happens not infrequently that we want to know how people will react to a particular idea or suggestion. The same general problem arises in diplomacy, courting, and negotiation of all kinds (see Pruitt 1981, pp. 93–101). A negotiator may be willing to consider particular concessions if they are necessary for settlement, and if the other party is also willing to make certain concessions. In exploring possibilities for concessions, one avenue is for them to offer hints of willingness to concede in a particular direction, without actually doing so. Peters recounted a case of a union–management negotiation where the management negotiator

> conveyed willingness to concede to a five cent raise by *denying* interest in this offer. '"Fifteen cents," he erupted. "You can't really mean it. Why, I wouldn't even offer you five cents."' (Pruitt 1981, p. 175, quoting Peters 1955; Pruitt's italics).

If he said more clearly at this point, 'I offer five cents', he may risk pressure for a higher offer, but he has now maintained a position that allows him to disavow any intention of making an offer, if there is no sign of acceptance from the other party.

Similarly, if we imagine courting behaviour, I might notice an attractive person somewhere nearby, we might exchange a glance or two, and I might then say 'Excuse me, but don't I know you from somewhere?'[6] There is an opportunity for the other to decline further exchange or to extend it, as preferred, but I can disavow any intention of making advances. From an ethical point of view, it is important to be sensitive to any possibilities of giving offence or causing distress, but in principle it is possible for the process to be done in a way that is quite ethical, while still saving my own face if the initiative is declined. Equally, while some writers have contended that the process of negotiation is outside usual ethical constraints (e.g. Dees and Cramton 1991), it seems clear that there are ethical constraints, which most negotiators tend to heed (see Provis 2000a and 2000b).

The same general kind of ambiguous 'signalling' process is common in politics at all levels. Negotiators between two countries at war may explore possibilities for settlement, or two others explore options for a free trade agreement.[7] In domestic national politics, a government may 'fly a kite': hint at possible policy initiatives to see how they are received, but do so in a way that allows them to disavow any intentions about that policy. In organisa-tions, managers may do the same sort of thing: moot a possibility, drop some hints, or the like, and see how people react.

In itself, there seems to be nothing objectionable to this strategy, in politics any more than in courting or negotiation. There seems to be nothing objectionable to seeking out possible reactions to a proposal before deciding to implement it. Nor does there seem to be a problem about doing so in a way that is vague or ambiguous, any more than in courting or negotiation. If someone asks, 'Why not be frank and open, and just put forward the proposal for discussion?', the answer is that often that may be the most appropriate course, and it may often be the best management course to follow, but the point here for the moment is that there is nothing inherently unethical in hinting at a proposal to see what response it receives.

It *can* be unethical, of course. It can be used as a tactic to identify potential opponents, and neutralise them. It can be used as a distraction from other proposals or events. Similarly, ambiguous communication can be objection-able and amount to sexual harassment in some circumstances: the studied *double entendre,* the suggestive gesture, or the like, can easily be offensive or distressing. Equally, a negotiator might hint at a concession as a means of working out the other party's interests, without any real intention of seeking agreement. In that case, the negotiator would violate a 'norm of truth in signaling' that is widely accepted amongst professionals (Pruitt 1981, p. 97, noting that 'bargainers who violate this norm endanger their reputation'). But the fact that it can be unethical does not mean that it is inherently unethical to explore possibilities with ambiguous communications.

If Simon had been doing so with Jennifer, there would still have been special ethical risk. Even if his approaches were less overtly threatening than the description of the case implies, asymmetrical power relationships can make overtures from the more powerful party much more threatening and more distressing than they might be otherwise. Being in a position of power requires sensitivity to such facts. But there are occasions when being in a position of power can make it more, not less, ethical to explore reactions with ambiguous communications. If we accept that it is common for those in a weaker power position to tell those who are more powerful what they think the latter want to know, then a manager who is trying to ascertain what people really think may do so by hinting at a possibility and thereby giving others a chance to respond without their opposing a definite proposal. While such a tactic could be used to identify and neutralise potential opposition, it could also be used to ascertain people's genuine wishes and interests as policy is formulated. That might be done on an individual, one-to-one, basis, or more widely. Equally, when we are working things out with colleagues, we may need to be aware of sensitivities they have, and tread carefully as we explore possibilities. In many ways, this is no more than ordinary tact. True, it might be good for there to be such trust amongst people in the organisation that all communication can take place openly and frankly. However, it is a fact of life that organisations do not always meet that ideal, and then we have to work how to act in an ethical way in an imperfect context. Ambiguous communications can then serve a worthwhile purpose in a range of ways.

AMBIGUITY AND INTERPRETATION

Then what is our position when we receive ambiguous messages? Assume that the situation is not presently affected by any power imbalance between the sender and the receiver of the communication, as it would be between Simon and Jennifer. Assume that you and I are on a more or less equal footing so far as that goes, but that there is some ambiguity in the message I receive from you. I may be the union negotiator to whom you say, 'Why, I wouldn't even offer you five cents', I may be the person to whom you say 'Excuse me, don't I know you from somewhere?', or I may be a fellow manager to whom you drop a hint about a new marketing plan. Are there any significant general ethical points to be made about my situation?

We have already alluded to ethical issues about weighing evidence. When we are receiving deliberately ambiguous communications, however, the situation is a little different, since *ex hypothesi* the full truth is deliberately reserved. To some extent, at least, the responsibility for my conclusions must rest with you, who kept the full facts back. If I fail to understand that you may have been willing to offer a five-cent rise, if I do not see that you may wish to make my further acquaintance, if I disappoint your hopes for advice about the marketing plan, then at least to a significant extent I can surely be excused. It is not clear that my failure is an ethical one even to the extent that I am obtuse or slow.

However, a moment's thought will bring to mind cases where we do have clear ethical obligations in the way we evaluate ambiguous communications. Othello is one classic case. Iago, Othello's lieutenant, is disappointed when Othello prefers Cassio to him for promotion. Iago secures revenge through convincing Othello that the latter's wife, Desdemona, has committed adultery with Cassio. Othello, despairing, kills first his wife and then himself. At first, Iago's sly hints and insinuations were ambiguous and disavowable, but nicely calculated to lead Othello by the nose to the point of tragedy, and Othello's fault was to let himself be thus led, to make inferences on the basis of ambiguous evidence to the detriment of another.[8]

Or consider the situation of journalists and other reporters of events. Politicians may give hints of policy change or intimations of other developments, with a deliberate intention that reports will be published along certain lines, perhaps to their own advantage and others' detriment. Not all such hints or leaks are wrong or bad: that is the point of saying that ambiguous communications have ethical as well as unethical uses. They may be used to gauge public opinion, to prepare the way for necessary gradual change, or for other worthy purposes. Equally, like other ambiguous or unambiguous communication, they can be used amiss. Because of that, journalists have a professional responsibility to check their facts and qualify their reports, so that they do not, through being led by the nose themselves, lead others by the nose as well.

In general, it seems as though when we receive some communication it is wrong to leap to conclusions that go beyond the evidence, and it is morally wrong to do so when the conclusions impugn or imperil others. More than that, however, we saw above that where our judgements impute fault to others, considerations of fairness and respect for them come into play, considerations reflected in the forensic idea of due process. In Othello's case, Desdemona effectively stood accused, and deserved the benefit of the doubt with opportunity to rebut allegations made against her, which in turn were obliged to be stated clearly and unequivocally. The same general principles seem to apply not only when people are accused of wrong-doing, but whenever conclusions may be drawn to their detriment.

In these cases, though, some thought has to be given to the responsibility of the person who sent the ambiguous message. Othello's actions were wrong and blameworthy, but blame falls also on Iago, and we are inclined to some extent to blame him more strongly, because his actions were deliberate and calculated wrongdoing, whereas Othello at least can call for partial exoneration based on his obtuseness and on Iago's promptings. If as a negotiator I fail to reach agreement with you, there may be some fault at your door for failing to be more careful in your assessment of what I would understand. And so on.

Clearly, we are in difficult territory. It is very hard in such cases to say where responsibility begins and ends. To some extent, the question is one about conscientious action. I may act in good conscience when I report to union members that you are unwilling to reach a settlement, that in your own words, 'I wouldn't even offer you five cents'. Comedy as well as tragedy can revolve around such misunderstanding, when parties fail to appreciate one another's hints and intimations. The tragic element can lie in the fact that my action is taken in all good conscience. Othello, after all, had no wish to be unjust to Desdemona, but had been so far misled that his beliefs were wildly awry.

Here, it may be suggested, we are too generous to Othello. C.D. Broad suggested that a necessary condition for an action to be labelled 'conscientious' is that

> The agent has reflected on the situation, the action, and the alternatives to it, in order to discover what is the right course. In this reflection he has tried his utmost to learn the relevant facts and to give each its due weight, he has exercised his judgment on them to the best of his ability, and he has striven to allow for all sources of bias. (1968, p. 506)

It is not at all clear that Othello's action would meet this standard. On the other hand, it is not really clear how many of our ordinary actions would meet it, or whether it is a practicable standard. If, for example, trying our utmost to learn the relevant facts meant doing everything possible, we might be involved in great commitments of time and effort; time and effort which after a certain point might better be employed on other things: 'better employed' in an ethical sense. It would be a flaw of character to be preoccupied with all remote possibilities, to the exclusion of good things we might be doing.

This, in fact, seems to be a common problem for ethical action: how well assured do we have to be about the facts of a matter before we decide on an action? By and large, in working out what we ought to do in some situation, we can come to an assessment of the facts that we can subscribe to with some degree of assurance, and consider whether that is enough, bearing in mind what is at stake. We condemn Othello not necessarily because every conscientious action requires us to do our utmost to learn the relevant facts, but because he did not do as much as the issue required.[9]

However, Othello's case may be distinguished from many others by the fact that the imputation of guilt to Desdemona should have made him especially wary, and required him to give her a chance to be heard. We have noted that as a usual requirement of such judgements, but there will be many ambiguous situations where that requirement will not be so salient. Where there is that requirement, it at least prescribes a way forward. Other cases are made difficult because considerations are more finely balanced.

Often, interpretations of ambiguous communications have implications for 'face' and 'position', partly because of the great difference between alternatives implied by different interpretations. As a union negotiator, the possible interpretations I can make of your action are opposites: when you say 'I wouldn't even offer you five cents', either you are hinting at an offer, or firmly ruling one out. At least in some such cases, it seems as though I have to seek some clarification before I can reasonably think that one option may be more reasonable than another. I might say, perhaps, 'Well, if I believed you then I would walk out of here right now!' But I would have to be careful, because if you do mean it then it is hard for me to remain without losing face, and I have to take that into account. Sometimes, the course of gaining evidence is rather like partners gaining information at one another's hands in a bridge auction, where each exchange of information ups the ante for the play of the hand.

As a recipient of an ambiguous message, then, I have two tasks. One is to perceive that there are indeed two ways of interpreting the message, and perhaps to embark on a process of clarification as to which is meant. The second is to assess the integrity and sincerity of the person sending the message. Difficulty arises because of the need to combine these two tasks. Clarification is often easy and straightforward if the parties are assured of one another's integrity and sincerity. If they are not, then the process is difficult because it may not be reasonable to expect the other to provide clear information without evidence of one's honesty, which it may be risky to provide without assurances of the other's own honesty (see e.g. Walton and McKersie 1991, pp. 356–8 and Rojot 1991, p. 143).

The sort of problem that confronts us has both an ethical aspect and a practical aspect: deciding first what it is proper to do and then working out how to do it. Like so much else, it involves skills that can be put either to ethical or to unethical uses. Various writers have given accounts of how we deal with the problems (e.g. Goffman 1970 and Ekman 1991).[10] As in so much else in organisational politics, there do not seem to be straightforward, routine solutions, but opportunities to develop experience and imagination.

AMBIGUITY AND CONFIDENTIALITY

In organisations, one particular difficulty that arises in interpreting others' communications is the need to respect privacy and confidentiality. Goffman notes the effect of conventions and norms that prescribe respect for another's private information:

In many informal social circles it is felt to be improper for one individual to doubt another's expressions or statements, or to probe intrusively into what might be called his informational territory. (1970, p. 45)

The idea of private information – information that one has some right to keep to oneself – raises particular ethical issues in this context. If we are confronted by an ambiguous communication from another manager, we might make some further enquiries from others. But in doing so we would have to be careful not to breach any confidence, or to ask others to do so.

Requirements of confidentiality are widespread in organisational life. In a case like that facing Tricia, the importance of confidentiality is clear. If Simon is innocent, it can do him unwarranted harm for it to be known that the allegations have been made. Even if they are true, Jennifer may have some reservations about them being made public, and it might be proper to keep the matter confidential unless she clearly agrees to it being made known.

Bok identifies several grounds for confidentiality. Some of these have to do with control over personal information and commitments created by relationships of trust or by promises (1984, pp. 120–22). There are other cases, which she refers to as 'administrative secrecy', which have to do with the need for privacy in processes of deliberation and planning, and possible harm to innocent people from inappropriate publicity (pp. 175–6). Underlying these considerations there seem to be three points, which are different but complementary. One is the importance to us of privacy and private information about us for maintaining our personhood in a world of other persons. This takes us into the nature of own individual psychology, and the fact that we are affected by people's observations, regardless of how they act towards us as a result of anything they learn: peeping toms are objectionable even if they do no more than look (see Benn 1988, pp. 270–78). A second is that people may indeed act differently as a result of things they learn, and do so to their own advantage or others' disadvantage, and others may have interests that are harmed as a result. If clients of the organisation were to learn about the allegations against Simon, then they might go to other firms, perhaps, without detailed regard for the truth of the allegations. They might do so because, after all, they have the right to choose with which other firms to deal, and simply decide to 'be on the safe side', and not deal with a firm where such things are said to happen. Finally, not quite unrelated to that, people's capacity to process information is finite and constrained by limits of ability and time. We act in many cases on the basis of 'being on the safe side'. Learning about accusations, or learning that certain issues or plans are being considered, may affect what we do, without us having the time to analyse an issue completely or wait for full information. The need for confidentiality of many issues reflects these fallibilities in our judgement.

Unfortunately, of course, we know that confidentiality can be a cloak for wrongdoing. We know of governments which claim that some matters need to be kept secret or confidential for reasons of 'national security', when what is mainly at issue is the security of the government's electoral majority. We know of cases where people's wishes to maintain confidentiality for the sake of victims of sexual harassment are turned to advantage by perpetrators of the harassment. A group of managers may wish to conceal blunders ostensibly to protect the share price of the firm, but in reality to protect themselves. In these and other sorts of cases, confidentiality is a vexed issue because sometimes it is a genuine concern, but sometimes used wrongfully.

In the sort of context we were considering where we receive some ambiguous communication, the situation needs particular care if the ambiguity results from the fact that decisions are not yet made and different alternatives are being contemplated. This can be the case in negotiation processes also. Although such processes often are depicted as ones where parties have well worked-out interests and positions, which they only gradually reveal as they become better informed about the party's interests and more confident of their integrity, they can also involve positions that are formulated only in vague terms, pending better understanding of the other party. We have noted that experienced and effective negotiators consider a wide range of options. Something similar is likely in organisations, as managers and others work out policies and proposals and moot them to others. Often, the ambiguous communication I receive from you will not be a carefully disguised or concealed statement of a detailed position, which you touch on ambiguously to me so as to see how it is received, but rather a partially formulated idea that will be further developed and refined depending on my and others' reactions. In that case, we may have a mixture or hybrid of different sorts of confidentiality. Some of the reasons Bok gives for what we might refer to as 'personal confidentiality' include reference to 'individual autonomy over personal information' (1984, p. 120). Reasons to be given for administrative secrecy may draw partly on such reasons for confidentiality of personal information, because 'a tentative process of learning, of assimilating information, of considering alternatives and weighing consequences, is required in order to arrive at a coherent position' (p. 175).

Such justifications for administrative secrecy have been debated as its proponents have been taken to task by others who believe that it is important for citizens to have a clear view of the process of government. A leading case was the publication first by the London *Sunday Times* and subsequently in book form of the diaries of Richard Crossman, a cabinet minister in the Wilson Labour Government in the 1960s (Young 1976). A good deal of the debate and the court case over the issue revolved around issues of confidentiality. Of the grounds put for suppression of the diaries, there were two major ones which are relevant here. One is that the diaries recounted advice and recommendations given in confidence by some individuals (public servants, in particular) to others (such as ministers). The other is that processes of deliberation in cabinet identified points of views and positions adopted by particular individuals, which were later sacrificed as part of the deliberative process and submerged into collective responsibility for decisions finally taken. Let us consider each of these two grounds in turn.

The fact that matters are put to others in confidence often raises similar kinds of considerations as keeping promises more generally. There can be similar reasons for maintaining undertakings of confidentiality as for keeping other promises, and the same sorts of mitigating circumstances that may be argued to free one from the obligation to keep them. If one person has promised another not to reveal something, and thereby incurred an obligation, then all the relevant considerations come into play: whether unforeseen circumstances or great ill consequences or some other conflicting obligations can free the other from the obligation or override it. Such a promise may be implicit rather than explicit, and yet be binding. On the other hand, promises may be made with qualifications ('I promise not to tell unless ...'), and such qualifications may also be implicit rather than explicit.

As we have noted, there are many situations in organisational life where we are tempted by self-deception, and the area of implicit promises or implicit qualifications are one category where this often beckons. It may be easy to convince ourselves that the other did not receive an implicit promise from us, or that we hedged our promise round with some implicit qualifications, but the fact that we can deceive ourselves does not mean that there are no obligations: only that like so much else in these matters, there can be disagreement and conflict over what they are. Clearly, of course, it is an area where it may be even more difficult for external observers to be clear about what transpires, and fruitless to offer opinions. But the fact that it is hard for an observer to be clear about such things does not imply that a participant has no idea of them.

At least in this sort of case, we have some idea what sorts of considerations are relevant: What were the reasonable expectations of the individuals involved? Is there a 'script' for these circumstances that make others likely to expect one thing rather than another? Is it taken for granted that recommendations about marketing strategy will go no further? Did Jones use terms or phrases that implied confidentiality, or lack of it? And so on. Bearing these in mind, we can make a start in deciding what our obligations are.

Then, also, there will be other categories of matters that will be treated as confidential because of the class of material they deal with, rather than because of any promises, explicit or implicit. Information about people's medical conditions, financial affairs, sexual inclinations or involvements, and the like, would commonly be regarded to be confidential in themselves, and any information one receives about them to be kept confidential unless some appropriate permission to the contrary is given. Again, these sorts of factors are well known, and come clearly into the categories of 'personal information' referred to by Bok and others. To a significant extent this sort of consideration applies in particular to information imparted by one person to another when they are in a special, intimate relationship, a point made in the legal case of *Argyll v Argyll* (1967 Ch 302), cited in the Crossman case (Young 1976, e.g. p. 67; and cf. Bok 1984, p. 120). At least sometimes in organisations, a similar consideration will be relevant (for example, because of the relationship between a manager and the manager's 'confidential' or 'private' secretary).

Thus, the fact that certain sorts of communication or information are confidential, either because of promises or because of the inherent personal character of the information, does not raise questions that are unusual. The ways to deal with them have been widely considered, even if the circumstances of organisational politics often raise some difficulties of practice. What has perhaps been a little less widely considered is the second sort of consideration raised in the Crossman case, as it relates to organisational politics. This is to do with the fact that people work through possible positions as part of a shared deliberative process.

Bok suggests that one consideration favouring a measure of organisational secrecy is that 'if administrators had to do everything in the open, they might be forced to express only safe and uncontroversial views, and thus to bypass creative or still tentative ideas' (1984, p. 175). Thus, at one point in the Crossman trial, during the examination of the Cabinet Secretary, Sir John Hunt, a question is asked by the Lord Chief Justice, Lord Widgery, who was hearing the case:

> 'Sir John, there is only one question I wanted to ask you. One talks rather loosely about the secrecy of Cabinet proceedings, but in the correspondence we constantly find in your letters a reference to a "blow-by-blow" description. That, as I understand it, means a verbatim account, or near-verbatim account, of the observations made by individuals as they were made. It is attributing a view to a person, and I have the impression – I just want you to tell me whether it is right or wrong – that so far as the general limitation of publication is concerned the most serious vice which can thrive if not checked is that opinions will be allocated to people after the event, inconsistently, as I think you would say, with collective responsibility. Is that right?' (Young 1976, p. 95)

Hunt went on to reply:

> 'The essence of my complaint, my Lord, is that he should not give his account in a way which makes it impossible for a Cabinet to work together in mutual trust, and I think this does not mean the revelation of detailed arguments between colleagues and the stands they took and the points they surrendered.' (p. 96)

The eventual decision in the case hinged on the fact that sufficient time had elapsed since the events recounted in Crossman's diaries for publication now to be allowable, but Lord Widgery expressed agreement for some general principle restricting publication, depending on details of the material in question (Young 1976, chap. 7).[11]

For us, the question by Widgery, and Hunt's reply, identify a consideration that is often significant in organisations. Often, people adopt positions in
deliberation or discussion that they would not subsequently wish to be
attributed to them. The deliberations or discussions may reasonably be
labelled 'exploratory' deliberations or discussions: they involve people exploring the implications of positions in a dialogue process where individuals
to some extent adopt positions 'for the sake of argument', as we say. To some
extent, information about such positions is like the thoughts we have in our
own minds, that we would not wish to be revealed to others, when they
amount to temptations or inclinations that on reflection we reject or overcome. My thoughts might turn to the possibility of the inheritance I shall
receive on my father's death, and wish for a moment that it might be so,
before recoiling from the thought. Our thoughts may flow along such lines as
we put ideas and possibilities to ourselves, and we might be horrified at the
idea of a public display of them. Similarly, in organisations, discussion might
flow over possibilities which eventually are rejected by all parties to the
discussion, even by those who mooted them.

Here, as so often, there are some hard distinctions to make. If we consider
just one individual's deliberations, moralists seem to accept that there is no
blame attached merely to having unpleasant thoughts. St. Ignatius Loyola
suggests that there is even merit to be acquired when a thought of committing
mortal sin comes to mind if it is immediately rejected, and that it is only a
venial sin if such a thought comes to mind and one heeds it for a while (1951,
sections 33–35). But how quick 'immediate' must be, how long it might take
us to appreciate the import of a thought, or to see it in its true light, as we
might say – these are still things to be conjured with. We may therefore be
uncomfortable if questioned on oath about our inner life, even when we are
confident that our actions would never reflect some thoughts we have.

Equally, in an organisation, discussions might touch on options for
decisions or policies that will never see the light of day, because, as discussions proceed, it emerges clearly that they have potential for harm or evil. But
the potential might not have been clear at once. Attributing a proposal to an
individual might then be quite wrong, even if it had been put forward as a
real option. Sometimes, we might feel that even thinking of something or
articulating a possibility betrays flaws of character or moral failings, but we
may also feel that it is primarily individuals' actions and considered positions
for which they should be held accountable.

To some extent, this approach may be justified on grounds of necessity for
effective policy-making, extending Bok's point about administrative secrecy
to organisational life more generally: if managers had to do everything in the
open, they might be forced to express only safe and uncontroversial views,
and thus to bypass creative or still tentative ideas. But it also has to do with
fairness and respect for the individuals in question. Apart from implicit understandings about confidentiality, it may simply be inaccurate and unfair to

attribute to individuals positions that they expressed tentatively in discussion or debate.

There are some immediate implications for the ethics of organisational politics. It is possible on occasion to use against people the fact that in discussion they took some position or other, and if we wish to act in an ethical way we ought to refrain from doing so to the extent that the position is one that they articulated in debate without demonstration of any continuing commitment to the position.

However, there are also some conclusions implied by way of a corollary about interpreting ambiguous communications. Just as in negotiation you may not have a fully worked out position when you indicate a willingness to consider some option or other, so on occasion vague or ambiguous communications from others in an organisation may be part of working out policies or decisions. To that extent, we ought to be circumspect about the extent to which we attribute positions to people on the basis of vague or ambiguous communications.

Here, we are accepting as very significant the 'positions' people take on issues. The particular importance of not attributing to individuals positions to which they are not reflectively committed springs from the fact that individuals' positions potentially figure in matters of praise and blame. To the extent that people's positions on things may give rise to action, they stand to be praised and blamed, rewarded or penalised, for those actions. But they may also attract praise or blame for the positions themselves. Positions people hold can be praiseworthy or blameworthy because they reflect admirable qualities like compassion, sympathy, honesty, and many others, or hateful qualities like envy, malice, and others. Also, praise and blame apart, attributing positions to people often ought not be done lightly because, as we shall see later, to adopt a particular position often is to align oneself with one group rather than another, and to be associated with one position rather than another is tantamount to be associated with one group rather than another, bringing into play sets of group loyalties and antagonisms.

POLITICAL WISDOM

These points have taken us away from Tricia's case to more general issues about organisational politics. While we began this chapter considering issues about Tricia's judgement in her case, we have moved now to more general points about communication and judgement as part of the political process. Points about confidentiality remind us that while issues of confidentiality can figure in matters to do with individuals like Jennifer and Simon, they are also important in many processes of policy development and collective decision-making. These processes often contain interplay amongst different people's positions, but people develop their positions on the basis of judgements they make about others' positions, so that there is complex interplay amongst people's positions and their judgements

Such processes of group decision-making and policy development turn our attention away from evidence on technical issues or forensic encounters, toward the idea of 'political judgement'. There has been significant controversy over the extent to which political activity requires some unique type of judgement, and what such judgement may be like. The controversy revolves around claims that political judgement is different from theoretical understanding, and that effective politicians use a different sort of skill than scientists and others use in coming to judgements.

One development of this view is that political judgement is similar to aesthetic judgement and that discernment of appropriate courses of action in politics is more like intuitive perception of colour or aesthetic merit than a form of step-by-step ratiocination. Elements of such a view may be found in Machiavelli and Nietzsche, amongst others (Steinberger 1993, pp. 22–42). It can be seen also in some political biographies, for example in the comment Ted Morgan makes about Franklin Roosevelt, that 'he had a "feel" for things that could not be rationally explained' (1985, p. 314). For our purposes the idea is essentially similar to the view Steinberger attributes to Oakeshott, that 'political or practical experience is concerned with a peculiar and unique kind of fact, practical fact' (1993, pp. 52–3).[12]

Writers who have denied the possibility of rational scientific judgement about political matters may partly have been affected by the complexity and haphazard character of political phenomena. That is not the whole story, however. There is some general difficulty about observations and judgements that must be considered part of the phenomena they seek to observe or judge,[13] but that sort of problem arises very acutely and pervasively in regard to political phenomena. It happens quite clearly in the case of self-fulfilling prophecies. In Kelley and Stahelski's experiment, someone's judgement that another was competitive gave rise to behaviour first on that person's own part and then on the other's, that confirmed the judgement. Many different studies have shown how people's behaviour and achievements can be led to conformity with others' expectations and judgements. Often there is a discernible mechanism that starts with behaviour by those making the judgement. Their behaviour is prompted by their judgement, but on being perceived by the other party that behaviour elicits a response which confirms the judgement and expectations of the first. Some such cases revolve around people's established expectations regarding social behaviour. For example, in conversation and discussion, there are conventions we have mentioned about turn-taking and feedback. One person's failure to give feedback to another can sustain behaviour by the other which confirms the first person's impression of the other.[14]

The intermingling of people's judgements, their own behaviour and others' judgements and responses, may be one of the distinguishing features of political judgements. It is important to bear in mind that many such processes are at work in organisational politics. We noted in Chapter 2 that our judgements are often shaped by schemas and scripts, and Werhane has developed the point that often in organisational life we need 'moral imagination' to take us beyond the 'mental models' that often circumscribe our thinking and judgements (see Werhane 1998, 1999 and 2002). For ethical action, it is important to be aware of the fact that our thinking and perceptions are circumscribed, and to seek ways to take them further. However, it is not only such mental models that limit our judgements in ways that have ethical implications. There are also those mechanisms where there are circles of interaction between our judgements, our behaviour, others' judgements, and others' behaviours, which can establish self-sustaining spirals, for good or ill.

Where such mechanisms occur, there are clear ethical implications. Judgements or expectations about people or situations do not seem to justify or excuse a course of action, even if those judgements or expectations prove to be correct, if their having been made plays a crucial part in bringing about the situation that proves them correct. An experimental subject's competitive approach, based on a judgement that another will prove to be competitive, is not justified just by the fact that the judgement proves to be correct, if the subject's judgement and consequent own behaviour elicited the competitiveness it predicted.

More generally, in complex political situations we know that behaviour of our own will probably affect the dynamics and outcomes. In coming to a judgement about the possibilities and likely developments in that situation, then, we cannot properly avoid taking account of our own behaviour as a factor. We cannot take the behaviour of others as essentially fixed or given, independent of our own. To the extent that we have an obligation to behave in such ways as will influence processes and outcomes for good, we therefore have an obligation to explore ways of seeing the situation that are consistent with beneficial action on our own part. The Kelley and Stahelski experiment demonstrates this with regard to competition and cooperation. To the extent that cooperative behaviour by all is generally beneficial, it seems plausible to suggest that I ought to explore the possibility that the other can be conceived as cooperative rather than competitive.

Of course, it may well be that there is some general requirement of charity on us to regard others as well as we can. For example, given what we also know of the Fundamental Attribution Error, our tendency to attribute shortcomings in others' performance to their character rather than their circumstances, it seems plausible also to suggest that where possible we ought to explore explanations for shortcomings in terms of others' misunderstanding rather than their dishonesty, their family circumstances rather than their laziness, and so on. However, the requirement emerges not only from a need to be fair in our judgements. How we regard others may also influence the way in which a situation unfolds. In forming judgements about others' intentions and expectations, we ought to have regard for the way our responses – past, present, and future – may bear on the expectations and intentions that others have. That may at least be one part of 'political wisdom'. Morgan writes of Franklin Roosevelt that 'he was in a high-level political sense a planner, always looking forward, calculating the future, but seeing the future in terms of a variety of alternatives always developing out of a set of current alternatives' (1985, p. 530). Few people can be planners on the national and international stage as Roosevelt was, but on a smaller scale in organisations we may need to integrate planning and judgement in a similar way. It may be that political wisdom and ethical political judgement consist partly of that integration between judgement and planning: seeing directions for development, bearing in mind partly what role one's own attitudes and judgements may play in the whole array of possibilities; acknowledging moral constraints and desirable ends in making choices; but realising also that one's own judgements can play a part in developments.[15]

SUMMARY

Often, our discussions of ethical action focus on questions about what we ought to do, given a particular set of facts. Often, less attention is paid to ethical issues in determining what the facts are. In organisational politics, however, this is very important, because of the ambiguity and vagueness that beset organisational life.

We considered some of the ethical principles that apply to us when in our organisational lives we are weighing evidence and drawing conclusions. We have noted that some well-accepted principles apply to judgements about technical matters. Organisational processes can inhibit detached, balanced judgements, but it is possible to remedy that to some extent.

When we move beyond technical matters, we find that issues are more complex. Some similar principles still apply, about assessing evidence, but there is now also some need to consider other individuals' rights to due process when there is some likelihood of conclusions being drawn to their detriment. We have already seen that differently from courts of law and other relatively formal institutional situations, there is some possibility that considerations of friendship or personal loyalty may properly have some part to play. However, in the present discussion the point to note is that forming judgements about other people may bring into play considerations of fairness and respect that are absent from technical judgements.

Moving beyond Tricia's case, we have noted also that many communications in organisations are vague or ambiguous. Ambiguity is all-pervasive in organisations. It is used as a political tactic for a variety of reasons, some of them similar to reasons for the use of ambiguous communication in negotiation. Confining our attention so far to ethical issues that may confront us as receivers of ambiguous communications, we have to bear in mind the need to be alert to the actual intentions and expectations of the other party, assuming neither ill will, nor good will, too quickly.

We also need to bear in mind that while some communications may be deliberately ambiguous in order to serve as a signal, or a 'trial balloon' (Strudler 1995, p. 817), others may stem from positions that are not fully worked out. Here, we confront issues of confidentiality, where considerations of organisational effectiveness and of fairness to individuals both counsel against attributing positions to individuals that they may articulate in deliberation and discussion, without thereby being reflectively committed to them.

The way in which organisational politics often may involve the interplay of positions, with people working out courses of action as they examine their own positions and others', reminds us also that others' behaviour is influenced by our own, and that we cannot justify judgements we make just by the fact that they prove correct, if our own behaviour has ensured that they do so. The possibility of self-fulfilling prophecies cautions us that often it will be an ethical requirement on us to consider whether other possibilities may be open if we ourselves act differently. Ethical political judgement may involve us envisaging complex arrays of emerging possibilities for development, remembering that our own judgements about them help create them for what they are.

At the same time, of course, we may also need to bear in mind that others may seek deliberately to influence our judgements. It is central to the ethics of judgement in organisational politics that very often the judgements we make about others have implications for their future. On the one hand, a judgement about others can bring them praise or advantage; on the other hand, it can bring them blame or disadvantage. It is then natural enough that we all may try to influence one another's judgements. In the next chapter, this takes us on to some of the ethical issues that arise as we make such efforts.

NOTES

1. See also Werhane (1999), chap. 3; we discuss the example further in Chapter 9.
2. See for example the account by Glazer and Glazer (1989) of the Ford Pinto case, pp. 18–20, and Jackall's account mentioned earlier of the cleanup after Three Mile Island (1988, pp. 112–19). However, Werhane casts some doubt on widely accepted accounts of the Pinto case: see Werhane (1999), pp. 71–5. Other examples which raise some similar issues may be found in Punch (1996), pp. 85–212.
3. For some, at least, one consideration was that they had given oaths when taking up the work: for C.P. Snow's depiction, see Snow (1972d), chap. 25.
4. For discussion of some of the possibilities, see e.g. Baron, Kerr and Miller (1992), pp. 72–3.
5. In some circumstances there may be other options, such as a company ombudsperson, but we ought not allow discussion to turn on the assumption that there is that sort of option.
6. Students tell me that this is very old-fashioned, but it will serve as an example.

7. A nice example of Stalin signalling to the US in regard to the possible cessation of the Berlin blockade of 1949 can be found in Isaacson and Thomas (1986), pp. 472–3.

8. For useful discussion see Porter (1991), who analyses the process in the play by which Iago gradually manipulates Othello.

9. The law may distinguish recklessness, negligence and non-culpable error partly on the basis of the extent of the enquiry and deliberation made before action and how reasonable it was given the circumstances. See e.g. Stanton (1994), pp. 62–4.

10. Classical accounts have also identified the importance of the issue: e.g. de Callières 1983, pp. 145–6.

11. Lord Widgery noted that the obligation of confidentiality went beyond what was established by explicit agreement or contract, and can arise from the nature of the information in question and the circumstances in which it is imparted: see Young 1976, p. 190.

12. Oakeshott says that 'there will always remain something of a mystery about how a tradition of political behaviour is learned': Oakeshott (1989), p. 151. In fact, modern work on Artificial Intelligence and analysis of processes of thinking and judgement does seem to cast light on some of these issues. For an analogous distinction between analytical and intuitive thinking in medical diagnosis, see Hamm (1988).

13. The point arises to some extent in economics, for example: see Sheffrin (1996).

14. See Button (1992) for an example of someone being misled by others' failure to give the feedback that normally would be expected.

15. Clearly, the point can be taken further still, if we acknowledge that our judgements may not only play a part in how events unfold, but also in the development of our own future capacity for judgement. Cantor and Kihlstrom cite Piaget in suggesting 'Wisdom, then, entails a tortuous process of finding and shaping a social environment that fits comfortably with one's current expertise and, simultaneously, developing new expertise to fit the demands of an everchanging social life' (1987, p. 71).

8. Communication, Influence and Ethics

I have argued that on many occasions in organisational politics there are no clear rules or routines to guide us in ethical decision-making. In working out what to do we may need to take account of a variety of factors, like consequences for stakeholders, the extent to which actions are governed by legitimate external authority, and obligations that arise out of close personal relationships. We may identify some factors that are often relevant in the social dynamics of organisations. Much of what is relevant revolves around forming judgements and communicating with others, and so those processes are worth special consideration. In the previous chapter we considered the former particularly. In this chapter, we turn to the latter: communicating with others. I shall suggest that there are still a number of different sorts of factors that will have to be taken into account in deciding what to do, including the need to treat others as responsible decision-makers, while remaining aware of their fallibility and shortcomings. Other considerations like fairness will also be important on some occasions, and it will still be necessary to come to balanced judgements amongst the various relevant factors.

Katz and Kahn note the centrality of communication in social organisations, and a sense in which we may say that 'communication – the exchange of information and the transmission of meaning – is the very essence of a social system or an organisation' (1966, p. 223). It is therefore not surprising that communication is a fundamental part of organisational politics.[1] For us, the issue is how to act in an ethical way in the communication process.

Emphasis is often placed on communication and information as a solution to problems, including problems that range from the effective functioning of public institutions in a democratic society to the conflicts that may occur on an industrial shop floor. However, Katz and Kahn express reservations:

> The glorification of a full and free information flow is a healthy step forward in intraorganizational problems as well as in the relations of an organization to the larger social system. It is, however, a gross oversimplification. Communication may reveal problems as well as eliminate them. A conflict in values, for example, may go unnoticed until communication is attempted. Communication may also have the effect, intended or unintended, of obscuring and confusing existing problems. The vogue enjoyed by the word *image* in recent years reflects in part an unattractive preoccupation with communication as a means of changing the perception of things without the expense and inconvenience of changing the things themselves. (1966, p. 224)

In that brief statement, there are several different points. The final one, about the use of communication to manipulate images as a means of influence, reminds us again of the idea of 'impression management'. Another point is that communication can unveil a conflict of values, and it is not difficult to think of everyday occasions that give examples of the point. The old adage not to discuss sex, politics or religion at a dinner party is based on the fact that doing so may bring to the surface some value conflicts that would otherwise remain unnoticed, with no benefit from unveiling them.

Unveiling a conflict of values can distract attention from other issues, and that is related to the point that communication can serve to obscure rather than to illuminate. We may be inclined to think at first of communication as tending to impart beliefs, be they true or false, but communication has functions that go far beyond passing information, from expressions of feeling to redirecting people's attention or framing things one way rather than another. In organisational politics, as in other politics, these functions are sometimes overwhelmingly important. Later in this chapter, and in the next, we shall consider some ethical implications.

First, however, we need to consider ethical issues that do arise in connection with communication as the straightforward transmission of information. These raise questions that are difficult enough, and only after considering them can we move effectively toward other aspects of communication. Considering communication as transmission of information, the most prominent issues are about deception. Punch comments that deception is one feature that 'unites most instances of business deviance' (1996, p. 215).

DECEPTION AND ITS COMPLEXITIES

Conceived most simply, the issue is about lying. In most contexts lying is condemned as unethical, but there are blatant lies told in national and in organisational politics. Many have been catalogued. So far as organisational politics goes, discussions of whistleblowing and business ethics are replete with accounts of false public statements, forged records, untrue denials, and the like. The political life of modern nation-states is no different. The Watergate scandal and the case of Kurt Waldheim's war service are only a couple of examples (see Vedung 1987, pp. 354–6).

Sometimes, there seem to be strong arguments to justify lying: for example, when a politician is asked about intentions to devalue a currency, where not lying would open the way for speculation and manipulation (Chapman 1993). Machiavelli went further than cases like that (1992, chap. 18). Nevertheless, even though Machiavelli argued that lying was often justified, he enjoined an appearance of virtue, and it seems clear that political actors try to avoid outright lies, because the latter are too straightforwardly identifiable and open to blame (Vedung 1987, pp. 353, 356).

However, lying blends into deception of other forms, as clearly noted by many writers, going back at least to Augustine (see St. Augustine 1847a and 1847b). Between outright lying and distraction from one issue by true statements about another there are such possibilities as giving a false impression, concealing the truth, or failures in candour and openness. Here we come upon complexities that have occupied theorists in a number of areas. One sort of question is when lying is justified. Another is how to classify types of deceptive conduct: What actually constitutes lying, or deception? Clearly, the two sorts of questions are linked. In medical ethics, for example, there are issues about the extent to which failure to reveal the truth to a patient constitutes deception, and whether there is an ethical difference between failing to reveal the truth and outright false statements. Are there circumstances that justify the one but not the other? Are there circumstances that justify either? What is the relationship between obligations of confidentiality to a patient and obligations of truthfulness to others? What obligations of truthfulness does a physician have to a patient, to the patient's family, and to other parties? Essentially similar kinds of issues arise in many areas: marketing, public relations, policing, legal practice, and many others.[2]

It is clear how some of these kinds of issues arise in organisational politics. In many cases, the ethics seems to be clear. Other things being equal, at least, it is wrong to lie about one's achievements to obtain appointment or promotion, it is wrong to falsify records in order to disclaim responsibility, it is wrong to lie to colleagues about one's intentions in order to disarm them or to obtain some advantage over them. In many cases, the salient issue is not what actions are wrong but how to encourage and support right actions.

As noted already, that issue, of how to promote right action, is an important one. For us, however, the question is how to distinguish amongst some problematic cases. It may generally be wrong to lie to a colleague about one's intentions, but what if I suspect that she intends to use the information for some hostile action: for example, to reveal them to a competitor? What if she herself intends to compete for the same position as I do? What if I merely feel that there are others who ought to be informed first? Clearly, I ought not forge a purchase record, but how careful do I have to be to record different people's comments in the minutes of a meeting? It may be wrong to lie about my past experience in order to obtain a position, but may I give an exaggerated impression of my competence at the work involved? Is there a difference between my giving the impression through the way I act as opposed to what I say?

Questions about deception in organisational politics are inextricably linked with questions about influence. Pfeffer's comment that 'knowledge is power' (1992, p. 111) was anticipated by Herbert Simon's comment that there can be 'no influence without communication' (1957, p. 7).[3] Our discussion about ethical issues to do with deceptive behaviour will mingle inexorably with issues about influence more generally. The area is vast, and we cannot hope to deal with all the points that arise. The general strategy for our discussion will be as follows. Firstly, to state an approach to deceptive conduct that I shall suggest is generally a reasonable basis for analysis and action. Secondly, to address some specific cases which are especially important in organisational politics, and which are not so much discussed elsewhere as to make treatment here unnecessary or irrelevant. These include the fact that often in organisations individuals mistrust one another, and the fact that 'impression management' often utilises non-verbal techniques of affecting others' beliefs.

A BASIS FOR ANALYSIS AND ACTION

Classical moral philosophy has often taken lying as an example, even using it as a sort of test case for accounts of morality, evaluating them in part by how well they account for our common intuitions about what is right and wrong in regard to deception. Thus, for example, proponents of utilitarianism may try to show that it gives a satisfactory account of when lying is wrong and when it is not, while critics of utilitarianism will argue that it fails to account satisfactorily for particular examples, and that it has counterproductive long-run implications (see e.g. Hodgson 1967, Smart and Williams 1973). Kant's views are sometimes criticised on account of the strong and exceptionless view he expresses about the wrongness of lying, on the grounds that it is contrary to our feelings about cases where lying can be justified. The best-known case is that where we are confronted by someone with murderous intent asking if we know the whereabouts of his intended victim. Kant denies that even here we can rightfully lie (Bok 1978, pp. 37–8).[4]

Unfortunately, of course, the evaluation of competing theories of ethics cannot be carried out in quite the way that scientific theories can sometimes be tested, by comparing implications of the theory with clear experimental outcomes. We may compare the implications of ethical theories with particular ethical issues or problems, and sometimes the implications of the theory may be so wildly at odds with what we generally accept that we have no hesitation in discarding the theory. But it is much more likely in evaluating ethical theory than in evaluating scientific theory that we shall have different opinions about some test cases and what an ethical theory ought to say about them. Here, all that is possible is to outline principles that I think will commend themselves to many, which give an account of what is and is not ethical in some specific cases. They include principles to do with fairness and avoiding harm to others, and a principle of respect for others as autonomous agents with scope to make responsible decisions.

That last principle is worth a little more comment at this point. One of the aspects of organisational politics which we need to take account of is the fact that other participants in the process are people like ourselves, and if we are to regard ourselves as responsible, autonomous decision-makers it is hard to see how we can avoid regarding others in the same light. That we normally regard ourselves in that light seems clear enough. However much we may recognise that we are biological creatures whose faculties are associated with biochemical functions of the brain and central nervous system, it is not straightforward to see how we can base our practical reasoning and decisions on that recognition. We have to regard ourselves as the authors of our decisions and as the deliberators who arrive at them, at least in those cases where we are free of coercion and clearly identifiable influence processes. But if we regard ourselves in that light, we seem committed to a similar regard for other people around us. Then, though, if we have to acknowledge others as self-conscious beings like ourselves, there seems to be some obligation implied to respect their need for an understanding of the world which is as accurate as our own, to allow them to make morally responsible decisions. Deceiving others about the facts of a situation can lessen their responsibility for decisions or outcomes, and reflects a lack of respect for them as capable of making responsible decisions.

On the other hand, our common experience and modern psychology both tell us of our susceptibility to influence in our deliberations and in our decisions. We know that there are systematic ways in which our reasoning may be distorted, and systematic ways in which our decisions may be influenced by others. The works we have referred to earlier by Nisbett and Ross (1980) and by Cialdini (1993) are only two summaries of the sorts of factors that impact on us to make our deliberations and decisions less sound than they might be. In Chapter 2, we noted the challenge posed for us to take realistic account of one another's limitations while still respecting one another as autonomous decision-makers. In communication, perhaps the best we can do is to refrain from deliberately manipulating others' beliefs in ways that we would in our own case regard as taking away our responsibility for the decisions we make.

Certainly, the approach being suggested here tries to avoid the assumption that people are ideal information-processors and decision-makers. It accepts that we have only finite capacities to assimilate information, process it, make decisions and implement them. It suggests that it is possible to be realistic in taking account of just how our limitations may affect our judgement. At the same time, however, it suggests that we can still regard one another as autonomous agents who within the constraints placed on us by our finite capacities can come to responsible conclusions and make responsible decisions.

It is still necessary to take account of a variety of factors in individual cases. There is wide agreement that many contextual factors determine what is acceptable in regard to deception. How important the issue is, what conventions apply to such matters, and other factors, all affect our assessment. With compliments to the host on the quality of the food, to the guests on their appearance, to the children on their achievement, and in many other cases, strict truthfulness may not be appropriate (e.g. Bok 1978, chap. 5, Kleinig 1996, p. 130). Much everyday deception is unobjectionable. In those cases, it does not detract from others' significant decisions. In cases where it is wrong, that may sometimes be on account of factors that are unsurprising and might affect the moral status of any action: for example, because the act violates some special relationship, because of its consequences, or for other reasons.[5]

On this account, some things are reasonably straightforward. For example, the wrongness of lying and deception do not have to do with the precise methods used to mislead others. It does not seem to matter whether I get you to believe falsely that it was John who took the money by saying to you 'John took the money', by nodding or remaining silent when you ask if it was he, or by deliberately reminding you of John's earlier peccadillo, if in each case I intend to produce that belief in you and am reasonably assured that in these circumstances what I do will have that effect. By and large, what I do is wrong to the extent that giving you a false belief impedes you from a responsible decision and tends to harm you or unfairly disadvantage you.

Returning for a moment to the considerations of the previous chapter, we may note that there can still be more blame attached to you yourself in one case than another: it may be that if you are told explicitly that John took the money, your belief is more excusable than if you jump to that conclusion when reminded of his past. Blame is not like a cake, that is fixed in amount, with only the proportions for each recipient to be determined. The blame attaching to me may be the same in either case, but yours may still be greater in one case than the other. (It is a theme of tragedy that sometimes a number of characters emerge badly, without any requirement for an overwhelming balance of virtue amongst others: in *Othello*, for example, Desdemona is perfectly virtuous, but no more so because of Iago's malice and Othello's jealousy). In some cases what I do may be unethical because it impairs your responsibility for your decision. In other cases, both you and I may have some responsibility, and some blame, for what transpires.

That is consistent with the central point in this account, the need to be realistic in our beliefs about others, about their capacities and about what conclusions they will actually draw from what we do. We cannot excuse ourselves by complaining that we did not actually say, in so many words, that John took the money, any more than we should be blameworthy for saying so if when we did say so we intended the comment as a joke and knew that it would be interpreted as such. Here, as so often, there is plenty of room for self-deception about what others are likely to believe or do, but the fact that we can deceive ourselves about our behaviour does not seem to count much in evaluating it as more or less blameworthy.

What is more relevant is not the scope for our self-deception or its actual degree, but the difficulty of actually being sure what effects our statements or actions will have. There is constant room for error about that (it is the constant room for error about that which seems to make self-deception all the more possible). Here again we face a variant of the issue we discussed earlier about conscientious action. How certain do we have to be, and how much effort do we have to put in at becoming certain, for our beliefs and related actions to be reasonable in the circumstances? If I mention John's past sins and you immediately infer his present guilt, going far beyond what I intended, how does the case differ from that where I make the comment knowing and intending that that will be your reaction? How far ought I have foreseen or taken care to anticipate how you might react?

Once more, the answers to these questions can only be vague. They are not questions that have to be answered only in the present context, but are quite general questions about conscientious action, and we may rest on the hope that any general answer to them will allow us some natural and reasonable policies and practices about our communication behaviour. What we can say, however, is that there are some general approaches that go too far in trying to remove from us any burden of investigation in ascertaining what others' intentions, expectations and likely reactions may be in such situations. An example is how we ought to act with one another when we do not fully trust each other.

AN EXAMPLE: TRUST AND MISTRUST

Trust is very important in organisations. Many writers have noted that it is important for people in an organisation to trust one another if the organisation is to perform effectively, and it is arguable that even apart from its effects, trust is inherently important as a good for people (Provis 2001). The importance of personal relationships was emphasised in Chapter 6. Trust enhances the depth and quality of our relationships, and thereby also our own self-understanding, as we see ourselves reflected in others. To the extent that trust thereby enhances our understanding and our decision making, accepting the importance of trust is part of accepting the picture of humans as members of communities of responsible decision-makers.

However, we do not always have good intentions, and even when we do we may fail to put them into practice, through shortcomings of skill or capacity. Knowing these things, we do not always trust one another. Organisations and organisational politics are littered with mistrust, and we have to ask what the implications are for our decisions about ethical action.

In the previous chapter, we noted a contention that the process of negotiation is outside usual ethical constraints.[6] Dees and Cramton have suggested that the absence of trust between parties removes ethical obligations to a significant extent:

> moral obligations rest, at least in part, on a foundation of mutual trust. When that foundation of trust is absent, the obligation is undermined. Specifically, to take

risky or imprudent action on the basis of moral ideals, when others cannot be trusted to do the same, may be admirable, but it goes beyond the obligations of morality in practice. (1991, p. 136)

They say elsewhere

In war there is, according to Hobbes a 'generall rule of Reason, that every man, ought to endeavor Peace, as farre as he has hope of obtaining it; and when he cannot obtain it, that he may seek, and use, all helps, and advantages of Warre' ... He explicitly states, 'Force, and fraud, are in warre the two Cardinall virtues.' ... On the Mutual Trust view, this translates into a general obligation to attempt to push back the moral frontiers, when this seems feasible. When it is not feasible to establish grounds for trust and reciprocity, one is entitled to use otherwise immoral practices. (1991, p. 147)

In particular, for example, we are entitled to bluff or otherwise mislead others about our intentions and what we would be willing to accept. This view might appeal to some practitioners of organisational politics, perhaps especially those who embrace a Machiavellian view of *Realpolitik*. However, the position seems clearly to be too strong. When there is no trust between ourselves and others, we may lack positive reasons to expect others to act rightly, but that is too weak a condition to justify immoral practices. Part of the requirement on us to treat one another as autonomous subjects and to allow one another to make responsible decisions, is that we are obliged to ascertain one another's actual intentions and expectations in each concrete situation, so far as we can do so without disproportionate cost. For otherwise immoral practices to be justified on our part, it seems as though principles of self-defence would require us to have reasonable belief that others will deceive us or otherwise attempt to do us harm: it is not sufficient that we merely lack reasons to believe that they will not try to do us harm. This is as true as ever when the otherwise immoral practices have to do with communication and deception.

This view is consistent with full acceptance of the point that in organisational politics there is often a lack of trust between parties. Perhaps that fact is part of the reason for adverse attitudes to organisational politics. But it seems a mistake to assume that the only possibilities are a fully cooperative environment where parties trust one another, and a wholly antagonistic environment where they do not. For one thing, as various writers have noted, trust and distrust are not always simple or straightforward: they can be matters of degree, and it is possible that you may trust me in one respect but not other respects (see e.g. Lewicki, McAllister and Bies 1998 and Baier 1994). For another thing, there are ways to try to work within an atmosphere of mistrust, and how to do so in an ethical way is an important issue of organisational politics. Carr tells of a businessman who believed that 'the golden rule, for all its value as an ideal for society, is simply not feasible as a guide for business' (1968, p. 146). However, suppose we take the classical statement of the

Golden Rule to be 'do unto others as you would have them do unto you'. It is not at all clear that this is impractical, if what we would have others do unto us is regard us as autonomous subjects, pay careful attention to our beliefs, expectations and interests, and seek to achieve a fair outcome on that basis. In organisational politics, even if we do not trust one another, our policies and strategies for action may include careful assessment of the circumstances of the particular case, including others' actual expectations and intentions.[7]

As senders of messages, the sort of situation we are in parallels the situation we are in also as receivers of messages. In the latter case, I have argued, we have some obligation to put in so much time and effort as is warranted by the issue and the possibilities we risk if we get things wrong. C.D. Broad's requirement, that we always 'do our utmost' to get things right, seems too strong. In sending messages, as in receiving them, we have some obligation to assess how others will interpret what we do or say, but the extent of our obligation depends to some extent on the nature of the issue and what is at stake. We may not be required always to 'do our utmost', but there is some obligation on us to try to discern what people's concerns and interests are, when we are communicating with them. Lack of trust between parties can make the process harder, but does not seem to take away an obligation to do what is possible.

When we do not trust those to whom we are making some communication, we still have an obligation to assess the realities of the situation, including the other party's expectations. We cannot just assume that they plan to do us ill, unless we have some evidence to that effect. We may be justified in not exposing ourselves to risk, but that is different from taking pre-emptive counter-measures against a party who may not prove to be a foe. We may be careful in just how much we say, and how we say it, but that is not necessarily the same as concealment or misleading behaviour.

In arguing that a lack of trust between parties does not remove their obligations to one another, I do not mean to suggest that they are not entitled to protect themselves from attack if they reasonably apprehend that such an attack is likely. But it can be all too easy to claim that an attack is likely as a justification for some action when the evidence is slim. In the politics of nation-states, we shall note that it can be a political tactic to draw people's attention to some external threat, in order to turn it away from domestic issues. But it may not only be others whom we deceive about possible threats, it can be ourselves as well. In organisational politics, it can be easy for us to persuade ourselves that others will move in some way to our detriment or contrary to principles we espouse, if we do not first take some pre-emptive counter-measures, and we have some obligation to be sober and realistic about what others are genuinely likely to do. Then, further, we have the same obligations as always to do no more than necessary to protect ourselves.

IMPRESSION MANAGEMENT

When we and others mistrust one another we can try to be realistic in our beliefs about others, not assuming hostile intent and taking pre-emptive action against them, while trying not to leave ourselves open to exploitation or harm, either. Our obligations in that situation are an example of the requirement on us to be realistic in our assessments of what is ethical, avoiding preconceived views and self-deception as far as we can. The general requirement to be realistic is bound up with our obligation to treat others as responsible decision-makers like ourselves who nevertheless have finite and fallible capacities to draw conclusions and make decisions. Our need to take into account our finite capacities and our susceptibilities are especially important when we assess the ethics of 'impression management'.

We noted above in Chapter 1 that 'impression management or image building' has been categorised as a tactic of organisational politics, and that there is room for discussion about how ethical it may be. It seems as though it may be ethical in some contexts: in Chapter 3 I suggested that one problem that may arise in organisational politics is how to act in an ethical way without flaunting the fact: while skills of impression management can often be self-serving, they need not be, and the same ability to cast oneself in a favourable light may also be used to disarm suspicion about the genuinely virtuous motives behind an ethical action. But in many other cases the ethics of self-serving impression management can still be questioned.

We shall see below that the term 'impression management' has a variety of uses, but for ease of discussion we can start with cases where impression management consists largely in getting others to draw favourable conclusions about us or matters we are involved in: often, a form of 'self-presentation', where 'one wants to convey an impression of oneself that the audience will regard favorably' (Baumeister 1989, p. 59). Undoubtedly, we can give others impressions about ourselves in a variety of ways. We do so in how we dress, in our manner and bearing, through our voice, in likes and dislikes we express, in the activities we engage in, and in many other ways. There is plenty of evidence about the effects such cues have on others, ranging from the fact that people's dress conveys information about their social class (Argyle 1988, pp. 239–240) to research suggesting that more attractive people are perceived as superior in a variety of other qualities (Zebrowitz 1990, p. 70). Deliberate attempts at impression management can be more or less successful, depending on their technique:

> verbal self-presentation is often unsuccessful, especially in claims to status, since it may be disbelieved and ridiculed unless done very subtly and indirectly. However, non-verbal methods, especially appearance, tend to be taken at face value. (Argyle 1988, p. 234)[8]

As far as ethics goes, what we can say about this form of impression management does not seem either complex or surprising. To the extent that the
ways we present ourselves are intended to convey information to others, they
seem to be subject to the same constraints as other communication. It is hard
to see what ethical difference it makes if on the one hand I falsely say that I
went to such-and-such a school, or, on the other hand, I lead you to think so
by wearing the old school tie. While some writers have argued that deception
by other means is less serious than by lying, it is difficult to see why this
should be so. As Kleinig says,

> The duty of veracity is concerned with straightforwardness in communication, and
> the person who deceives, *no less than* the person who lies, is not being straight-
> forward. In both cases, our interest in having others deal with us openly is deliber-
> ately subverted. (1996, p. 129)

We can think of a number of considerations that might affect the manner in
which deception is carried out. Most obviously, some are more reliable than
others. Reliability may itself be affected by a number of factors. Wearing the
tie may be more effective, because it is harder to obtain the right tie than just
to make a verbal claim, but others may be less likely to recognise the tie than
a verbal claim. Verbal claims may just be processed differently in the brain
than visual images and associations. But that does not clearly make a difference to the ethics of what I do.

It may be suggested that if others infer from the fact that I am wearing the
old school tie that I went to the school, then they have to accept more responsibility for their belief than if I make the verbal claim: 'After all, they jumped
to that conclusion', we might feel. In some cases, even after reflection, we
may be inclined to maintain that view. But in others, more careful consideration may be necessary. It is sometimes true that people jump to conclusions
to an extent that moves the responsibility to their own shoulders and frees
others from blame. In some cases, though, where others contrive to bring
them to those conclusions, things are not quite so clear. Cialdini recounts the
following story:

> At the height of his wealth and success, the financier Baron de Rothschild was
> petitioned for a loan by an acquaintance. Reputedly, the great man replied, 'I won't
> give you a loan myself; but I will walk arm-in-arm with you across the floor of the
> Stock Exchange, and you soon shall have willing lenders to spare.' (1989, p. 45)

There is a narrow line, and a difficult one to evaluate, between cases where
the Baron and his friend walk across the floor deliberately intending to influence others' impressions, and the case where they do so unreflectively, with
the same effect. In the second case, we might indeed say that others have the
responsibility for any conclusions they draw. Is there anything ethically more
problematic about the first case than the second? Can we not say in both
cases that the responsibility for their conclusions and decisions rests on those

who jump from seeing the Baron and his friend together to believing that his friend is affluent and a good credit risk? Might we not regard the case in the same way as courts regard cases of contributory negligence? Do not those who are exposing themselves to risk have the responsibility to acquaint themselves carefully with the reality of the situation?

The question is difficult because there are some apparently similar cases where our inclinations seem to be different. Suppose that I am dressed for my appearance in a theatrical production. If someone jumps to the conclusion that I really am the character I shall portray later in the evening, the conclusion may well be their own responsibility. But if I know that they have come to that conclusion, and know that they are likely to use the belief as the basis for action which is to their detriment or to my unfair advantage, then in most circumstances I have some responsibility to disabuse them. The situation then seems no different in principle than the responsibility I have to warn people who falsely believe that a crocodile-infested river is safe for swimming.

There seem to be a number of relevant factors. One is the intention that I have, or that the Baron and his friend have. If I set out deliberately to deceive, that is different than if I unreflectively do something that others use as a basis for inference. Another is the accuracy of the conclusion others draw. If the Baron's friend really is a good credit risk, then it is hard to see how the two are to be criticised for either deliberately or unreflectively allowing others to draw that conclusion.

What of the case where I intend the other to come to a false conclusion, but the other has to accept some responsibility for the inference? We should bear in mind the point made above that if the other person does have to accept some blame for their conclusion, that does not in itself relieve the first person of responsibility. We are nowadays quite familiar with stories of confidence tricksters whose technique involves their victim doing something unethical in an attempt to gain some advantage, only to fall into the trickster's trap. I may believe that I am getting a watch at a low price because it is stolen, whereas in fact it contains no working parts. You may believe that you will be paid for allowing some shady customers to use your bank account to launder money, only to discover that your own funds have gone. In such cases, we are inclined to apportion some blame to the victim: 'it was their own fault', at least to a significant extent. However, it is not clear in such cases that the blame deserved by the confidence trickster is proportionately less. As we noted earlier, it is not clear that blame is like a cake, that is fixed in amount, with only the proportions for each recipient to be determined. If anything, we may be inclined to think that the confidence trickster like a blackmailer is all the worse for preying on human weaknesses and shortcomings. Equally, in cases of impression management, if we take advantage of others' weaknesses and their tendencies to draw unwarranted conclusions on too little evidence, that does not seem to lessen any responsibility we ourselves bear.

We can see various reasons why it may be wrong for me to lead others to false beliefs. Sometimes, what we do will be questionable because it reduces others' responsibility for what they do. In other cases it may be problematic because of harm or unfair disadvantage it brings to them. But granted that for some such reasons it is usually wrong to bring others to false beliefs, the key factor seems to be the extent to which I act to bring about the other's error, not the means by which I do so. In general, when I deliberately act to influence others, the fact that my influence relies on some faulty decision or action on their part does not seem to cancel any blame due to me. By and large, when my actions or behaviour lead someone to a conclusion, a belief about the facts that may affect decisions they make, it seems as though my intention to produce an inaccurate conclusion is the key factor. Undoubtedly, there are other relevant sorts of considerations to be taken into account, such as the importance of the issue and the potential for harm and the rights of self-defence I have if I genuinely apprehend a threat. But if I set out deliberately to get another to have a false belief, then it does not seem to matter very much whether I try subtly to inveigle them into drawing a conclusion or just use a bare-faced lie.

This point seems clearer still if we notice that even if I have not set out to deceive, but become aware that others have a false impression that may harm them, I may still have an obligation to correct them. As in response to Dees and Cramton, it seems reasonable to suggest that we have to take account of the reality of the actual situation we are in. I do at least have the same sort of obligation to disabuse others of false impressions about me that may disadvantage them, as I seem to have to disabuse them of misconceptions about the safety of swimming in the crocodile-infested river. As always, the seriousness and likelihood of the consequences are relevant, as may be the cost to me of telling them. But, other things being equal, it seems reasonable to suggest that I have a duty to correct others if they have a false impression that may lead them into any sort of harm. More strongly, if others know that I am aware of their impression, and I do nothing to correct it, then they may take my silence as confirmation of their impression. The situation is similar in some ways to the one we discussed earlier regarding consent. Just as there are circumstances where silence amounts to consent, so are there cases where silence amounts to confirmation.

The general point is that impression management is not somehow exempt from the ethical constraints that surround our other actions. It may be more tempting to wear the school tie than to say I went there, perhaps because it will be harder to prove my intention, but whatever the difficulties of proof may be, if I do in fact have the intention, then other things being equal there seems to be no great ethical difference. If someone makes an assumption I know to be false, it may be more tempting to leave them with the assumption than it would have been to induce it in them, but I seem to have some real obligation to them in either case. We have obligations to allow others to maintain responsibility for their decisions, but also to stop them from being avoidably harmed or unfairly disadvantaged.

Cases of 'impression management' like Baron Rothschild and his friend form one class of cases where these issues can be important in organisational politics. Another class, perhaps even more common, revolves around uses of language and tendentious 'formulations'.

INFLUENCE AND PRAGMATIC RULES OF LANGUAGE

The idea of a 'formulation' rests on the fact that parties to a conversation share quite a large and complex set of background knowledge and assumptions. Some of these are about the way things are, some of them are about how things ought to be, and some of them are about how language is used. Often, our expectations and beliefs are built into our utterances, by virtue of 'rules of discourse', also referred to as the 'pragmatic' as opposed to 'semantic' or 'syntactic' rules of language. For example, the forms of address and idioms that you and I use in our conversation reveal our understanding of our relationship. We reveal expectations or understandings not necessarily by direct affirmation, but by presuppositions underlying what we say and how we say it. My question, 'When is the next train for Brighton?' presupposes that trains from Brighton leave from this station. If I ask you whether it is raining and you reply 'It is expected to rain tomorrow,' the implication is that it is not raining at present, even though that is not logically entailed by what you say.

The importance of background knowledge and assumptions about how language is used has been most clearly articulated by H.P. Grice. He has noted a number of maxims or pragmatic rules about language use which guide our interpretations of what others say, such as expectations that their statement is relevant to what has gone before, that it is as informative as required but not more so, and so on. Thus, he gives an example where B approaches A, who is standing by a clearly immobilised vehicle, and A says 'I am out of petrol'. When B responds 'There is a garage round the corner', Grice comments that 'B would be infringing the maxim "Be relevant" unless he thinks, or thinks it possible, that the garage is open, and has petrol to sell; so he implicates that the garage is, or at least may be open, etc.' (1989a, p. 32).

In such cases, it is arguable that it is A's decision to infer that the garage may be open, but to the extent that B is a usually competent language user he cannot dissociate himself from responsibility for A's inference. The same would be equally true for many other cases. If I say 'Jack is late today', and you respond 'He walked this morning', our conversation is built on shared knowledge and understanding about Jack's habitual use of a bicycle and the fact that walking is slower than cycling. In general, what is implied depends on the shared assumptions of those involved. If at a committee meeting you say 'The number of units sold in the third quarter more than doubled the numbers for each of the previous two quarters', there may sometimes but not always be a tacit implication that the value of sales has increased comparably. When there is, the communication may be a deceptive attempt at influence.[9]

Clearly, these examples are vast over-simplifications of what can happen in reality. The complex and subtle depth of actual exchanges is brought out to some extent in Walker's analysis of part of a transcript of a negotiation where participants include Andy (management) and Pete (union):

> Andy explicitly identifies what he is doing as *just clarifying*. However, in the process of being reconfirmed, the activity the union are purported to be doing has been somewhat modified. Pete is initially asked to confirm a description which categorically identifies his action as a proposal (i.e. it is *a suggestion that you're making*). But in the reconfirmation it is described in terms of a request (*that's what you're asking*). This modification may be immaterial, but there is a significant difference in negotiations between 'proposing' (or 'suggesting') and 'requesting' (or 'asking'). If an activity is explicitly identified as a 'proposal', this precludes the interpretation that the turn constitutes a concession: 'proposals' certainly provide an opportunity for *an exchange* of concessions to be made, but they do not in themselves constitute a concession made by the speaker. On the other hand, such an interpretation is permissible if the activity is described as a 'request'. (1995, p. 108)[10]

More generally, Walker shows how negotiators use 'formulations' of preceding discussion as a way to elicit concessions. A common part of conversation and discussion is to formulate the general sense or direction that it has taken, but negotiators do this in specifically tendentious ways, in order to elicit concessions. Referring to detailed analysis of transcripts of union–management negotiations, Walker says:

> 'Optimistic formulations' are transparently being used as a strategic device to seek a concession and they are designed to maximize the recipient team's acceptance of it. It is in the speaker's interests to furnish a low-key description of the concession initially and to disclose the hidden 'extras' once it has been accepted by the recipient team as a way forward. (1995, p. 123)

In organisational politics, the pragmatic rules of communication are an equally potent source of influence. The sorts of 'formulations' discussed by Walker are specifically about the course of some discussion. Other formulations can be similarly applied to one's own or others' past or proposed behaviour, implicitly redescribing it in favourable or unfavourable terms, or in terms that imply certain other actions as required by it, consistent with it, or incompatible with it. 'Why are you leering at me?' is ostensibly a question seeking reason or explanation, but contains a formulation that describes the other's expression and manner in a particular way. Appropriate formulations may conjure up one 'frame' or another, as did young Brother Gregory's redescription of his own proposed behaviour, in the story recounted from Solso (Chapter 2 above). And as we shall note further below, they may signal affiliation to a particular group or party. Often, skilled use of the pragmatic rules of communication can be used to do a number of these different things at once.[11]

What are the ethical implications of such tactics? In a formal negotiation involving professional negotiators, the tactics seem generally unproblematic, because the possibilities are understood, and where necessary the other team's natural response is to enter a *caveat* before the discussion goes further. But in formal negotiations people are usually aware of a need to be on their guard, professional negotiators are alert to the processes involved, and negotiations are often over relatively well-delineated issues. Norms of behaviour tend to discourage personal criticism or attack. None of these things is necessarily true in organisational politics. As a result, the use of 'formulations' or the equivalent is not only a potent but also a sometimes problematic source of influence in organisational politics.

These various interwoven aspects of communication and impression management are bound up with techniques and tactics of organisational politics that can be subtle but all the more in need of ethical consideration. Just as it might be argued that responsibility for inferring the creditworthiness of Rothschild's friend lies with those who make the inference, so it may be argued that responsibility for coming to beliefs on the basis of background assumptions or 'frames' submerged in the pragmatic rules of communication must lie with those who draw the conclusions. But as in the case of the Baron's friend, any responsibility that others may have for inferences they draw does not necessarily take responsibility away from those who deliberately set out to give one impression rather than another. More important, it does not diminish the responsibility they may have for deliberately 'submerging' assumptions beneath the surface of discourse. Bowers and colleagues (1977) note that pragmatic rules can be exploited to send 'devious messages', when the speaker avoids direct lying but gives a misleading impression. If one manager asks another if the new product line will be ready for sale the following week, and the other answers that they are just preparing the packaging, there is an implication that the products are ready, but that is not actually stated. That can be a form or corollary of impression management, and to the extent that it involves inducing false beliefs in others then it is open to the same sorts of ethical concern as other forms of impression management that are used for that purpose.

Submerging assumptions into the background presuppositions of statements or questions is a well-known tactic in tendentious communication. The classic example is perhaps the old question 'Have you stopped beating your wife yet?' Research by Snyder and Swann suggests that background assumptions have great power to influence opinion. Their research suggested not only that observers will often uncritically accept background assumptions put to subjects, but that the subjects themselves often will fail to contest such background presuppositions, despite those presuppositions being contrary to the subjects' own sound self-understanding (Swann, Giuliano and Wegner 1982). Sometimes, perhaps, people use heuristic assumptions that usually serve us well ('they wouldn't make the assumption implicit in that question unless they had some evidence for it'). Sometimes, perhaps, the implications of an utterance are deeply enough embedded for the mental resources used to unravel them leave the hearer less well able to analyse the assumptions critically. Thus, for example, Porter notes that even Iago's simple use of 'My lord, I see y'are mov'd', can have that effect:

> For one thing, the clause embedded may be thereby partly insulated from denial. 'You are mov'd,' is open to an unambiguous 'No [I am not],' but the same reply to 'I see you are mov'd' is ambiguous, as it stands, between 'I am not mov'd' and 'you do not see.' (1991, p. 82)[12]

The ethical problems of such devious communication emerge most clearly when it is made clear what effort and persistence may be necessary to 'surface' the assumptions. Often, it is only an alert and persistent interlocutor who will continue. Bowers and colleagues recount the exchange between UPI reporter Helen Thomas and White House Press Secretary Ronald Ziegler, where she asks 'Has the President asked for any resignations so far, and have any been submitted or on his desk?' He replies 'I have repeatedly stated, Helen, that there is no change in the status of the White House staff.' When she says 'But that was not the question. Has he asked for any resignations?', he reiterates 'I understand your question and I heard it the first time. Let me go through my answer. As I said, there is no change in the status of the White House staff. There have been no resignations submitted' (Bowers, Elliott and Desmond 1977, p. 239, citing Walters 1974).

We may admire Thomas' professional skill at detecting Ziegler's implied evasion, and her persistence in continuing to 'probe' him. Bowers and his colleagues note that the failure of someone to explain clearly in response to a probe often suggests devious intent (p. 239).[13] Often, though, such persistence at probing carries costs. Some of these are straightforward: it consumes time and mental resources. In addition, however, it risks disapproval. Sometimes it may even risk being labelled incompetent or mad ('Don't you understand English?'), or malicious ('You are badgering me!') (Bowers, Elliott and Desmond 1977, p. 239, referring to Watzlawick, Beavin and Jackson 1967).[14]

In some circumstances, background assumptions may not be intended deceptively, but still may influence listeners, and may be used either consciously or unconsciously to exert such influence. The response can still be to comment on the assumptions, to 'surface' them, and perhaps bring them into question. In *Corridors of Power*, C.P. Snow depicts a meeting of officials discussing the proceedings and potential outcomes of a scientific committee set up to consider British nuclear weapons policy. One view, about a possible system that would be powerful but very costly, is dismissed, and then discussion turns to the possibility of forsaking any independent nuclear deterrent. Douglas Osbaldiston, the meeting convenor, comments that 'As I said, this is the other extreme. But I ought to say that it seems to be held by chaps who are usually level-headed, like Francis Getliffe and our scientific adviser, Walter Luke.' While he seems to put the issue in an even-handed way, Lewis Eliot is dissatisfied, and gains an opportunity to speak, although more junior than others at the meeting:

> Wasn't Douglas pre-judging the issue when he talked about Getliffe's view as 'the other extreme'? Wasn't this view, in fact, deliberately conceived as a means of taking one first step? Did they assume that no first step could ever be taken? Were they all accepting that the entire process had got out of conscious control? (Snow 1972b, chap. 13)

He 'takes none of them with him', but warns them that others are thinking differently and that what they might have been inclined to take for granted should not be.

Again we may ask, What can we say about the ethics of these processes? The use of 'formulations' to elicit agreement from others in formal negotiation or less formal interaction, and inducing the acceptance of beliefs or frames by importing them into the background assumptions behind questions or statements, are all processes of influence. Some similar issues arise as in acknowledged cases of deception, as we shall note in the next section. They will also emerge in cases we shall come to in the next chapter, like processes of distracting people or putting choices to them when they cannot bring reasonable psychological resources to bear on them. Such tactics are often problematic, whether the specific tactics trade on background assumptions of discourse or otherwise.

DECEPTION, FAIRNESS AND RESPECT

To a significant extent the issues that arise in influencing people through use of the pragmatic rules of discourse are similar to cases like that of Baron Rothschild and his friend or that where I give you a false impression through wearing some particular tie. The person who is the object of influence is manipulated into drawing some false conclusion or accepting some dubious assumptions. At one extreme are the sorts of cases that Cialdini discusses, which we noted in Chapter 2. We may recall his use of the '*click*, and *whirr*' imagery to emphasise the almost automatic, machine-like response we tend to give to some forms of influence such as reciprocity and expert authority, and his use of the term 'trigger principles' for the explanation of our responses. We also noted his suggestion about ethical requirements on the use of trigger principles, when he contrast cases where people 'smuggle' influence triggers into a situation, with other more legitimate cases where we act as 'detectives' to discern what triggers of influence already exist in the situation. For us, the question is what general ethical principles account for the difference between the different sorts of case Cialdini identifies. How can we give some less metaphorical account of smuggling triggers of influence into a situation?

Consider the particular example of smuggling Cialdini gives: a waiter who relies on his expertise-based credibility to influence diners' orders, but does so to elicit orders that will be most to his and the restaurant's advantage, without any particular reference to the merits of the dishes they order. This, he suggests, may be contrasted with the case where a waiter again influences diners in what they order, again perhaps to his own and the restaurant's advantage, but only after taking some trouble to ascertain what will actually be best for the diners that night, making the order equally good for them also (1987, pp. 158–9, 162–3).

One approach would be to say that in the first sort of case the reason why the waiter's smuggling tactic is wrong is just that it harms the diners, because they pay for poorer food than they would have otherwise. However, this does not deal with cases where others are not led to act to their detriment in any clear or obvious way, but the way they are led to act nevertheless gives some unfair benefit to the person influencing them. Perhaps because there are such cases, fairness is sometimes taken to be the basic issue in cases of deception (see e.g. White 1980, p. 928). Then unfair benefit to the person who exerts deceptive influence might be the main thing that makes for the wrongness of deception. Such an approach might be taken to cases of influence like that by Cialdini's waiter. In this view, what explains the wrongness of smuggling in triggers of influence and other similar ways of manipulating others is not the fact that others are harmed in any discernible way, but the fact that the perpetrator somehow uses unfair means to gain an undeserved benefit. Such cases may be labelled 'exploitation', or more fully, perhaps, 'noncoercive exploitation' (see e.g. Feinberg 1983). Such cases are in some ways like those where one person can be said to 'use' another (see Blum 1973). In explaining what is wrong in such cases also, it may be contended that the issue is about fairness. In this view, the point about Cialdini's waiter is that he takes unfair advantage of his position and credibility and his action would be wrong even if the diner would otherwise have ordered a meal of similar quality and price, because the waiter has taken unfair advantage of his opportunity to guide them to a dish with a greater profit margin. Similarly, for example, in organisational politics it might be wrong for us to use a special advantage we have because of privileged sources of information.

If that is correct, similar considerations of fairness might often explain the wrongness of deception. However, it seems likely that we shall still be left with a question about some cases of impression management where this does not seem to be the whole story. It may seem as though in many common sorts of impression management in organisations there is no clear unfairness at issue. If, as a candidate at a job interview I give you, the interviewer, the impression that I have vast experience at certain work, it may be that your belief will do you no harm (assuming that I can in fact do the job competently). Is there anything unfair in what I have done? I have done you no harm, and it is not clear in what other ways I may be said to have taken any unfair advantage of you.

Admittedly, there may be a question about fairness to other applicants for the position, or harm to them. But even there it is hard to identify any clear unfairness. They have similar opportunities from impression management. There is in that respect a 'level playing field', and it might be argued that there is to that extent no 'unfairness' involved.[15] Nor is it quite clear in what respect it harms them, since at most it deprives them of some benefit that they had some imponderable chance of acquiring.

The same kind of viewpoint might be considered in regard to linguistic 'formulations', influencing people by getting them to accept some idea or position through using pragmatic rules of discourse. It can be suggested that the opportunities for influence through the use of such mechanisms is equally open to all, since there is widespread knowledge of how they work. Indeed, in some sense the pragmatic rules of discourse are known to all competent users of a language.

There is some room for argument about those issues.[16] Overall, though, it is not clear that considerations of fairness are all that is at issue in cases of deception or withholding information. It is quite possible that different sorts of consideration are important in different sorts of case. In the case of the swimmers in the river, a crucial reason for me to tell them of the danger may just be to avert the potential harm to them. If I could instead put in place a net to protect them, then my obligation might be just as much to do that. In other cases, fairness may be a key issue. In many cases to do with the ethics of communication I think that a fundamental consideration will also be the principle that we have an obligation to treat one another as autonomous subjects and to allow one another to make responsible decisions.

Consider impression management in an interview. If I know that you, as interviewer, have some clearly false impression that may affect your decision, then I may have some obligation to correct you just because you have a right to make a decision based on the best information available. This seems largely independent of the extent to which I have deliberately contrived to produce your false impression. Such contrivance would be wrong, but even if you have gained a false impression without contrivance on my part then when I become aware of it I seem to have some obligation to disabuse you, subject to various qualifications we have alluded to before, about cost, importance, and so on. This sort of obligation does not seem to have anything especially much to do with 'fairness', but rather to do with a requirement that we ought to treat one another all as autonomous subjects with the right to make responsible decisions. There will be many cases that can certainly be understood in terms of fairness, because often it will be unfair for me to make a decision on the basis of better information you have available to you to in making yours. But there are some cases where the idea of fairness does not clearly have any implications, where nevertheless it is questionable whether I ought to withhold some information I have available that you do not, because withholding it treats you as unworthy of making decisions on the basis of the best available information.

A principle like this may also apply to the sorts of cases discussed by Cialdini. Where there are 'natural' triggers of influence then people may be able to take account of the sorts of things that they know tend to influence them, and make allowances accordingly. To that extent, they can remain autonomous subjects.[17] Where such triggers are smuggled in, people are unable to make a realistic estimate of the influences on them in a way that allows them to take account of those influences and decide accordingly. It may be that fairness is a relevant consideration of many such cases of influence, but another consideration is our obligation to acknowledge other self-conscious subjects as beings like ourselves, to respect their need for an understanding of the world which is as accurate as our own, and to allow them to make morally responsible decisions. Where there are 'natural' triggers in Cialdini's sense, there is nothing about the situation which is known to us but concealed from others, which they might reasonably want to take account of in choosing what to do. Where triggers are smuggled in, others might have chosen differently if they had known more. Their ignorance detracts from their moral responsibility for what they do, and our maintaining their ignorance implies low regard for them as active subjects.

ETHICS AND INFLUENCE IN GENERAL

If these arguments are sound, then even though we began by considering influence through communication, the arguments apply to many other forms of influence that may be used in organisational politics, such as those identified by Cialdini. Many specific points that can be made about influence through communication can also be made about influence strategies more generally.

For example, just as mistrust of others' communications does not necessarily justify us in deceptive communications of our own, so mistrust of them in other respects does not necessarily justify other unethical behaviour by us. Being wary of unscrupulous meeting tactics by others might justify us in seeking the postponement of an issue to allow full discussion, but not of using similar tactics to theirs for a contrary end. Believing that a colleague plans to finalise some arrangement with the boss may justify me in having the arrangement discussed openly, but not necessarily in making some contrary pre-emptive and covert arrangement of my own.

Again, for example, just as my own fault may lessen some obligations you have toward me, it does not eliminate them all. If it is through laziness that I am late for a meeting, that may lessen your obligation to postpone items of business, but not your obligation to let me speak on other items when I do arrive. If I have unfairly promoted someone else over your head, that does not justify you spreading unsavoury rumours about my private life. Nor does the fault of some third party exempt us: it may have been bad of the boss to accept some covert arrangement with you, but that does not eliminate my obligations.

As in other parts of the discussion, these judgements rely on the belief that there will be some degree of consensus about the cases referred to, so that we can use them in trying to analyse other, more difficult cases. There may be differences of intuition amongst us about some of the cases referred to. In general, however, any particular case can be discussed in detail if it is contentious, and the line of argument here tries to avoid too much reliance on judgement about any single case.

At the same time, it is a recurrent theme of the discussion here that often our ethical judgements in particular cases rely on matters of concrete detail about the situation in question. We cannot say 'lying is wrong' without the qualification that some circumstances may make it otherwise. We cannot say even that 'lying is wrong unless done to protect the innocent', because the detail even of particular cases where lying is done to protect the innocent may be relevant (what they are to be protected from, perhaps, and what other effects the lie may have, or whether they have voluntarily and knowingly accepted the risk). A philosopher's way of making this point might be to say that our discussion can only refer to situations and cases 'under a description',[18] whereas practical ethical judgements are made in concrete situations. By describing such a situation in one way or another we may remind ourselves or others of some of its salient characteristics, but the decisions we make about how to act need to take account of all relevant features, whether included in the description or not.

Another way of putting this point as we discuss communication and influence is to say that often it is not what is done so much as how it is done that may be a matter of ethical concern. We commented earlier on Fairholm's identification of 'developing others' as a tactic of organisational politics. As thus described, it does not seem problematic or objectionable. If, however, you were to allocate development opportunities unfairly, that might be of concern. It might also be problematic if you expect those favoured to repay you with loyalty in matters where you do not deserve it. A similar point can be made of a number of other tactics Fairholm identifies: 'brinkmanship', 'rationalisation', 'dispensing rewards' and others may be entirely ethical in some circumstances, problematic in others. Likewise for other mechanisms that shape influence and power in organisations. It seems reasonable to suggest that French and Raven's 'coercive power', 'expert power' and other forms of power can all have both ethical and unethical uses. Our discussion is an attempt to say what aspects of situations may be relevant for the ethical assessment we wish to come to about them. Most especially we have noted our obligations to avert harm to others where we can do so at little cost to ourselves, our obligations to treat others fairly, and our obligations to treat them as autonomous agents like ourselves, who deserve opportunity to make responsible decisions. In making concrete judgements about specific situations, these are the sorts of considerations that are relevant. Our discussion is an effort to display just how they may be relevant in certain recurrent sorts of cases.

SUMMARY

The ethics of communication in organisational politics takes us quickly into issues about lying and deception. It seems reasonable to take a basically similar approach to various sorts of deceptive behaviour, ranging from lying or concealment to forms of impression management. Various factors will be relevant to determining what is ethical in our communications with others. One especially notable consideration is the need to treat others as responsible decision-makers. Nevertheless, we ought to be realistic about people's limitations and susceptibility to influence.

We also need to be realistic in protecting ourselves from harm or exploitation, not making *a priori* assumptions either about others' dishonesty or malice, or about their honesty and benevolence. Such a need to be realistic extends to guarding against self-deceptive efforts to lay the responsibility at others' feet when they have a false belief we could correct at little cost to ourselves. Sometimes, in that context it will be necessary amongst other things to bear in mind requirements of fairness.

Similar considerations apply also to influence tactics which rely for their effect on pragmatic rules of discourse, where people are led more or less covertly to conclusions *via* unstated background assumptions and tendentious formulations. In broad terms, they apply also to influence tactics that rely on triggers of influence like those described by Cialdini. One approach is to consider what is fair, but sometimes that will not determine the issue, and we need to consider what course most fully allows others to make responsible decisions.

Thus, we can deal with a number of situations that recur in organisational politics, and although there is no recipe for how to deal with them in a routine way, nevertheless there are considerations and principles that we can bear in mind to help us avoid some tempting errors. We turn now to some further cases of communication and influence, to see whether the same considerations will help us there also.

NOTES

1. Pfeffer emphasises that 'knowledge is power' in organisations, and that power therefore comes from being well situated in the organisation's 'network of communications and social relations' (1992, p. 111).

2. For an overview, see Bok (1978). For the example of physicians, see e.g. Bok 1984, chap. 9, Jackson 1991 and 1993, Bakhurst 1992 and Gillon 1993. For examples of discussion in the other areas, see: on marketing, Gundlach and Murphy (1993), Zeckhauser and Marks (1996) and Strutton, Hamilton and Lumpkin (1997); on public relations, Englehardt and Evans (1994); on policing, Kleinig (1996), chap. 7; on legal practice, White (1980), Williams (1983) and Applbaum (1998).

3. Simon suggests that the principle is analogous to the natural science principle of 'no action at a distance'.

4. Kant's 'On a Supposed Right to Lie from Altruistic Motives' forms an Appendix in Bok.

5. On the violation of a special relationship, see Bok (1978), chap. 11, Jackson (1993), p. 185 and Englehardt and Evans (1994), p. 263. As with a number of other ethical issues in organisational politics, there are problems with the view that the consequences of deceptive action are alone sufficient for its ethical evaluation (see e.g. Bok 1978, chap. 4), but it is consistent with that to suggest that consequences are one factor to be taken into consideration.

6. Above, p.130. In what follows I draw on Provis (2000b).

7. For some general discussion of how an ethical stance may have a realistic orientation to actual practice, see Boatright (1992).

8. Nevertheless, non-verbal methods can certainly be overdone: see e.g. Baron (1989) and Rosenfeld (1997), pp. 802–3.

9. Or consider this example:
   '"Yes, I've been talking to Commander Vimes, and now I would like to see the room where the crime was committed." William had great hopes of that sentence. It *seemed* to contain the words "and he gave me permission to" without actually doing so'
   — Pratchett 2000, pp. 113–14.

10. The first three italicisations are used by Walker to identify passages from the transcript she has presented earlier, with underlining to show speaker's emphasis; the other italics are emphasis by Walker.

11. The force and effect of the influence techniques that revolve around such rules cannot be emphasised too strongly. In some contexts, they are even the basis for induction of hypnotic trance: see e.g. Bandler and Grinder (1975), pp. 15–20.

12. The reference is to *Othello*, Act III, scene 3; Porter's brackets. In fact, the character Othello deals well enough with this particular sally by Iago, although eventually succumbing.

13. Hence, perhaps, Lewis Eliot's wish that a witness would 'answer a straight question fast': Snow (1972a), chap. 28.

14. For related but more general material see also Kipnis, Schmidt and Braxton-Brown (1990).

15. For more detailed discussion of how unfairness may be involved in some such cases, see Feinberg (1983), pp. 219–24.

16. For further discussion about the specific case of impression management in a job interview, see Rosenfeld (1997).

17. For general discussion of such issues, see Benn (1988), chap. 10.

18. Complexities of this notion are discussed in Anscombe (1979), but we may disregard them here. For more discussion of this general point, see Cullity (2002) and references therein.

9. Impression Management and Reality

We have been considering cases of influence, especially influence through communication, but also some other forms of influence that raise similar ethical issues. Various considerations are relevant, but in working out what is and is not ethical it will often be important to regard one another as autonomous agents who within the constraints placed on us by our finite capacities can come to responsible conclusions and make responsible decisions.

We have considered in particular how to evaluate cases where people use some techniques of 'impression management'. In the cases we have examined so far, impression management often consisted of giving to observers some true or false impression about pre-existing facts, such as my experience at the type of work I am being interviewed about. In other cases, however, it is not so clear that impression management leads others to true or false beliefs. In these cases, one person may perhaps be said to give others some impression, but there are no clear-cut facts that the impression is about. In this chapter, we consider some specific ethical issues about these latter sorts of cases. In some ways they resemble cases where people influence others' decisions by redirecting or distracting their attention. However, I shall suggest that we may not come to similar ethical evaluations of all these sorts of case. Once more, a dominant general requirement will be to take realistic account of others' abilities, needs and expectations.

We shall move on then to yet another form of impression management, which consists of a cooperative effort by a number of people jointly maintaining an impression which is required as part of some current social 'performance'. Consideration of this form of impression management may involve elements of deception, but also raises some ethical questions about forms of influence that we shall consider in the following chapter.

IMPRESSION MANAGEMENT AND FRAMING

Some of the linguistic 'formulations' we referred to in the previous chapter could have been efforts to deceive or mislead people: to lead them to false beliefs. But in many cases it is open to question whether people are misled about any factual issue. In cases like the 'optimistic formulations' discussed by Walker, what seems to be at issue is more to do with how people see the facts: how they 'frame' them, perhaps. The work on framing which was mentioned in Chapter 2 gives some clear examples of how people's attitudes toward facts can be influenced without any apparent difference in the facts themselves. Consider the classic experiment by Kahneman and Tversky:

> A group of subjects was presented with the following problem:
> The United States is preparing for the outbreak of an unusual Asian disease that is expected to kill 600 people. Two alternative programs are being considered. Which would you favor?
>
> 1. If program A is adopted, 200 will be saved.
> 2. If program B is adopted, there is one-third probability that all will be saved and a two-thirds probability that none will be saved.
>
> Of 158 respondents, 76% chose Program A, whereas only 24% chose Program B. The prospect of being able to save 200 lives for certain was more valued by most of the subjects than a risky prospect of equal expected value. Thus, most subjects were risk averse.
> A second group of subjects received the same cover story and the following two choices:
>
> 1. If program A is adopted, 400 people will die.
> 2. If program B is adopted, there is one-third probability that no one will die and a two-thirds probability that 600 people will die.
>
> Out of the 169 respondents in the second group, only 13% chose Program A, whereas 87% chose Program B. The prospect of 400 people dying was less acceptable to most of the subjects than a two-thirds probability that 600 will die. Thus, most subjects were risk seeking to the second set of choices.
> Careful examination of two problems finds them to be *objectively* identical. However, changing the description of outcomes from lives saved (gains) to lives lost (losses) was sufficient to shift the majority of subjects from a risk-averse to a risk-seeking orientation.
> (Neale and Bazerman 1985, p. 42, drawing from Tversky and Kahneman 1981)

The experiment is well known, and often cited. It shows how people's attitude to risk can change when the description of an event is changed even though it does not seem as though there is any change in the factual situation the description would apply to. In Chapter 2 we referred to the well-known joke that a pessimist is a person whose cup is half empty whereas an optimist's is half full, as an example of possible attitude and behavioural changes in people depending on how they 'frame' a situation. In wage negotiation, it could make a difference whether union representatives conceive of an offered increase as 3 per cent better than they are getting now, or 3 per cent less than the claim they made (or 3 per cent less than the rise obtained by some other group). And so on. There are various cases where the same situation or events may be described in more than one way, and the different descriptions then affect people's response. Techniques of framing can therefore be significant means of influence.

A related but slightly different form of influence redirects people's attention. We noted above that our practical decisions are made in real situations, and our descriptions of them can only ever be an abstraction from their full complexity, focussing on characteristics which are salient and relevant to our deliberations. In many situations, it is a challenge for us to drag back our minds from some features that preoccupy us for the moment, to consider some others. Often, processes of communication and influence get us to focus on some features that that we have neglected or to look away from some that have gripped us.

Such processes of framing and directing people's attention are very common in processes of persuasion. In organisations, for example, Bies has noted the importance of giving 'accounts' for actions, and impression management often is associated with providing 'excuses' for some action or outcome (see Bies 1989, Higgins and Snyder 1989, McLaughlin et al. 1992, Buchanan and Badham 1999, pp. 71, 201–04). Accounts and excuses often involve drawing people's attention to new aspects of a situation. What ethical issues arise about such processes?

Certainly, such processes are often ethically quite proper. An excuse may just be a genuine reason or justification for what was done, and an account may just highlight actual reasons and justifications. Sometimes, giving accounts or making excuses may be uncontroversially reasonable, when, for example, they consist of pointing out facts that others may simply not have known otherwise. If I explain the increased resource allocation to one production facility by referring to a new order you did not know about, or if you explain the failure of the marketing initiative by the unforeseeably mild winter that I did not previously know of, and if that account or excuse allays concerns, then there seems to be no reason for ethical disquiet, providing that the truth has been told and no relevant facts withheld. On the other hand, accounts or excuses people give may involve lying or concealment, and then the ethical issues are similar to those in other cases where deceptive accounts or conclusions intentionally lead people to false conclusions.

The difficult case is where giving an account or making an excuse does not involve truthfully adducing new information or deceptively telling lies or concealing relevant facts. Sometimes, it involves 'reframing' an issue, to have the same facts seen differently. Thus, for example, Higgins and Snyder note that some excuses 'capitalize on the fact that some acts or outcomes are more negative than others', so that 'with a bit of massaging, some negative outcomes can be made to look a lot better'. This 'massage' need not involve lying or concealment:

> A clear-cut example … can be seen in the routine trotting out of safety statistics comparing airline and highway travel following air tragedies. Also, charges that the air traffic control system is in disrepair have been refuted with the argument that the growing number of 'near misses' being reported is partly due to better reporting – a good thing! (1989, p. 79)

This kind of excuse-making seems often to be an exercise in 'framing'. It can change how things are seen, more than changing people's beliefs about what has actually happened. Similarly, when a manager gives an 'account', in Bies's terms, there may be no new facts adduced, but a different 'frame of reference' invoked, say, by pointing to other people who fared worse: 'For example, a manager could point out that "your 10% budget cut is a lot less than the company wide average cut of 20%"' (1989, p. 86). This could be new information, but may be only a matter of emphasis.

In cases like this, if Singh persuades Ali to see something in one way rather than another, we cannot condemn Singh's effort because it leads Ali to a false conclusion. If we persuade others to think of Kahneman and Tversky's case as saving 200 out of the 600, rather than as letting 400 die, or if we persuade the pessimist to think of his cup as half full rather than half empty, we cannot be criticised because the beliefs we have led them toward are false. In this, there is a contrast with other cases of deception. Whatever we may think about metaphysical and epistemological issues regarding objectivity, truth and reality, there seems to be a clear difference between the case where I frame something differently, on the one hand, and the case of such claims as that 'textile workers suffering from pulmonary problems are all heavy smokers', as mooted in legal argument by one of the companies Jackall studied (1988, p. 157). In the latter case, but not in the former, there are facts about the world that make one point of view veridical and another not. As an excuse, the company statement can be compared with evidence and evaluated as true or false, whereas in many cases there seems to be no truth or falsity about how things are framed.

Nevertheless, despite the fact that different frames may not correspond to any fact of the matter, in some cases a decision can certainly depend on seeing something one way rather than another. The term 'framing' is associated with the idea of a 'decision frame', used by Tversky and Kahneman to refer to 'the decision-maker's conception of the acts, outcomes, and contingencies associated with a particular choice' (1981, p. 453). How we 'frame' such acts, outcomes, and contingencies can affect our attitudes and inclinations in a variety of ways. In many ways the idea is an old one. Aristotle noted that we can excite admiration by giving our speech a 'foreign' air, and that whether we refer to someone's act as 'making a mistake' or 'committing a crime' can affect our attitude towards it even though each description may be true (1926, III, ii, p. 357). Such effects on attitudes can then flow on to our decisions and actions.

Political rhetoric is not the only area where those kinds of effects are well known. It is the stuff of literary criticism. Ideas like metaphor, tone, allusion, euphemism, and many more, make up an armoury of critical apparatus that can be brought to bear in analysing how writers and speakers contrive their effects on an audience. The use of 'association' and 'framing' were well known in practice, even before modern experimental testing identified some of the mechanisms clearly. For us, the general question is whether it is possible to give any clear ethical evaluation of such 'framing' when it is used as a tactic in organisational politics.

Some ethical problems seem clear enough. I have suggested that deliberately inducing false beliefs in others in some controlled way can be liable to blame, whether it consists of a false statement in words – lying – or by some other mechanism such as wearing a particular tie. The same principles will apply to such cases as concealing certain information, if we have some reasonable belief about what conclusion someone else would arrive at with the information, and that concealing it will induce a different belief. It will also apply to 'distortion', if that includes revelation of some facts but withholding others. But is it 'distortion' to refer to something as 'making a mistake' rather than as 'committing a crime', when each description is a true one?

There seem to be many variations of these processes in organisational politics. We may recall Allen and colleagues' finding that 'attacking or blaming others' and 'selective use of information' were among some of the most frequently mentioned tactics of organisational politics. The use of 'excuses' as part of impression management overlaps very much with blaming others or using information selectively. There are many ways that these tactics can be put into practice. 'Blaming' does not have to take the form of saying 'so-and-so was to blame'; it can be implicit in our description of events. If we revert for a moment to our earlier example, to say that Simon 'made advances' to Jennifer has a connotation of blameworthiness not present in 'asked out on a date', or to say that Tricia 'left Jennifer in the lurch' has an implication absent from 'decided not to act on Jennifer's allegations'.

Analysis is made especially difficult because there are some cases where accounts and excuses involve misrepresentation of some facts, but facts that are hard to evidence. For example, there are cases where there is some element of deception in our use of language to impute blame. If I blame Rhonda by saying that she victimised Jeff, then I imply not only that Rhonda treated Jeff adversely, but that Jeff was in some way especially picked out or was treated in some identifiably wrong ways. I might accuse Rhonda despite knowing that she had endeavoured to act fairly and reasonably. To that extent, my accusation is deceptive: it distorts the facts. However, in this case, even there though there may be some facts that make my accusation false, it is likely to be contentious to what extent the treatment was wrong or Jeff especially picked out, and for that reason the claim may escape any clear identification as deceptive conduct.

It may well be that clear cases of deceptive conduct blend gradually into cases where 'distortion' occurs, not through clearly identifiable mis-statement but through choice of language. In some cases, there are clear facts that are mis-stated. In some others, like an accusation of 'victimisation', the facts are hard to get at. For our purposes, though, going back to the idea of 'framing', the important thing is that there are some cases where imputations of blame may escape the label of deceptive conduct not because the facts they imply are contentious, but they have no clear factual implications at all.

Something similar can be said about selective use of information. There are occasions where selective use of information consists of revealing some facts but concealing others. If I mention to the boss that you failed to get the contract, but omit to mention that the reason was that the other company went out of business, I may do so with the deliberate intention of doing you down in the boss's eyes, and imputing some blame to you, contrary to what is reasonable, thereby using information selectively, acting deceitfully, and blaming others, all at once (we should never be lulled into thinking that the processes and tactics we are thinking about cannot co-exist). If, at a meeting, I reveal some figures but not others that I know would lead people to a different overall conclusion, I have acted deceptively. We may condemn such conduct for the sorts of reasons we have discussed in the case of other deceptive conduct: it deprives others of the opportunity to come to responsible decisions of their own. But there are other cases where it is not clear whether 'selective use of information' amounts to deceptive conduct. Imagine the case at the same meeting where the figures are available to everyone, and I have concealed nothing, but make a case which emphasises some at the expense of others. We can equally well refer to this as selective use of information, but here where the selective use lies in emphasis, the case seems to be different from that where the selection lies in concealing some facts and revealing others.

From an ethical point of view, the case is made more difficult because it seems as though any presentation or statement does in one sense involve selective use of information. We never tell all the facts: time does not allow it. Just as descriptions of ethical problems abstract from the complexity of any real situation, so does any statement of fact. The question seems not to be whether one selects, but how one does.

Effectively the same point can be made in response to a suggestion of Aristotle's. He acknowledges the finite capacities of humans as something that we have to take realistic account of, and suggests that this 'corruption' alone explains the need for attention to matters of rhetorical style:

> For justice should consist in fighting the case with the facts alone, so that everything else that is beside demonstration is superfluous; nevertheless ... it is of great importance owing to the corruption of the hearer. (1926, III, i, p. 347)

But consider once more the experiment by Kahneman and Tversky. What were 'the facts alone' in the situation described to subjects? What are 'the facts alone' of the cup: is it half full, or half empty? It is not clear that it is always possible to find a statement that avoids any 'frame'. At least in some situations, there may be no straightforward and comprehensible way to state things without choosing one frame or another. We are confronted here by aspects of human beings that cannot reasonably be labelled 'corruption',[1] but only reflect our finite and imperfect capacities for processing information and making decisions. For us, then, the question is whether there can be any ethical concern about what frame is chosen, provided it is consistent with the facts.

ATTENTION, RESOURCES AND RESPONSIBILITY

We can approach this same point from a slightly different direction if we consider the virtue of tact. This revolves around the fact that communication not only conveys information, but turns people's attention in some directions rather than others. We noted Katz and Kahn's suggestion that 'communication may reveal problems as well as eliminate them' and that 'a conflict in values, for example, may go unnoticed until communication is attempted'. To possess the virtue of tact requires us to be aware of the effects that our communications may have, quite aside from their truthfulness. Tact at a dinner party may require us not to mention that Ted is a socialist, even though that may be true. Often, the most important requirement of tact is to consider the effects of our communications on people's attention, whatever the truth of them may be. Others may know that Ted is a socialist, but that fact may not have been at the forefront of their minds during the hitherto pleasant conversation. More simply, that I have a boil on my nose does not mean that you have to point it out. A tactless communication may direct our attention in ways that are both unnecessary and unwelcome.

The result of communication can be to divert our psychological resources from considering one issue to considering another. The point is a fundamental one in all kinds of politics. In wider politics, the term 'khaki election' can be used to refer to efforts by one party – often an incumbent government – to focus electors' attention on one problem or issue, such as a tense international situation, so that they attend less to other problems, such as social or economic conditions. But the same technique can be used in organisational politics, at all levels. A Board of Directors may focus attention on new initiatives to divert people from existing problems. A manager may raise an issue about car parking in order to distract staff attention from bonus arrangements or departmental restructuring. A section leader may talk about the Christmas party to distract people from problems with the computer upgrade. The possibilities are endless.

Most importantly, there is no need in these cases to assume that people are lying in what they say about issues. There may actually be a tense international situation. The Board may have genuine interest in the new initiatives. There may be some real problem about car parking, and there may really be a need to consider the Christmas party, before it is too late to make a restaurant booking.

Just as in cases where the same facts are 'framed' one way rather than another, there is little room to raise ethical concerns about such tactics on grounds that people are brought to false beliefs. The case where people are distracted from one issue by true statements about something else are perhaps at one end of a spectrum that has outright lying at the other. We may then ask whether there are ways for us to come to reasonable conclusions about the ethics of such processes.

I suggest that there is an obligation to consider others' state of attention, and the understanding that they will have of an issue, and that it stems from the same general obligation we have discussed before, the obligation we have to acknowledge other self-conscious subjects as beings like ourselves, to respect their need for an understanding of the world which is as accurate as our own, and to allow them to make morally responsible decisions. We noted in Chapter 5 that parties may not reasonably be held to consent to a proposal if their agreement is obtained by deception or fraud. We have argued in the previous chapter that there are often reasons to condemn actions that deliberately induce false beliefs in others, at least in part because such actions can diminish those others' responsibility for consequent actions of theirs. That point is tied to the idea that consent based on deliberately induced false beliefs is not binding. We might more strongly argue that people's consent to a proposal is not binding unless it has been presented to them in a way that allows them to understand and consider it. Various factors can detract from their doing so. One of them is for other issues to be presented to them that distract their attention. Another, closely related, is just for the issue to be presented to them when their attention or cognitive resources are already preoccupied. The concrete ways in which these sorts of tactics may be manifested is limitless. They often intermingle with other slightly different tactics, such as presenting issues when people are fatigued, under time pressure, with others whose presence will affect their decision, and so on.

In this view, our obligation to allow others to make responsible decisions requires us to take account of factors that may inhibit them from doing so, such as fatigue or distraction. That obligation is not limited to simple face-to-face communication between individuals. It includes other forms of communication, and cases where numbers of people are involved. It also goes beyond simple forms of distraction of attention to other issues about people's ability and opportunity to deal with an issue. For example, consider the design of a meeting agenda. We have several items to consider. We can make some estimate of how contentious each may be, and – what is not necessarily the same thing – how much time each may take. We may know also that one or two members probably will not be able to attend until part-way through the meeting, that others may have to leave early, and that most will have to leave at the scheduled finish time. We could if necessary alter the meeting time, and within limits also, we can decide on the venue. We can decide on additional items if we wish.

Given that situation, we might consider how best to organise things. If we are trying to present items in a way that allows those considering them to make considered, responsible decisions, then we may have to take account of the items' relative importance and urgency, or which members have the greatest expertise and interests in different items. It could be tempting to put some contentious items late on the agenda, so that perhaps some who would have opposed the course we desire may have left the meeting and others will be under time pressure when it is being discussed. Or we might deliberately include some item that can reasonably be expected to attract extended, detailed discussion, and immediately afterwards schedule the item in which we have an interest. (Of course, in many cases the early discussion in a meeting can be about how to order the business to be dealt with, but even assuming that, there is some room for manoeuvre, in a variety of ways.)

What are the ethical constraints on us? If we extrapolate from our earlier discussion of misleading or deceptive behaviour, we can take it to be clear that we ought not lie to people about what the agenda of the meeting will be, when it will take place, or what the order of items will be. (Even clearer, if anything can be, we may not lie in any background information given to people at the meeting about the items under discussion.) But may we refrain from indicating in positive terms what the agenda will be? May we send out the agenda as late as possible, in order to ensure that people will have as little time as possible to change other commitments? Can we use abbreviated or guarded language in the terms of the agenda, in order not to alert people to the full detail of what is to be discussed?

Here, we come to some precisely similar issues as those which arise about communication. When one person is communicating with others, lying is generally condemned, but there are question marks over some other forms of behaviour like impression management. While lying is generally wrong, there are cases of impression management where it starts to become unclear whether responsibility lies at the door of the person giving the impression or the person gaining the impression.

Sometimes, people may gain an impression through their own lack of care. Not immediately, but eventually, there comes a point where we are no longer obliged to cater for others' possible shortcomings. In the present case, if full notice of a meeting has been given, with a clear agenda and ample time for discussion, then if one or more of those opposed to a proposal absent themselves for reasons to do with their own pleasure or minor convenience, then there seems no obligation on us to postpone discussion of the issue. This is not to say that all cases are straightforward. What if someone goes to sleep in the meeting? Is there an obligation to wake them up? Does it make a difference if they are tired for laudable or for culpable reasons (working late for charity, or up all night partying, for example)? Once more, we can point to sorts of considerations that may be relevant, without identifying rules.

With communication in general, I contended that if people through errors of their own assist others' attempts at deception or influence, that still does not in itself free others from blame. However, there are limits to the obligations we have to cater for others' errors or shortcomings. We cannot pretend that they do not exist, and we ought to take reasonable steps to assist others when they falter, but our obligations are not limitless. If our intentions are straightforward, we have done nothing to evoke the others' failure, and we have acted in ways that would be appropriate given reasonable effort by the others, then the only question seems to be what cost there is to us to make further allowances for them. If the cost is significant, then it might be good but does not seem obligatory for us to do so. We ought not pretend that things are different than we know them to be, or assume things that we can easily check, and we ought not take advantage of others simply because we cannot be sure that will not try to do the same to us. But we do not have to go indefinitely far out of our way to compensate for failings of others which it is open to them to remedy.

Clearly, these things may be true and it still be hard to work out what is required in any concrete case. There will be difficult questions about the extent to which others might have avoided their error, or were responsible for it, and about the cost that I may incur by trying to make further allowances for them. But that is only to say as we have said elsewhere that often there will be no rule that we can follow blindly in determining what to do. Each case is likely to have its own complexities, and the basic ethical requirement on us in all cases is to heed the details that are relevant and try as far as we can to decide accordingly.

SOME PRINCIPLES FOR AN ETHICAL APPROACH

Clearly, it is not hard to replicate examples which raise the same general issues. In face-to-face communication between two people, in telephone conversations and by electronic mail, in written reports and oral briefing sessions, emphasis can be given to some points rather than others, issues raised to distract attention from others, or the timing and arrangement of the communication designed to enhance or inhibit critical thought.

In organisations, a perennial issue is that the plethora of information available to be communicated constantly means that selection is necessary. The idea of an 'executive summary' of a document reminds us that busy managers cannot assimilate all the detail about a matter, and that the author of a document is expected to identify some details as crucial, conveying an understanding to executive readers which is sufficient for their purposes. The implication is that the author can ascertain their purposes and then decide well enough what is relevant. The principle can be taken further to other situations, involving not executives but other managers and staff: often, when deciding what to communicate, we can decide what is relevant given the purposes and interests of the audience. Sometimes, that is not clear to start with, and it may require effort and time to work it out, but we may have obligations to commit that effort and time. More generally, we have some obligation to take account of people's limitations: the fact that we are finite in our capacities and resources, and thereby constrained in dealing with information and issues that are presented to us.[2]

If this is correct, we can find some grounds for ethical evaluation of tactics like drawing people's attention to one thing rather than another, in the general obligation to respect others as responsible decision-makers, but decision-makers whose capacities are finite and fallible. The question we always have to consider is whether people can reasonably be held responsible for the decisions they are induced to make: Would we say that they are the authors of the decisions, or would we hold others responsible? That question is not always an easy one to answer, but we have to answer it in many contexts in ethical and legal decision-making, so that calling on it in organisational politics is at least using a tool with which we are familiar from other contexts, however imprecise a tool it is. The situation is one that Benn referred to as 'heterarchy' ('rule by others'), saying that this is a condition

> in which a person's preferences, his beliefs, or his capacity to act on his belief commitments have been rigged or impaired by methods that intentionally circumvent or block his rational decision-making capacity. (1988, p. 167)

If I construct an executive summary of a document which I know omits certain information that you, the reader, would take to be important, and that you will rely on the summary, there is a strongly arguable case that you are not responsible for the decision you take: that I am the one who is responsible, not you. In some cases there will be room for argument about the extent to which I ought to have relied on the summary, but the general kind of argument is one we are familiar with in a variety of contexts.

Techniques of influence can be questionable when they involve distracting people in order to influence their behaviour by taking account of our fallibility and finite capacity for absorbing and reflecting on information. But that is not to say that there is anything inherently problematic in redirecting people's attention. What we normally attend to is a matter of what we hold to be important, and what we hold to be important is discernible from our decisions and courses of actions in a variety of situations. If I direct your attention to an oncoming vehicle, I am only helping you to attend to what you hold to be important, and there is no ethical question about the case.

Some difficult questions arise where there might be argument that I ought to hold something to be important, even though I do not. However, these are again questions that arise in a variety of contexts, and we cannot hope to deal with them in the context of organisational politics independently of answers we may wish to give to them in other contexts. The general issue is that of 'paternalism': how far am I justified in influencing others' decisions in their interests or in the interests of a good outcome, even though I do so contrary to their own preference and judgement? The answer may depend on what is at stake, for them and others, and on what other options I have available. But we can at least say that it is unethical to influence others toward decisions to the extent that they can no longer be said to be the authors of the decisions, unless there is some strong and worthy reason so to influence them.

If that line of argument helps us to deal with examples of influence that involve directing people's attention one way or another, it also helps us deal with cases that involve 'framing' or getting people to see things in one way rather than another. To the extent that framing is associated with decision-making – that is, to the extent that frames are 'decision frames' – we can look here also to whether the framing in question detracts from people's responsibility for their decisions. That will again require us to look at whether they are induced to see things in ways that run contrary to what they hold important, as evidenced by their decisions and actions in other contexts.

There seems to be more room for legitimate influence through getting people to frame things in a new way, than through distracting their attention, or seeking decisions from them when they are tired, unwell, or the like. Consider the case of the *Challenger* disaster. Robert Lund was the vice-president of engineering at Thiokol, the company that made the rocket boosters. At first, he would not approve the launch, agreeing with the company engineers that conditions were dangerous.

> However, feeling pressured by NASA's anxiety to launch the *Challenger* and reassured by NASA's confidence in the launch's success, Jerry Mason, to whom Lund reported, told Lund, '[T]ake off [your] engineering hat and put on [your] management hat ... Lund capitulated, agreed to the launch, and Kilminster, senior vice president at Thiokol, signed off for the company. (Werhane 1999, p. 49, citing Vaughn 1996, pp. 318–20)

The invitation to look at the situation from the point of view of a manager rather than an engineer, seems (as Werhane points out) to be an invitation to frame the decision differently: to attend to different considerations and to weigh risks differently. But it is not clear that it was unethical of Mason to try to influence Lund in that way.

Undoubtedly, the ultimate decision was a mistake. Werhane suggests that 'if managers in Lund's position are supposed to take into account overall conditions, facts, and likely outcomes, Lund failed' (1999, p. 59). Just here, though, the question is whether there was anything unethical in Mason's influence. It seems hard to say that there was. There is no reason in the situation as we have outlined it to assume that Mason was not being reasonably conscientious in what he did, or that he was bringing unreasonable pressure to bear on Lund, beyond the sort of persuasion that is necessary in organisational life. In this case, the outcome was appalling for all concerned, but that may simply show that not all bad outcomes are the result of unethical action, which seems uncontroversially true. It is not to say that Mason's action or Lund's decision were good, or sound. Often, in organisations, people will fail to live up to the highest standards of action, but in our ordinary lives we do not condemn as unethical or morally wrong all failures to achieve the highest standards of conduct.

In some ways, this point is reminiscent of one discussed by Riker in *The Art of Political Manipulation* (1986: see esp. pp. 31–3). Where members of a group have varying preferences amongst different outcomes, and have to decide on a course of action by voting, the decision will often be affected by how the issues are separated and ordered. But they have to be separated and ordered in some way or other, and to arrange things in a way that is likely to produce a particular outcome is not necessarily unethical, if done openly and in ways that are consistent with fair procedural rules. Undoubtedly, it is possible to manipulate a meeting agenda covertly, or in ways that do not give different points of view a fair chance to be heard, or to attain outcomes that are unethical for some other reason, such as producing harm for third parties, treating individuals poorly, or the like. But the mere fact that the agenda is arranged in a way that makes one outcome more likely than another is not inherently unethical, even if that outcome is the one favoured by the person making the arrangement.

Equally, a choice will often have to be framed in one way or another, and there seems to be nothing inherently unethical in a person framing it in a way that promotes a favoured outcome. At the very least, we can say that if there was anything wrong about Mason's influence of Lund, it was not inherent in the way he got Lund to frame the decision differently. If there was anything unethical, it must be found in background detail such as what was at stake, what were accepted standards and contractual obligations, and the like. If we condemn as unethical the way that Mason influenced Lund, by openly and straightforwardly getting him to reframe the decision, then we tend to lose the distinction between this sort of case and cases that we wish to condemn more forcefully: cases where influence is 'smuggled in', to use Cialdini's term, where the reframing is achieved subtly and covertly, like Iago's success at getting Othello to see Desdemona quite differently than before.

Overall, there does not seem to be any single, general answer to the question whether it is ethical or unethical to influence others by getting them to frame things in one way rather than another, or by directing their attention one way rather than another. Whether it is ethical depends on detail of the concrete situation. We can point to relevant sorts of considerations, but we shall need to evaluate different cases one by one in the light of those sorts of considerations. We can at least see that it would be an over-simplification, and an error, to suggest that all these sorts of cases are a matter of deception, or of manipulation, and equally an error to suggest that none are.

IMPRESSION MANAGEMENT AS PERFORMANCE

These points and some others can be seen in the example of job interviews, which we have alluded to already. We made mention of some issues that arise, such as the possibility that I as an applicant for a position might deliberately give you the impression that I have much greater experience of some work than I actually do have, or that I fail to disabuse you of some clearly false impression that you have gained. It would be wrong deliberately to give you a false impression by making a false claim on a résumé or a false statement in the interview, but it seems to be equally wrong to contrive a straightforwardly false impression by other means such as wearing a particular old school tie.

However, there are other sorts of impression management in interviews. Impression management may involve 'framing' or direction of people's attention in ways that affect their conclusions or decisions, but this sort of impression management blends into another form, where the impression management that we undertake is more in the nature of a theatrical performance. Here, people convey their ways of seeing a situation to others by their verbal and non-verbal behaviour, and others respond so as to confirm and perhaps extend that way of seeing. This sort of reciprocated impression management may be relevant to job performance, because the ability to perform it is relevant to people's ability and willingness to perform the job itself (cf. Rosenfeld 1997, p. 804). Jackall refers to this sort of case when he comments on the change that comes over students who are being interviewed for the sorts of jobs he studied:

> Every spring at elite colleges and universities throughout the land, a small but instructive transformation takes place when corporate recruiters from a wide variety of large companies descend on campuses to screen graduating seniors for entry-level managerial jobs. The jeans, ragged shirts, beards, mustaches, and casual unkemptness of youth that typify college life, particularly in rural areas, give way to what is called the corporate uniform – three-piece, wool pin-striped suits or suited skirts; button-down collars or unfrilled blouses; sedate four-in-hand foulards for men and floppy printed bow ties for women; wing-tipped shoes or plain low-heeled pumps; somber, straightforward hues; and finally, bright, well-scrubbed, clean-shaven or well-coiffured appearances. It is, in short, a uniform that bespeaks the sobriety and seriousness appropriate to the men and women who would minister to the weighty affairs of industry, finance, and commerce. (1988, p. 46)

More junior students who have not yet reached that point look on bemused and disapproving, but the interview candidates 'know that managers have to look the part and that all corporations are filled with well-groomed and conventionally well-dressed men and women'. Because of the need 'to look the part', 'they consciously decide to alter their external appearance to fit these well-known and widely disseminated criteria' (p. 47).

In such cases, there does not appear to be any harm done by one party to another, nor any deception of one party by another, and in terms of fairness to other candidates for employment or promotion, using one's proficiency at such impression management at least does not seem any more unfair than it is to display any other job-relevant proficiencies and skills. Nor is there any lack of respect for others as responsible decision-makers. One is simply displaying one's skill at discerning what sort of 'performance' is required and at participating in such a performance. To that extent, it is hard to see what might be ethically objectionable.

Nevertheless, the sort of 'performance' that Jackall describes as part of employment interviews can be found elsewhere as well, and in some cases there may be some other issues that need ethical exploration. Let us therefore consider more closely the idea of impression management as performance.

The idea of a need 'to look the part' in the way Jackall describes is an aspect of Goffman's wider idea of impression management. The 'performances' that Goffman discusses are endemic to social life. His accounts point out that in most social settings we have some appreciation of what is and is not expected of people like us in that setting, and that we use that understanding to guide and regulate what we do just as actors in a theatrical production use a variety of means to get an impression across to an audience. In conveying a character's affluence, the actor will dress appropriately as well as moving and speaking with an appropriate air of confidence, in conveying affection an actor on stage and we in our own interactions may speak with tender voices, touch another gently, ask considerately what we can do to help them, and so on. In everyday life, we may sometimes act in those ways spontaneously out of affection, but sometimes will do so intentionally to let our affection be known, and to that extent what we do is a 'performance'. As a performance there need be nothing about it that is insincere or misleading. It may be distinguished as a performance by just the same sorts of characteristics as H.P. Grice noted are part of 'meaning' something by what we say: we say it with the intention that it will be recognised as being said with that intention (Grice 1957). If I tell you that it is raining outside, then I mean you to understand that by what I say I intend you to understand that it is raining. Equally, when I gently touch your arm as a sign of affection, I may mean you to understand that I do it as a sign of affection. As a performance, everything that I do may be clear and open, and yet be done deliberately as part of a set of accepted conventions and 'scripts'.[3]

Goffman has been criticised for over-emphasising the 'ritual' aspects of social life,[4] and it seems clear that sometimes our behaviour is less self-conscious or reflective than the term 'performance' suggests. On the other hand, however, it reminds us that there are many pieces of social behaviour that have important aspects of performance about them. One of these is the need for the hopeful applicants for entry-level managerial jobs to 'look the part'. There is no suggestion that the graduating students are trying to convince their interviewers that their dress and demeanour are always as they present it for the interview. The interviewers are not so naïve as to believe that, and the students are not so naïve as to think they would. The students are showing to the interviewers that they understand what is expected and can meet the expectations.

To that extent, it is too narrow to suggests that it is just in 'sales settings' and the like that the ability to undertake effective impression management is important in its own right, and so something that a job interview may quite reasonably wish to assess (Rosenfeld 1997, p. 804, citing Lautenschlager and Flaherty 1990). The skills demonstrated in an interview can be more general skills of social perception, expression and interaction. Jackall suggests that within corporations self-presentation and associated forms of impression management are important because of the skills and dispositions that they signal to others:

> Businesses always try to epitomize social normality, and managers, who must both create and enforce social rules for lower-level workers and simultaneously embody their corporation's image in the public arena, are expected to be alert to prevailing norms. ... Anyone who is so dull-witted or stubborn that he does not respond to social suggestions and become more presentable is quickly marked as unsuitable for any consideration for advancement. If a person cannot read the most obvious social norms, he will certainly be unable to discern more ambiguous cues. (1988, p. 47)

This is the sort of impression management emphasised by Goffman in *The Presentation of Self in Everyday Life*. It is not a unilateral effort by one person to produce an impression on another, but a cooperative effort by a number of people to maintain an impression which is required as part of some current 'performance'.

This sort of impression management can be very important in organisational politics, and raises some new ethical issues, as emerges in the comments by one of the managers interviewed by Jackall, who referred to 'the game' that it is necessary to play:

> 'What's the game? It's bringing troops home from Vietnam and declaring peace with honor. It's saying one thing and meaning another.
> 'It's characterizing the reality of a situation with *any* description that is necessary to make that situation more palatable to some group that matters. It means that you have to come up with a culturally accepted verbalization to explain why you are *not* doing what you are doing. ... [Or] you say that we had to do what we did because it was inevitable; or because the guys at the [regulatory] agencies were dumb; [you] say we won when we really lost; [you] say we saved money

when we squandered it; [you] say something's safe when it's potentially or actually dangerous....' (1988, p. 145; ellipses and brackets in Jackall)

He goes on to say that 'everyone knows that it's bullshit', and there may then be some question about the extent to which the tactics are deceptive, in the sense that they are intended to induce false beliefs in the audience. However, discussing bullshit in general, Frankfurt notes that 'however studiously and conscientiously the bullshitter proceeds, it remains true that he is also trying to get away with something' and it is at least 'unconnected to a concern with the truth' (1986, pp. 122, 124). Further still, perhaps, in the cases recounted by Jackall's interviewee, it is at least likely that while there is no expectation of deceiving those who know the game, nevertheless there is some intention to deceive any who are not amongst the *cognoscenti*: junior workers, outside observers, and the like.[5] In some cases, at least, this sort of social impression management is ethically questionable because it is deceptive.

Nevertheless, the fact that some people may be deceived by the bullshit that is part of the game, does not identify all the dimensions of it that raise ethical issues. The idea of the game draws us further into Goffman's account of impression management as part of a 'performance'. The idea of a performance builds in the idea of a theatrical role, with associated scripts. It was mentioned in Chapter 2 above that subsequent social psychology has taken up the idea of a 'script', and has acknowledged that often our actions are guided by what we take to be appropriate in a situation, given established patterns of expectation by ourselves and others. Often, these scripts are shared amongst a number of participants, who have to cooperate in joint 'impression management'.

It should be clear how this form of impression management as conceived by Goffman goes beyond the forms we have previously considered, where one individual tries to influence others' impressions to obtain some advantage. Some authors imply that impression management is almost exclusively a form of behaviour dedicated to self-advancement and pursuit of advantage. Baumeister seems to suggest this:

People's own individual goals typically involve the pursuit of self-interest. In work organizations, such goals include protecting one's job, maintaining and increasing one's salary, and advancing one's career. Increasingly, these goals depend on how the individual is perceived by other members of the organization. Thus, for individuals to pursue their goals in an organizational context, it becomes vitally important to communicate certain information (or misinformation) about themselves to others. Thus, self-presentation, or impression management, is of central importance. (1989, p. 57)

We have questioned the extent to which it ought to be assumed that self-interest is a predominant motive people have in their organisational behaviour, but we can certainly agree that self-interest is common. It is not clear, however, that we need even that point as a basis for the claim that impression management is important or common. It would be a mistake to believe that only the pursuit of self-interest leads to impression management. It is too limited to view it as 'analogous to an advertising campaign on behalf of a commercial product' (Rosenfeld 1997, p. 801). Manning notes that while parts of Goffman's work might suggest that this is the main function of impression management, some of Goffman's articles clearly have a quite contrary implication: 'Instead of analyzing people as calculative manipulators seeking personal gain, these papers suggest that we are all guardians of face-to-face situations' (1992, p. 38, referring in particular to Goffman 1955 and 1956). In many contexts, joint impression management activities seem to be very much a matter of mutual cooperation rather than individualistic pursuit of advantage.

This guardianship of face-to-face situations (and perhaps of other social situations) can require us to acknowledge others' expectations as reasonable and legitimate, and to be consistent in the expectations and intentions we ourselves express, so as to allow this joint enterprise to continue. We have alluded above to the ethical requirement that we ought to take realistic account of others' expectations, but the present point goes beyond that. For us to make our social life mutually comprehensible we often need to take account of one another's expectations and make decisions about courses of action that are at least broadly in accordance with them, including the general expectations people have of one another, and the more specific expectations we have induced by our prior actions. In particular, to the extent that we induce a well-defined set of expectations in others by what we say or how we act, we can be said to establish a particular 'line' of action, and there will then be pressure on us to act subsequently in ways that are consistent with the line, to avoid disappointing others or eliciting accusations of inconsistency from them. Goffman contends that

> Regardless of whether a person intends to take a line, he will find that he has done so in effect. The other participants will assume that he has more or less willfully taken a stand, so that if he is to deal with their response to him he must take into consideration the impression they have possibly formed of him. (1955, p. 5)

The ideas of 'taking a line' and 'taking a stand' are both fundamental to accounts of organisational politics, and taken further in the work of positioning theory, mentioned earlier. In the next chapter we consider how they can play a significant part in some techniques of influence.

Social life often involves people understanding one another's mutual expectations, acknowledging them and taking account of them in what they do. Often, they are thereby involved in a type of performance and an activity of joint impression management where it is too limited to confine ourselves to such ideas as that 'shrewd impression managers will seek to learn what kind of person the boss likes and then try to act accordingly, in order to get the boss to think of them as that kind of person' (Baumeister 1989, p. 59), or the idea that 'pleasing the audience tends to make people become almost social chameleons, who change their behavior and appearance depending on the preferences of their social environment' (ibid.). Goffman's emphasis on impression management as part of a performance is that a number of people tend to find themselves together in a situation where each has some role to play, and poor performance will impact adversely not just on the actor but also on the others involved. The performance people give is not just a matter of the 'preferences' of their social environment, but of the mutual expectations of the people in it. We have so far discussed some of the ethical issues that are raised by impression management when we conceive it just in terms of one person producing an impression on others. We turn in the next chapter to some ethical issues about impression management as social performance, and further implications about obligations derived from others' expectations.

SUMMARY

In this chapter we began by noticing forms of impression management that go beyond inducing beliefs in others about some fairly well-defined facts, to cases where there does not seem to be any fact of the matter at all. When such impression management is used as a means of influence, it in some ways resembles influence through redirecting or distracting others' attention. The latter form or influence may be ethically questionable even where people's attention is affected by pointing out things that are true. Ethical communication can require us to take realistic account of people's capacities to process information, and their interests, as well as the truth of what we communicate.

On the other hand, there is no general presumption that it is wrong to direct people's attention in one way rather than another, or to get them to frame things one way rather than another. To do those things is often an unavoidable part of communication. Whether our communication is ethical depends upon the extent to which we try so far as we can to take account of others' priorities and resources, to allow them once again to make responsible decisions.

A somewhat different form of impression management is to be found in cases of social performance. Here, there is a cooperative effort amongst different people to maintain a good impression, both for themselves and other observers. Sometimes, again, there is no false impression conveyed, but only a true demonstration given of participants' skills and capacities. In other cases, the joint performance may give observers a false and misleading picture, and in those cases it is as questionable as other deceptive conduct. However, there are some other ethical issues that arise about impression management as social performance, apart from issues to to do with deception. In the next chapter, we shall consider some of the other ethical issues that arise when social impression management is used as a means of influence.

NOTES

1. We may note that μοχθηριαν can also be translated as 'hardship' or 'wretchedness', which perhaps connotes only the finitude and limitations of human nature that we recognise.
2. Arguably, the whole profession of accounting is devoted to presenting information in ways that satisfy these constraints. See for example MacNeal (1939).
3. And, even more subtly, perhaps of non-verbal 'idioms': Goffman (1971), p. 80.
4. For discussion of some such criticisms, see Branaman (1997), pp. xlix–li.
5. Thus Punch's comment that most instances of business deviance are united by deception (above, p. 147) adds reference to 'the accompanying necessity to engage in institutional impression management' (1996, p. 215).

10. Influence, Expectations and Legitimacy

In the sort of 'game' described by Jackall's manager, there is more to impression management than just self-advertising or trying to please an audience, and the performance people give is a continuing reciprocal response to one another's expectations and behaviour. In the earlier cases we considered, when impression management is a matter of conveying some particular impressions to others, there are some ethical issues about truthfulness and deception. There can be similar problems with impression management as social performance. The examples given by Jackall's manager paint things in a false light, and may deceive outsiders, if not insiders.[1] But there are cases of impression management as joint performance which need not involve any false impressions. A performance by host and guest may display their abilities to give and receive hospitality in a graceful way: they are not falsely pretending to be graceful, rather their successful display of grace is truly graceful because it is successful. Sometimes, such performances are given for their own sake, or for the mutual satisfaction of participants; sometimes, they are given for others. In either case, often there is no intention to convey a false impression of people's abilities or dispositions, so much as a true impression of their capacity for perception and expression. The display can then reflect skills people have at social perception and communication and responsiveness, which are relevant to many types of work in organisations and which it is important for others to be able to assess.

To that extent, impression management as performance does not seem to raise ethical concerns. However, performances which require cooperation from a number of participants can result in pressure from others for each to play his or her part. Because of that, the sort of impression management that consists of a social performance can be used as a means of influence. In what follows, we explore some ethical issues that emerge from that fact. They take us back to ideas we touched on earlier about the extent to which people can be influenced through their perceptions of what is 'legitimate'. The exploration draws us into the significance of people's expectations. We shall consider the extent to which some course of action may be constituted as legitimate or illegitimate by what others expect. One party's actions can require complementation by some specified actions of another party in order for the whole episode to conform to an accepted script. Others' expectations most clearly give me genuine obligations when I have myself instilled or maintained those expectations, but I may have obligations as a result of others' expectations even when someone else has created those expectations. It is possible sometimes to manipulate people's expectations in ways that affect a whole array of rights and obligations, their own and others'. To use the term we took from writers about 'positioning theory', that can constitute manipulation of a 'local moral order', and may give people problems of conflicting obligations.

IMPRESSION MANAGEMENT AND INFLUENCE

Goffman's insight about impression management is that performances often involve a number of people in a process of continuing response to one another's actions and expectations. Often, these performances will be in small-scale, face-to-face situations:

> For the participants, this involves: a single visual and cognitive focus of attention; a mutual and preferential openness to verbal communication; a heightened mutual relevance of acts; an eye-to-eye ecological huddle that maximizes each participant's opportunity to perceive the other participants' monitoring of him. Given these communication arrangements, their presence tends to be acknowledged or ratified through expressive signs, and a 'we rationale' is likely to emerge, that is, a sense of the single thing that *we* are doing together at the time. (1972, pp. 17–18; see also 1971, chap. 3).

Performances do not all need to be face-to-face.[2] However, face-to-face examples are the most straightforward to consider: Goffman documents cases in hotels, hospitals and elsewhere. Hospital staff will cooperate not only to sustain patients' welfare, but also the appearances and standards that are generally expected within the hospital. Similar processes have been described by Hochschild, in her accounts of 'emotional labour':

> [F]light attendants typically work in teams of two and must work on fairly intimate terms with all others on the crew. In fact, workers commonly say the work simply cannot be done well unless they work well together. The reason for this is that the job is partly an 'emotional tone' road show, and the proper tone is kept up in large part by friendly conversation, banter, and joking, as ice cubes, trays, and plastic cups are passed from aisle to aisle to the galley, down to the kitchen, and up again. Indeed, starting with the bus ride to the plane, by bantering back and forth the flight attendant does important relational work: she checks on people's moods, relaxes tension, and warms up ties so that each pair of individuals becomes a team. (1983, p. 115)

In this case, as in many others, social impression management does not have the overt appearance of formal ritual. In others, it does. But the general point is that participants attend and respond to one another in ways that conform to people's shared expectations: participants' expectations, at least, and often other observers' also.

People's attention and responsiveness during social impression management includes attention to possible faults in performance. If one person makes a *faux pas*, then typically others will help to cover it over or brush it aside. If a guest takes up the wrong fork for the entrée, then a tactful host may follow suit. If a manager forgets a meeting with a customer, a colleague may step into the breach and explain that the other was unavoidably detained. More than that, however, skilled social agents will try to avoid others being placed in situations where they may commit *faux pas*. The sales manager will give the technical manager a briefing before a meeting with a client that includes not only facts about the potential deal, but any relevant information about the client that may help avoid social gaffes ('She's a great baseball fan, but she hates the Yankees: be sure not to say anything good about them.'). In Goffman's account, this general kind of activity is an important part of impression management (see e.g. 1971, pp. 204–5). It is essentially a cooperative activity, in which a number of participants jointly manage the activity in which they are engaged. We tell one another of a mutual friend's divorce, or bereavement, or the like, so as to avoid troubling references in conversation. We alert one another to issues that may be contentious. Often, if there is an interpretation that we may give to someone else's utterance to avoid making them look foolish, we shall do so. If one manager refers to sales in Taiwan, where none have been made, another may seamlessly pick up the reference as though it was one to Thailand. And so on.

All of these processes assist participants to engage in a shared social 'script'. As a result, however, there are kinds of pressures in this sort of social impression management that are important in organisational politics. People's expectations about cooperative impression management take us back to issues about 'legitimacy' in organisations. Goffman suggests that it is 'morally proper' to expect others to sustain us in a particular appearance (1955, p. 7), or, as he also puts it, in taking a particular 'line'. This is because of participants' dependence on one another: 'each team-mate is forced to rely on the good conduct and behaviour of his fellows, and they, in turn, are forced to rely on him' (1971, p. 88). He says that 'if a team is to sustain the line it has taken, the team-mates must act as if they have accepted certain moral obligations' (1971, p. 207).

Why should we say that there is any 'moral' issue in regard to such matters? We might in many cases label them as matters of mere etiquette, to distinguish them from more important ethical issues. The answer seems to be that often the issues will not be important enough to warrant moral censure, but the difference is one of degree, not of kind. Sometimes, the issues will be about minor, low-key matters, such as which fork to use. Sometimes, though, they will be of greater moment. The distinction between courtesy and respect for others is a nebulous one. Departures from the accepted script can sometimes be amusing for others, but sometimes distressing. Tactless comments can sometimes embarrass, but sometimes wound. Unsavoury tactics of organisational politics can even involve someone deliberately exposing another's shortcomings in a way that is quite deliberately calculated to embarrass or humiliate.

Ethical analysis of those latter cases is not difficult.[3] There could be situations where such behaviour was justified, perhaps in self-defence or where the other was intent on some morally repugnant course of action, but there would need to be no better options available. The situation does not seem very different from the use of physical violence. We have obligations to avoid inflicting either physical or mental harm on others,[4] and the extent of our obligations is affected by the significance of the harm and the context of the action. It seems clear that only in extraordinary circumstances may we be justified in deliberately embarrassing or humiliating others by exposing the shortcomings of their social performance.

Less straightforward are cases where one person trades on possibilities of embarrassment as a means of influence. Goffman discusses various ways in which impression management can be used as a means to influence others (e.g. 1971, p. 15). At the simplest level, one may use a particular accent to get others to accept one as a person of a certain background, social class or degree of sophistication (1971, p. 215). In more sophisticated cases, Smith may contrive to put Jones in a situation where embarrassment can be avoided only if Jones acts as Smith wishes. For example, Smith may simply give Jones an instruction. Jones's refusal may embarrass Smith, Jones and onlookers.[5]

One way of explaining this mode of influence is by saying that one person contrives to have others accept some shared script about a situation, so that the others will suffer distress or embarrassment if they do not comply with the script. For example, Smith's instruction may be intended to claim expertise that would make it appropriate for Jones to comply with the instruction. Here there can be overlap between impression management as simply giving an impression to others, and impression management as joint participation in a shared script, since the impression given to others will sometimes have as its point to conjure up some accepted script. The ethical issues about such influence through impression management can overlap with the ethical issues about deception. Sometimes, when Smith contrives to get others to accept a certain definition of a situation – for example, one where Smith is accepted as an expert on a particular type of matter – the contrivance is wrong because it simply gives others a false impression. In other cases, however, Smith may not get others to accept that he really is an expert, but they may be able to call into question that definition of the situation only at the cost of embarrassment for all concerned.

In those sorts of situation a number of factors seem relevant to ethical evaluation. It may be important whether Smith really is an expert and whether the issue is one where expertise is relevant. It might be an issue whether Smith has official authority to give instructions to Jones about the use of computer equipment, if Smith is the IT Manager and Jones is the Production Manager. If there is nothing in those arrangements that renders Smith's instruction an exercise of official authority, then there may still be some kind of social pressure on Jones: there will be embarrassment if Jones does not comply.

Suppose, however, that Jones is considering whether to comply with Smith's instruction. Suppose also that Smith does not actually have relevant expertise, or official authority. Perhaps Smith expects compliance from Jones because Jones is young, or black, or female, for example. Even if Jones dislikes the embarrassment caused by refusal, that refusal may be justified simply because it was Smith's decision to construct the situation in that way: Smith, not Jones, may reasonably be held to blame for the embarrassment.

One thing that seems to matter most in this kind of situation is the extent to which people's expectations are 'legitimate' expectations. There may always be some degree of obligation on us to avoid embarrassing others if we can, but the strength of the obligation seems to depend on how reasonable or legitimate the expectations are which others have, when it is contravening those expectations that creates the embarrassment. The obligation we have to cooperate with others in sustaining a particular impression may depend on the legitimacy of their expectations. That possibility takes us back to some of the issues of legitimacy which we considered in earlier chapters, and we turn to them again in the following section.

CONSISTENCY, NORMS AND EXPECTATIONS

Before proceeding further, we ought to note that there are various sorts of influence which are based on eliciting consistent lines of action from people, not all to do with the social expectations of impression management. Cialdini notes that becoming committed to behaviour that is consistent with our past lines of action can be used as a means of influence which has been labelled 'the foot-in-the-door technique' (1993, p. 62). Pfeffer has discussed this as a means of influence within organisations (1992, pp. 192–200). He uses analogies like those of a door-to-door salesperson who tries to get a prospective customer to evince some interest in a product, and then take advantage of that to build increasing degrees of commitment. Or people may get others to assist them by eliciting one favour first, so that more will follow, as a result of the commitment that has been built by the first. He notes a number of factors that promote our tendency toward such commitments, including some internal factors such as cognitive economy as well as other external ones like social norms. There is a similar kind of '*click,* and *whirr*' mechanism at work in this mode of influence as in others like reciprocity. It may be possible to resist, and Cialdini makes some suggestions about how to do so (1993, pp. 86–90), but the effort required and the fact that many people are at best only vaguely aware of the mechanism at work on them, implies that we can say some similar things about this form of influence as about others that diminish people's status as autonomous agents who have responsibility for their actions.[6] There are ethical concerns about inveigling people into courses of action through a 'foot-in-the-door' technique if it would be possible to afford them opportunity to assess the whole prospect from the start, and make a considered decision about it.[7]

In this case, however, that is not the end of the story. One set of ethical issues arises from the pressures we have on us to maintain commitments and lines of behaviour for reasons of internal psychological consistency and cognitive economy, but another set of ethical issues arise from the pressures we have on us in organisations to take lines that are consistent with others' expectations. The first sort of pressures raise issues that are essentially similar to cases like Cialdini's waiter where people trade on others' susceptibility to '*click,* and *whirr*' responses. The second set of pressures are those where others have expectations of us, expectations that we will continue a line of action that we or others have mapped out as appropriate in the circumstances. In this sort of case the issue of legitimacy does not seem to be about the extent to which '*click,* and *whirr*' mechanisms detract from our responsibility for what we do, so much as about the extent to which explicit, undisguised social pressures can be a legitimate source of influence.

It is possible that the two sorts of influence may go together. When Smith gives Jones an instruction, Jones may comply through a '*click,* and *whirr*' response to perceived authority, rather along the lines seen from Milgram's experimental subjects (Cialdini 1993, chap. 6). At the same time, Jones is under pressure not from any such quasi-automatic response mechanism, but because failure to comply will result in embarrassment (and possibly in some social disapproval). When they go together, the two sorts of influence may be especially potent. In principle, however, the two processes are separable, and separating them is necessary for ethical analysis. The first can be evaluated along the same lines as the example of Cialdini's waiter. Here, it is the second that needs more careful attention.

At the end of the previous section it was suggested that the obligation we have to cooperate with others in sustaining a particular impression may depend on the legitimacy of their expectations. The most obvious situation in which they may have legitimate expectations of us, which impose on us some derivative obligation, is the case where we have given our explicit consent to those expectations. If we have given an undertaking to play a particular role, and the requirements of that role are reasonably well defined, then others can legitimately expect the actions from us that the role requires. If Smith were a mediaeval lord, and Jones had freely sworn fealty to him, then the pressures on Jones to comply with Smith's instruction would seem legitimate.

In many cases, however, the situation will be much less clear-cut. While Smith's effort to influence Jones might be an exercise of legitimate authority if Jones had consented to the set of arrangements of which Smith's authority is part, we know from our discussion in Chapter 5 that it is not straightforward to say in what circumstances people give consent to organisational arrangements.

We should note here once again that sometimes organisational purposes will determine what can reasonably and legitimately be expected of organisational members. Some expectations of an operating room nurse, a company secretary, or the mate on a fishing boat will be fairly clearly linked to patient welfare or shareholder understanding or crew safety. But in many cases there will be more than one way to achieve organisational purposes, and often expectations will be more to do with how those purposes are achieved than whether they are.

We noted in Chapter 4 that often people will have expectations about how things are to be done which are associated with norms that apply in that group. However, we also noted that while norms play an important part in organisational arrangements, it is questionable to what extent norms ought to be accepted as a basis for legitimacy in themselves. We noted in our earlier discussion that official rules in an organisation are often vague or ambiguous, and that local norms may resolve that vagueness and ambiguity. Such norms 'bring order and predictability to a person's environment' (Brown 1988, p. 44; see Chapter 4 above, p. 79). We noted also that what is sanctioned by such norms is perceived as legitimate, at least in some respects. However, the question remained to what extent such perceived legitimacy coincides with genuine legitimacy. I suggested that we can classify cases into three categories: where perceptions of legitimacy reflect some general moral principle; where they reflect some rule or norm but that rule or norm does not seem to be associated with any general moral principle; and where perceptions of legitimacy reflect some fairly explicit agreements or understandings amongst individuals. I suggested also that it seems clear how the first and the third are cases of genuine legitimacy, but less clear how the second is. Where general moral principles are involved, there does not seem to be an issue. Where there are fairly explicit agreements or understandings, then it seems clear enough that obligations follow. The situation which is unclear is the second, where there are local rules or norms, but they do not seem directly to reflect any general moral principle.

If we now return to that point, we may consider the situation where the sorts of local rules and norms under consideration are ones which embody standards and scripts for social impression management. By and large, these will not directly reflect general moral principles and often will not reflect explicit agreements. Nevertheless, they can reflect expectations and understandings that people have of one another. Perhaps they embody expectations that members of the group have of one another that have emerged gradually over time, or which members of the group import from other contexts. However they have arisen, we may have cases of norms which in effect are constituted out of people's continuing mutual expectations. In whatever way these expectations have emerged, we can ask whether they are legitimate, and whether there is any moral obligation on others to comply with them.

In some cases there can be, because people often maintain expectations in one another to some extent or other by reciprocal action and response. The simplest case is that where I instil or maintain expectations in you about my own future behaviour. There may be no explicit undertakings or agreements, but my past behaviour may have created expectations in you, and as a result, I may have some corresponding responsibilities.

I suggested earlier that it is the expectations and intentions that we convey to one another that are a more direct source of moral praiseworthiness and blameworthiness than norms that may create or sustain those expectations. In the processes of social impression management, we convey such expectations and intentions to one another, and we thereby incur obligations. Conveying expectations by actions and non-verbal behaviour gives us obligations in the same way as an explicit verbal understanding, just as inducing a belief by wearing the old school tie can make us liable to blame in the same way as an explicit verbal statement. We have obligations that emerge from others' reliance on the expectations we instil or maintain in them by our behaviour. In simple cases the process verges on explicit agreement, as people quite clearly give one another a shared understanding about what is to be done, as we beckon and nod, or shrug and smile, or let one another believe that we shall go on as we have started. In these and other cases, we may have some responsibilities because we have instilled or maintained others' expectations. While consideration of social impression management shows how the process can occur, the point is a wider one, that applies generally to situations where people have expectations of one another.

EXPECTATIONS AND OBLIGATIONS

People's endorsement of others' expectations can be shown in many ways, and therefore so can the norms that emerge from coalescence of people's mutual expectations be transmitted and affirmed in many ways. My manner and bearing, and my tone of voice, all may convey something about my self-image, about what organisational norms are about particular issues, and about the line I am taking. We know that interpersonal communication is a complex process, with participating individuals using multiple 'channels' to convey and receive messages, which include not only factual information but expressions of emotion, including approval or disapproval, like or dislike, and indefinitely many others. We can reasonably expect that in small groups, all these channels are used in conveying and receiving information. In addition, as others speak, we constantly tend to give back-channel confirmations of what they say, or by withholding responses where they are expected, thereby give disconfirmation (Krauss, Fussell and Chen 1995, p. 139; also see above, Chapter 2, p. 46). The pragmatic rules of discourse discussed in Chapter 8 can have similar functions.[8] Even where behaviour departs from what might have been expected, there will be pressure to give excuses or accounts that are consistent with local norms, and to that extent serve to maintain them (see e.g. Bies and Sitkin 1992). In all these ways, we can signal our acceptance of others' expectations, and it is important that we can do so without explicit agreement. In such cases, others' expectations still seem legitimate, even without formal or explicit agreement. It was accepted in Chapter 5 that possibilities for genuine participation in organisations can allow a reasonable inference of consent to a proposal when people do not oppose it, and it seems similarly clear that we can have obligations based on others' legitimate expectations, when we have led them to those expectations, even though there has been no explicit, open agreement.

It is undoubtedly a matter of degree to what extent people can be taken to incur obligations through their participation in organisational practices that sustain continuing expectations in others. Their participation may be qualified to an extent that ranges from mild detachment to cynical and grudging compliance However, it is also important that as a result of others' expectations, we may sometimes have obligations even when we have not signalled agreement at all. While the simplest case is that where I instil or maintain expectations in you about my own future behaviour, that may not be the only case where I have some obligations. There are certainly cases when one individual incurs an obligation through inducing an expectation in others: promising is the basic (albeit not the only) case, and has attracted so much analysis by moral philosophers just because it is such a basic case. But knowing others have expectations and doing nothing to discourage them can equally leave us with obligations, in many circumstances. Some of these are the obligations we have to avoid discomfiting or humiliating others if we can avoid doing so. When Smith unreasonably gives Jones an instruction, Jones may have little obligation to avoid some mild embarrassment to others, but sometimes Jones will have to choose between compliance and some more tangible harm to others. Obligations may emerge from others' expectations about our behaviour, even when we have not instilled those expectations, if on the basis of those expectations others have formulated significant plans or intentions.[9] If Ingrid plans to lodge a job application because Omar told her I would act as a referee for her, I may have at least some obligation as a result, at least to warn her if I cannot.

While such obligations may be all the stronger if we have some responsibility for others' expectations, the expectations alone seem to create some obligations for us, if failing to conform to them will indeed result in others' harm or discomfiture. It is relevant whether others' expectations are reasonable, but someone else's expectations about what I will do may be reasonable even if it is not I but others who have instilled and maintain those expectations. If others by their behaviour have instilled and maintained your expectations about what I will do, I may have some obligations toward you not because I am responsible for your expectations but because I have obligations toward anyone who may incur harm or suffer distress if their reasonable expectations are not fulfilled. It may well be that such obligations can be outweighed by other factors, but that is not to say that they are of no weight at all. Such factors can account for many obligations in small-scale groups and organisations, since people's expectations of one another are all-pervasive in them.

The sort of obligation here in question has its roots in the sort of case we discussed earlier in connexion with Baron Rothschild and his friend, where I have some obligation to disabuse you from a false impression you have, if you may be harmed by acting on the basis of that impression, and I can disabuse you without great cost to myself. If I know you plan to swim in a crocodile-infested river, I have some obligation to warn you, even if it is not I who led you to believe it would be safe to do so. The case seems to be the same if your impression is an impression or expectation about what I plan to do. The obligation I have will be greater if my behaviour has played a part in causing you to have your expectation or impression, and sometimes my failure to disabuse you of the impression you have will be enough to maintain or strengthen your expectation. It is where one person has allowed another to maintain some expectations, and then acts contrary to those expectations, that there can be such accusations as 'backstabbling'. But even in other cases, I may have some obligation to you.

Overall, it seems reasonable to suggest that we have obligations associated with others' expectations, which range from strong obligations when we are directly responsible for instilling or maintaining their expectations, through weaker but significant obligations when their expectations are reasonable but we have little responsibility for them, to obligations that are weaker still but nevertheless real ones, when others have expectations but no good grounds for them. In each case some other factors will be relevant, such as organisational purposes and the degree of harm that will befall the others if their expectations are not met, the cost to me of meeting your expectations, and the further expectations that may be created for the future. However, that just reflects the point we have noted before that concrete details will be relevant to particular situations.

Those sorts of obligations we have in virtue of others' expectations then go some distance to explaining what obligations may be associated with group norms. To the extent that norms and standards are associated with others' expectations, I may have obligations that emerge from those expectations. Such obligations are often associated with processes of social impression management. There is an intimate connection between processes of impression management in social performances, and the acceptance and transmission of group norms. The relationship revolves around the expectations that organisational members maintain in one another about how things are to be done and the attitudes that are to be expressed. The maintenance of such expectations serves to 'bring order and predictability to a person's environment', as reflected in Glazer and Glazer's comment on the problem that is caused by dissent within the organisation: 'central to management's dilemma is the need to repair the rupture of "mutual pretense" which helps managers sustain the belief that all is under control on matters under their jurisdiction' (1989, p. 135). The social performances that Goffman describes as impression management involve mutual expectations that through repetition coalesce into norms that are maintained by a variety of interpersonal communication and feedback processes. Failure of a person to conform to others' expectations in one respect can disrupt those processes and so impact on a variety of social performances. However, the point is a general one, not confined solely to social impression management: it applies whenever social arrangements embody people's expectations of one another.

EXPECTATIONS, INFLUENCE AND LOCAL MORAL ORDER

We have now established more clearly how the mutual expectations of people in an organisation may be associated with norms and can reflect obligations they have, based to a significant extent on their continuing to maintain those expectations in others. Clearly, the obligations which these kinds of processes give rise to are not absolute, even when we participate in them fully and enthusiastically. It is easy enough to imagine all sorts of cases where they are outweighed by other considerations. Jean's obligation to respond politely to Gido's thoughtful enquiry is blown away by the news that the building is on fire. Henry's obligation to maintain Geoff's self-esteem may be outweighed by the need to be fair to Dorothy. There will be many cases where prescriptions of local norms may be outweighed by more general moral principles. The obligations in question seem generally to be like others: they vary in content and weight, and what will outweigh them often will depend on the details of the case. Considerations to do with fairness and with consequences will be relevant, for example.

What of the case where Smith gives Jones an instruction? Sometimes he will have no background justification in terms of their history, organisational roles, relative expertise, or the like. Other things being equal, there might be some moral reason for Jones to avoid embarrassing Smith or others, but it may be a weak obligation compared to such factors as the encouragement it gives Smith to repeat such behaviour on other occasions.

On the other hand, Smith may not be so naïve as to expect Jones's compliance without further ado. Smith may take action beforehand, such as getting agreement from some others that he should take prime responsibility for the project. Sometimes, such arrangements are unobjectionable. Smith may openly discuss the issues, the reasons for him leading the project, and let the implications of others' agreement be clear. Sometimes, though, such arrangements resemble forms of deception and concealment we have discussed above. He might get agreement from some by falsely implying that others had already done so, or he might get agreement while concealing its implications. In the first case it is questionable to what extent those others are bound by the arrangement. If the arrangement were then used to coerce them, then the coercion would *prima facie* be illegitimate. In the second, what he does is ethically questionable to the extent that it deprives others of the opportunity to consider issues that are important to them and make a responsible decision about them, and once again any power he attains through what he does seems to fall short of legitimate authority.

However, the sort of ethical problem that can arise is that Smith may induce expectations in others on which they base some plans or actions, so that if Jones does not comply then the others suffer embarrassment, distress or harm, through no fault of their own. The sort of moves we are thinking of by Smith may be described in the terms of positioning theory, considered as the study of 'local moral orders'. To a significant extent, the mechanisms of influence that emerge from the dynamics of impression management discussed by Goffman and the conversational logic analysed by Grice are mechanisms that revolve around acceptance by participants of some 'local moral order', where local moral orders are conceived as 'ever-shifting patterns of mutual and contestable rights and obligations of speaking and acting' (Harré and van Langenhove 1999, p. 1). In the case touched on above, where Smith moves to get agreement for his leadership of the project, we might describe his moves as attempts to enhance his position, changing people's rights and obligations, as they emerge from their shared expectations.

Such rights and obligations are real rights and obligations, that people must take account of, but that is not to say that they have absolute or overriding force. We noted that in his account of impression management, Goffman suggests that it is 'morally proper' to expect others to sustain us in a particular appearance, and that there are myriad ways that people convey to one another what is acceptable or proper behaviour according to mutually accepted scripts. These scripts define the sort of 'local moral order' that positioning theory deals with. But what is accepted as morally proper within some local moral order does not necessarily imply any generally acceptable legitimacy or ethical propriety. We know too well of Milgram's experiments and the sort of 'local moral order' that obtained in concentration camps, and we understand that many groups can embrace norms that we generally would consider improper and unethical. Indeed, as we have noted, we generally consider that there are norms that have been widely accepted in our own society – homophobic or other discriminatory norms, for example – that did not reflect sound ethical standards. That people expect one another to discriminate against some group does not make it right to do so. Whatever we may wish to say about the possibility of universal or absolute ethical norms, it seems clear that we at least wish to be able to judge the norms that obtain as part of any local moral order by some wider and more general standards, standards that we can envisage applying to all responsible agents.

This is particularly important for us because of the importance of local norms and standards in organisational politics. We have noticed types of influence that are associated with impression management, where there is normative pressure on individuals to be consistent with past behaviour and to maintain the shared script for an occasion, related types of influence that rely on our tendency to accept background assumptions behind questions and utterances, and questions or manoeuvres that push people to make a commitment in one direction or another. All of these and many other tactics make use of 'legitimate power', in French and Raven's terms: the fact that people perceive certain actions or policies to be required by norms and rules that they accept as legitimate. We have now seen how local norms and understandings of what is legitimate can be associated with genuine obligations. It is important that even though such obligations can be genuine ones, nevertheless they can be over-ridden by other more fundamental obligations.

Some of those influence tactics are used on a small-scale interpersonal level, as in the sort of case that Goffman refers to where one person manipulates another by influencing the definition of the situation which the other accepts. Smith does so if he gets Jones to comply with his instruction just to avoid embarrassment. He does so also in a slightly more elaborate way if he arranges support for his leadership. But they can be used also on a larger scale, by manipulating the local moral order throughout an organisation. Hence the emphasis that has been placed by some management theorists on managing organisational culture. Deal and Kennedy refer to 'strong culture companies':

> They communicate exactly how they want their people to behave. They spell out standards of acceptable decorum – so people who visit or work in any of their places of business can know what to expect. They call attention to the way in which procedures – for example, strategic planning and budgeting – are to be carried out, so the fault if the procedures fail is substantive, not just a failure to follow prescribed process. Often they also establish ways, or at least the settings, in which their people can play and have fun – so that people will know they belong to a functioning and complete society. In short, strong culture companies create the rites and rituals of behavior in their corporate life – the rites and rituals that

exercise the most visible and pervasive influence on, as Bower says it, 'the way we do things around here'. (1988, pp. 59–60, referring to Bower 1966)

In many cases, there may not be anything ethically problematic in trying to 'manage culture' within an organisation. Indeed, to a significant extent this is precisely what is suggested by authors whose aim is to foster and improve ethical behaviour within organisations (e.g. Treviño and Nelson 1995, chap. 9). But there does not seem to be any general presumption that to create a 'strong culture' of this sort is always good. Whether it is, seems to depend on its content and ends. It is quite possible for 'rites and rituals of behavior' to be unfair and discriminatory, or otherwise problematic. Whether or not they are the outcome of deliberate, systematic management, there is still the need for organisational norms to be evaluated by reference to general moral and ethical standards.

WHEN OTHERS MANIPULATE NORMS AND OBLIGATIONS

The sort of culture management described by Deal and Kennedy can amount to manipulation of an organisation's 'local moral order'. For better or for worse, it can affect people's mutual expectations and the norms of behaviour within the organisation. Then there is a matter of ethical concern where the resulting norms are problematic in themselves or serve ethically questionable ends. The problem is especially acute because we can have obligations to others on account of expectations they have which we ourselves are not responsible for. In some organisational politics, moves will be made to affect people's shared expectations and the obligations they have to one another as a result, even though those making the moves have no concern about the wider context of the obligations, or their relationship to other obligations people have that emerge from general moral principles. People may be led to expect certain pay arrangements even though the arrangements are unfair to some individuals. Expectations people are encouraged to have of one another may create obligations that conflict with obligations they have to their families. Norms and expectations that prescribe the highest possible return on investment for shareholders may conflict with obligations to other stakeholders.

We might say straightforwardly that it is unethical to manipulate the local moral order for ends which will not themselves stand ethical scrutiny. But can we say any more?

In this chapter, we have focussed especially on influence which is exercised through people's expectations of one another. That can be reinforced though other mechanisms, which also have ethical implications. In some cases, the influence may use a '*click*, and *whirr*' mechanism, by calling on people's judgement about what they ought to do, influencing them by playing on their sense of obligation. In such a case, there can be something particularly objectionable about the means of influence. It can blur the distinction between felt and genuine obligation, and undermine respect for genuine obligations, undercutting the distinction between virtue and inclination, obligation and preference, ethics and interest. Such means of influence can be paradigmatic cases of treating others as means rather than ends. They can manifest an 'emotivist' approach to ethics, as though moral judgements are only expressions of preference or feeling; MacIntyre contends that emotivism 'entails the obliteration of any genuine distinction between manipulative and non-manipulative social relations' (1985, p. 23). By its denial of any important difference between genuine obligation and personal preference, it obscures any distinction between persuading others through identifying real obligations, and manipulating them through inducing felt obligation. If we accept that there are some genuine obligations, we have great concerns about that manipulation. But we have now seen also that there are problematic ways of influencing people which do not so much work through manipulating people's sense of obligation, but rather through manipulating actual obligations they have. These means of influence be of concern for some of the same reasons, potentially undermining our respect for the obligations we have.

This is not to say that manipulation of people's obligations will always be ethically problematic. It is possible for development of people's mutual obligations in a local moral order to be done constructively, for quite worthy reasons. A team coach may generate mutual expectations of team members for the benefit of the team and derivatively of its individual members. In an organisation, managers may generate employees' generalised expectations of one another's high performance, or more specific expectations about how organisational processes will be carried out.

As an example of the latter, suppose that there are several Departments in a particular Division of some organisation. Suppose also that the work of this Division involves it in frequent correspondence with outsiders (suppliers, customers, government officials, media outlets and others, perhaps). Hitherto, we may suppose, the people who work in these Departments have authored and sent most of this correspondence under the general supervision of their Department Heads. The Division Manager now determines that all outgoing correspondence must be signed by the relevant Department Head. This effects a change in the rights and obligations of the Department Heads and their subordinates. It does so in part at least by altering people's expectations about one another's intentions and actions. The Department Heads now are expected often to scrutinise the letters and discuss any matters of concern. Their subordinates are expected to submit the letters and make required alterations. Their obligations emerge at least in part from the expectations they now have of one another. Some such obligations emerge quite directly, and others less directly, such as obligations to deal with draft letters in ways that respect one another's workload and task commitments.

There is nothing improper or ethically problematic about the action of the Division Manager, in itself. It is the sort of thing that is entirely common within organisations as more senior managers determine the rights and powers of others below them. But there are several important issues that arise about the general type of case where changes to arrangements affect others' obligations. They do not always involve objectionable manipulation, but sometimes they do, and it is important to see in more detail just how they do.

Sometimes, managers may get compliance with their wishes through perceptions of legitimacy that work in Cialdini's '*click,* and *whirr*' fashion. The staff who write letters might unthinkingly accept that they ought to comply with the terms of the organisational directive, as a result of the same sorts of factors as led Milgram's subjects to comply with the experimenter's instructions: some uncritical acceptance of authority, perhaps. If the managers deliberately trade on uncritical acceptance of their authority, then they may be relying on the fact that our perceptions and reasoning are often imperfect. This is one form of 'manipulation'. Like a number of the other problems we have identified, that is an example of a wider problem, and not one that is unique to this context. It may at least signify once more the importance of opportunities for contest and debate in organisational politics, since it is when people have to defend courses of action that there may be opportunities to test local normative requirements against wider points of view, and probe behind the normative façade.

It may also be that changes to organisational arrangements can be deceptively contrived. Again, we touched on this in the previous section, as we noted that Smith's moves to get endorsement of his leadership might be covert or deceptive. The same general possibility is shown in this fictional case:

> 'Yes,' said Dawlish doubtfully, and then he was away into the administration: this is what he was so good at – the tactics of bureaucracy – and don't ever imagine it's not important. 'The Board will appoint four specialized committees: Communications, Finance, Training, and a Control Structure Committee. Now we won't be able to control all of those, so what we do is this. Let the Ministry people grab anything they want, in fact we'll nominate a few of them, lavish compliments on their suitability. Incidentally,' Dawlish blew his nose loudly on a big handkerchief, 'don't overdo the compliments; they're beginning to suspect you of sarcasm over the other side.'
>
> 'No', I said.
>
> 'Yes,' said Dawlish. 'Now; when they are committeed up to the armpits you will suggest a fifth committee: a Compatibility Committee – for co-ordination...'
>
> 'Very neat,' I said, 'just as you did on the Dundee Report – you ended up in control – I've often wondered how you did it.'
>
> 'Mum's the word, old boy,' said Dawlish. 'I'd like to do it again before they tumble to it.' (Deighton 1963, chap. 34)

The others have not fully anticipated what the process will involve and what its dynamics will be. If they do, it will be hard for them to change it without impugning the motives of Dawlish and his allies, something which carries the same sorts of costs as persistent 'probing' questions: motives being hard to evidence one way or another, challenging them exposes one to charges of malice, madness, or the like. The case is like others we have discussed which involve deceptive behaviour, where some people do not have a full opportunity to make a responsible decision or give considered agreement.

Nevertheless, even when arrangements are made for unworthy motives, or are deceptively contrived, they may still impact on other people's actual rights and obligations. In the case from Len Deighton's novel, once the extra committee is agreed on, parties to the process have obligations to deal with matters according to the various committees' terms of reference. The obligations that members of the different committees have to one another to discuss proposals, to weigh evidence and listen to one another's points of view, are not taken away by the fact that the committee arrangement is contrived to advantage Dawlish.

In general, the sorts of actions that effect alterations to others' rights and obligations can be ethically sound or ethically questionable. Even if they are not deceptively contrived, they may be ethically questionable in other ways: for example, if they impose costs on some individuals primarily to serve the interests of a different individual or group.

But then we come to the further point, that when people have contrived some normative commitments from others, it will not always be clear what ethics may require, even when those arrangements may be liable to question and criticism.

Various writers have adapted Hume's view that much of morality is built on 'convention' as a basis for arguing that moral commitments are relative to social context,[10] and there is no doubt that established conventions have to be taken account of in moral decision-making. It is a convention whether we drive on the right-hand side of the road or the left, but once that convention is established, then in many situations it is not only unconventional and contrary to the rules of the road, but imprudent and morally wrong not to conform with it. To ignore it in situations where there is other traffic places both oneself and others at serious risk. That is true even if I think that the convention ought to have been otherwise, and if I accord it no inherent moral authority or other normative force. When conventions have grown up, they affect others' expectations and patterns of action, and I often need to take account of those patterns of action and expectations if I am to avoid behaviour which is imprudent, offensive, or harmful to others. Even if you were to believe that other things being equal there is something superior about driving on the right, nevertheless if you and others expect one another to drive on the left (perhaps because we know one another to have those expectations), it would be wrong to drive on the right. Further still, even if I believed that the rule that we drive on the left had been contrived by auto manufacturers for their benefit (perhaps to cut costs by producing similar cars in all plants), nevertheless it would still be wrong to do otherwise. The fact that others had contrived this normative benefit for their own ends would in certain respects invalidate it. But once participants had established mutual expectations, it would be wrong to ignore them, however much the situation has been arranged by some third party for their own ends.

A central theme of this chapter is that the same general point can be true in organisations. Some group with the power to do so may contrive some local moral order which has no intrinsic force or merit of its own, but which nevertheless involves mutual, interlocking expectations by participants. One manager's bonus depends on meeting a target; to meet the target she needs the cooperation of another, who expects her to argue for the necessary resources, and so on. The permutations and combinations are limitless.

In these and related situations, others' contrivance of a local moral order for their own ends could incline us to say that the normative requirements have no inherent force, but to the extent that the contrivance affects people's expectations of one another it may result in them having real obligations they would not have otherwise. The 'manipulative' element of the contrivance consists not just in getting others to believe they have certain obligations, but in making it really the case that they do so.

Then, we may think that people's exploitation of others through contriving that they have real obligations to one another seems a matter for even greater ethical condemnation than merely eliciting a false sense of obligation. Our real ethical obligations at least in part serve to reflect an appreciation of one another's value as being worthy of respect for our own sakes, and exploiting others through the use of moral commitments turns the whole idea of morality and ethics on its head, undermining our trust in one another and any belief we have in the importance of an ethical life. Nevertheless, while that may strengthen our condemnation of such contrivance, it does not eliminate the fact that contrived or not there are real obligations we may have to one another as a result of our mutual expectations.[11]

Whenever people do contrive obligations on others in order to satisfy some ulterior purpose, this may result in those others being involved in a 'dirty hands' problem. Sometimes, it will not. Sometimes, it may be unfair to them, and involve them being exploited, but not involve them in any conflicting obligations. But on other occasions, to comply with these contrived obligations will involve contravening some other value or commitment, and however they act they will be involved in 'a violation and a betrayal of a person, value, or principle', to recall Stocker's words. If there are overriding moral principles that would be violated by local norms, then I may be right to heed the former, but still thereby violate some obligations to my fellows. At least in some cases, certainly where you have contrived an obligation for me which emerges from the expectations that I and others have of one another, there will be real obligations that I can only satisfy at the cost of violating some other commitment. When organisational arrangements mean that members of a work group are dependent on one another for effective task completion, their obligations to one another may well conflict with the obligations they have to family members. Or it may be that effective completion of a group task will require turning a blind eye to some standard requirements of accounting or safety. Group members then have to choose between those values and principles, and their obligations to one another. Is there anything they can do to avoid the dirty hands problem?

IS THERE A WAY OUT?

What ethical options are there for people have who have obligations to one another which have been contrived by a third party? In the simplest case, where one party, X, contrives mutual expectations in A and B, those mutual expectations may result in them having obligations to one another, but it may be possible for them to unravel the knot that binds them firstly by exposing it and then by agreeing on a different arrangement. Perhaps Bob through some fraud or deception gets Tricia to agree to water the garden if Pat weeds it, and Pat to agree to weed it if Tricia waters it. Then all three will be able to share the produce. If either Tricia or Pat fails to do what the other expects, then the garden fails. Tricia would be letting down Pat if she did not do her part, and vice versa. If they both play their part, there will be enough for each of them; if either of them fails, there will be nothing. Assuming deception or fraud on Bob's part, we can assume that the others have no obligation to him, but that still they have an obligation to one another. They can straightforwardly discuss the situation with one another, expose Bob's fraud, and agree to an arrangement that satisfied them both (in this case, perhaps, a two-way division).[12]

A somewhat similar case occurs when people have some obligations to one another as the result of there being some norm or convention in their community, and they cannot immediately change the norm but can change their own obligations. Schiffer comments on the convention (perhaps no longer so widespread) that men open doors for women:

> What is not so immediately clear … is why one should do what one is expected to do. Perhaps women expect men to open doors for them because it is the precedented thing to do; men continue to open doors for women because they do not want to upset women by acting contrary to their expectations; and the fact that men continue to open doors for women secures that women will continue to expect men to open doors for women, which secures that men will continue to open doors for women… (1972, p. 152)

Here are mutual expectations that create pressure for their own reproduction. Arguably, though, the convention has had an ulterior function of reinforcing women's subordination to men. Whether for that general reason or for reasons to do with their specific personal relationship, it would be quite open to particular women and men to decide to act differently, through some appropriate communication. That communication would have to take account of one another's real expectations, and be sensitive to possible misunderstanding; it might require people to know each other in order safely to avoid offence on one side or the other.[13] However, for us the important point is that if two people were able through communication to disabuse one another of their convention-induced expectations then there would be no genuine obligation on either of them to act in accord with the convention.

We argued in Chapter 4 that there can be room for members of a group through communication amongst themselves to override the expectations that tend to be induced by some wider norm, and thereby other things being equal they can avoid the obligations that their mutual expectations might induce. The possibility here is closely similar. If people's expectations of one another are the source of their obligations, then there is potential for them to change those expectations by communication amongst themselves. A number of conditions must be satisfied for this possibility to hold: in particular, there must be no general moral principle that grounds or explains the obligations independent of their mutual expectations, and it must be possible for the communication to involve everyone directly affected. Where significant numbers of people are involved, such communication will be difficult.

In complex cases, unravelling the knot will be difficult, and perhaps impossible, but as a matter of general principle it appears that that approach would be ethical, and it is hard to see what other approach would be. The practical difficulties stem from the complexity of multi-party arrangements, problems of communication, and in many cases the contestability of whether a certain set of norms or conventions or otherwise imputed obligations actually does have intrinsic merit. There will be cases where other obligations simply override the expectations people have of one another, but that is not to say that the latter have no weight: only that their weight is not so great as other considerations. It will at least be necessary to try to disabuse people of the expectations they have, and not just ignore them.

For practical purposes, therefore, two points seem to be derivable. One is the importance of discussion and open consideration of the degree of genuine force behind any normative injunction. The other is the need to take real account of what other individuals' expectations actually are in any particular situation, quite apart from whether the normative claims that ostensibly justify the expectations have any intrinsic merit.

If, for example, we are members of an organisation that ostensibly values reliability and precision, and we are sceptical about whether those qualities have any intrinsic merit or widespread commitment from members of the organisation, nevertheless we ought to pay real attention to what other members of the organisation actually expect. Sometimes we can discount others' expectations as sources of obligations: for example, when they are blatantly unreasonable. But people's expectations can be reasonable to the extent that they know others, too, to be expecting certain patterns of behaviour, even if it is only knowledge of one another's expectations that makes the expectations reasonable. At the same time, however, we ought to be open to discussion of those patterns of behaviour, to consider whether they have any real normative force, and whether our mutual expectations might not arrive at some better equilibrium. Ultimately, if we pursue those points, we shall confront issues about organisational culture, and the responses that people can properly make towards culture management, and about how we may properly respond to dictates of official authority which are exploitative or ethically questionable.

SUMMARY

There can be pressure on people to satisfy the requirements of impression management as part of a social performance. This pressure is all the stronger because such requirements are often seen as 'legitimate' or 'morally proper'. It can be used as a means of influence, often conjoined with pressures for people to be consistent with their past commitments. To the extent that such pressures derive from others' expectations, they can reflect genuine obligations. Such obligations are strongest when we have voluntarily fostered or maintained the expectations others have of us. However, we can have some obligations to others in the light of expectations they have, even if we have no responsibility for instilling or maintaining those expectations.

Sometimes, people can jointly foster or maintain expectations in one another and the outcome can be norms of behaviour. These norms reflect genuine obligations to the extent that those who participate in sustaining them can be held responsible for one another's expectations. But through manipulation of norms and otherwise it is possible for such obligations on people to be contrived, as a means of influencing them. This raises concerns about the extent to which hypocritical contrivance undermines respect for ethical constraints, and about the fact that it can lead to a dirty hands problem for those involved. Where obligations are based on interlocked mutual expectations, it may be possible for people to find a way out through communication with one another, but that will not always be possible. The result will sometimes just be a moral dilemma to which there is no easy solution. In the next chapter, we shall see how group alignments can sometimes add further complexity.

NOTES

1. For more examples see Goffman (1971), pp. 70–73.

2. Some labour–management negotiations provide examples where parts at least are not: see Friedman (1994).

3. Often, one reason to condemn such tactics is on the simple ground that they are cruel: cf. Shklar (1984), chap. 1.

4. For discussions of physical and non-physical 'harms' which cast light on their possible similarities and differences, see Kleinig (1978) and Feinberg (1984), pp. 45–51.

5. Cf. Goffman (1955), p. 10: 'Salesmen, especially street "stemmers," know that if they take a line that will be discredited unless the reluctant customer buys, the customer may be trapped by considerateness and buy in order to save the face of the salesman and prevent what would ordinarily result in a scene.' For a more up-to-date commercial example, see Leidner's description of a technique insurance agents were trained to use in an organisation she studied (1993, p. 152).

6. Baumeister reports empirical findings about the mental energy required to maintain or adapt one's self-presentation (1989, p. 64).

7. It would be compatible with this to point out to people that some course of action would be inconsistent with what they have done in the past: that is different from coaxing them into some action so as to elicit subsequent behaviour which we envisage but they do not. We seem to have diminished their responsibility for their course of action significantly more in the latter case than in the former.

8. Goffman's 'face-work' seems partly to be acceptance of rules of discourse that allow people to maintain a reputation for competent social interaction: see Goffman (1955), pp. 33–40.

9. For extended discussion about obligations we have to others to prevent them coming to harm, see Feinberg (1984), chap. 4 (although most of Feinberg's discussion is more directly about the extent to which such obligations ought to be enforced by criminal law).

10. Hume's view is contained in the *Treatise* (1897), Book III, Part II. A useful exposition and discussion of Hume's account is to be found in Harman (1977), chap. 9.

11. This is a problem that courts of law sometimes have to deal with: for example, when A and B have entered into arrangements about some property received from X, not knowing that X had stolen it. But the legal solutions to such difficulties will not readily generalise to complex multi-party situations, and may often be based more on legal precedent than on clear moral intuitions. For some cases of that general type, see e.g. Atiyah (1971), pp. 22–3, 44–5.

12. We can also imagine cases where there has been no deception or fraud on Bob's part, and his contribution does entitle him to some return: perhaps on the basis that he has identified an opportunity, provided training, or the like. Clearly, there is room for discussion about what sorts of contributions entitle someone to a proportion of the benefits of the activity, and wider implications to such discussion.

13. For an comparable example where people may offend one another, see Davies and Harré (1999), pp. 45–9.

11. Groups and Positions

We have discussed ways in which one party may contrive real or apparent obligations for another. In some respects, there is a much simpler way to do so than those we have suggested so far. It is to link the other with some group commitments. The case where one party manipulates a local moral order so as to contrive obligations for others can be difficult for them to deal with. The difficulty for them in that case is often to deal with conflicts of genuine obligation, commitment and interest. The case is especially difficult where genuine obligations have been created, because those others are likely to be involved in a form of 'dirty hands' problem. In this chapter, however, we consider a slightly different case which can also be difficult, where there is an association between normative commitments and group membership which means that espousal of one implies espousal of the other, and the fact is used to manipulate people's commitments or group alignments. Group alignments are clearly important in political processes where voting determines outcomes. However, even though many organisations do not rely on democratic internal processes or other voting processes to make decisions, group alignments can still be important, and so can people's associated commitments.

A number of points in our discussion have alluded to the relation between group membership and a commitment to certain lines of action. In Chapter 2 we referred to 'social identity theory' and some effects of our tendency to identify ourselves with groups. Associated with this is our tendency to espouse and support those groups' shared values, norms and beliefs. Examples have been seen in groups' 'impression management'. Glazer and Glazer's reference to the '"mutual pretense" which helps managers sustain the belief that all is under control', and the example of 'the game' which one of Jackall's interviewees recounted, both draw our attention to this factor. One sort of pressure on individuals to conform to others' expectations is pressure on fellow group members not to call group beliefs or values into question.

When people use the 'formulations' we discussed earlier, that are common in persuasive discourse, they tend to call on such shared norms, values and beliefs. In doing so, they often espouse some group membership or accuse others of membership of a different group. In the 1950s, if you suggested that my advocacy of welfare rights was communist, then you would be contending that my position was contrary to our listeners' values, and also trying to associate me with communists, an out-group as far as our listeners were concerned. Such formulations are common in many rhetorical contexts. I might say 'Would any reputable accountant accept that assets should be valued according to the owner's unconfirmed estimate?', and the other's social identity as an accountant is being called on. The tactic effectively puts the other in a position either of agreeing with the interlocutor, or of standing at odds with others' expectations and group norms. Examples abound of cases where one party draws another into agreement in that way. The other has three possible responses. One is to stand against group norms and values ('I don't care what other accountants do, I believe this is appropriate here'), a second is acceding to the opinions or proposals contained in the formulation ('You're right: I shall change the report'), and the third is some 'reformulation', to demonstrate that the first formulation is somehow at fault: either it does not accurately represent group norms and values, or there is some other formulation available of what is proposed ('There is confirmation from a reputable valuer').

COMMITMENT, ALIGNMENT AND INFLUENCE

In many cases, espousal of some normative commitments is associated with the existence of groups in a political environment. The previous chapter emphasised the importance of the expectations people have of one another. These are signalled partly in people's discourse. Their discourse simultaneously can signal normative commitments and group membership. Ruth Grant suggests that

> A political community cannot exist without some shared morality and some common standard for honor or respectability. Public discourse is conducted in moral terms, and that shared language is itself part of the constitution of any particular public. (1997, p. 49)[1]

In a political environment, any group is usually to some extent a 'public' for itself, and efforts to influence others' group alignments will commonly use the shared discourse that both maintains group identity and reflects certain normative commitments. Hence, Grant suggests, there is a Machiavellian argument for the inevitability of hypocrisy in politics. Rather than showing genuine normative commitment, espousals of norms and values are likely just to signal group membership and acceptance of what it entails. The same can be true for beliefs: espousal of a belief can function primarily to show group membership, rather than genuine commitment to the content of the belief. Bar-Tal suggests that 'group beliefs serve as a foundation for group existence' (1990, p. 105), and that 'group beliefs provide the psychological framework that allows group members to structure their social reality about the group' (p. 106). The fact that members of a group share a belief not widely held by others may help them to see themselves as members of the same distinctive group.

On the one hand, when one acknowledges membership of a group, one can thereby justify some expectations by others about various beliefs that are commonly upheld by members of the group. If I acknowledged membership of the Communist Party, I might have made it reasonable for others to expect me to be optimistic about the Soviet Union, even though that was not part of the definition of being a Party member. Conversely, someone can give an intimation of group membership through affirming a belief that is a core belief for a group, in the sense that it is common or official amongst group members, but not amongst others.

Sometimes, as a result, a position on an issue is like a flag, or rallying-point, for group members, something for them to gather around, and defend. Such a symbolic rallying-point can be important because it is thought important, however separable it may really be from the life of the group. In that situation, it can be hard to discern whether affirmation of a belief shows sincere commitment to it. There is an old saying that 'If the Archbishop of Canterbury says he believes in God, then that's by way of business, but if he says that he doesn't believe in God, then you can believe him.' The basis for the aphorism is that people do on occasion affirm beliefs for the sake of acknowledging group membership, and that when they do so it can be hard to evaluate their sincere commitment to the belief (whereas, on the other hand, if they affirm a belief contrary to what is expected of their group, the only plausible explanation is genuine commitment to the belief).

Group beliefs have multiple functions, from rationalisation of action to reinforcing group solidarity, and affirming a belief can equally play multiple roles, from reassuring others about reasons for action to giving information about group strength (Bar-Tal 1990, p. 107). We know from many sources that affirmations of belief can play multiple roles even for individuals, and that contextual factors can play an important role in how such affirmations are to be interpreted (see e.g. Austin 1975 and Grice 1989b). A number of authors have analysed political implications (e.g. Bell 1975 and Riker 1986). The relationship between affirmation and alignment can figure in a variety of political tactics. One such tactic is to put others in situations where they will be forced to make an affirmation that will align them with one party or another. Perhaps the most famous and clearest example is the Gospel story of Jesus:

> And they sent to him some of the Pharisees and some of the Herodians, to entrap him in his talk. And they came and said to him, 'Teacher, we know that you are true, and care for no man; for you do not regard the position of men, but truly teach the way of God. Is it lawful to pay taxes to Caesar, or not? Should we pay them, or should we not?' (Mark 12:13–15 RSV; cf. Matthew 22:15–17, Luke 20:20–22)

Jesus has three options. One, refusing to answer, seems to renounce claims to wisdom and authority. The others, to answer either 'yes' or 'no', each threatens to compromise him by aligning him with one party or another. For the 'positions of men' referred to by his interlocutors are well-established political positions:

> if he advised payment of the tax he would discredit himself in the eyes of all the nationalist groups (here perhaps symbolized by *the Herodians*, v. 13); for such advice would be regarded as a betrayal of the national cause, and no one who gave it could expect much support or acceptance of his messianic claims from the crowds. If he pronounced against payment he would offend those (represented in v. 13 by the *Pharisees*) who were prepared to tolerate the *status quo*, and he might even be reported to the Romans for inciting to rebellion. (Nineham 1969, p. 315)

In fact, of course, Jesus exits neatly between the horns of the dilemma. By getting them to show him a coin and drawing their attention to the image on it, he moves the onus of proof back to them: if the coins they carry bear Caesar's portrait, the onus is on them to show why they do not thereby acknowledge their duty to pay taxes, and to admit the role they had themselves played in bringing about Roman rule (Nineham 1969, p. 315; see also Cox 1952, pp. 135–6).

Some similar kinds of cases have been analysed by Riker. One is a similar tactic to that used by the Herodians and Pharisees, but used this time by Abraham Lincoln against his political opponent Stephen Douglas (Riker 1986, pp. 1–9). In this and other cases, Riker shows how political tactics often aim to compromise opponents by forcing them into positions that will alienate some or other of their allies.[2] The importance of a position on an issue as a symbolic rallying-point is one reason why in negotiation it may sometimes not be a good idea to focus exclusively on 'interests', rather than positions, as some writers recommend (Fisher, Ury and Patton 1991, cf. Provis 1996a). Where a group is party to negotiations, its position on an issue can be important for its members' solidarity and commitment.

The link between a position on a specific issue and group beliefs in general, may be quite clear-cut, or less so. There is no difficulty about seeing the relevance of an Archbishop's position regarding the existence of God to the beliefs of the Church he leads. The legality of paying taxes to Caesar needs more explanation for us to understand its relationship to group allegiances. These may have been quite clear to people at the time, but the relationship nevertheless depends on their array of background beliefs and knowledge. There are a range of cases where such relationships are more subtle still, down to cases where a proposal is put only for the sake of inviting people to come down on one side or another, explicitly to test their allegiance and perhaps to offer a forum for debate and manoeuvre. C.P. Snow depicts a nice example:

By the end of the month, Roger was due to make his speech on the White Paper. We were all lulling ourselves with work. All of a sudden the lull broke. It broke in a fashion that no one had expected. It was a surprise to the optimistic: but it was even more of a surprise to the experienced. It didn't look much, in the office. Just a note on a piece of paper. Harmless looking, the words.

The Opposition had put down a motion to reduce the Navy vote by ten pounds.

It would have sounded archaic, or plain silly, to those who didn't know Parliament. Even to some who did, it sounded merely technical. It was technical, but most of us knew it meant much more. (1972b, chap. 36)

In a budget of millions, ten pounds off the Navy vote would be neither here nor there. But a Parliamentary debate has to have a motion as its object. Here, the real object would be the degree of support that Roger Quaife, the Minister, could summon up for his defence policy. When the debate came, how many of his own party would defect?

While this is an example drawn from parliamentary politics, with clearer conventions than usually found in organisational politics, writers on organisations often stress the importance of symbolism in political processes (e.g. Jackall 1988, chap. 6, Pfeffer 1992, chap. 15). Such symbolic issues can become the object of political contention in exactly the same way as a motion to reduce the Navy vote by ten pounds. At the other extreme may be issues that wear on their face the importance they have, such as who the new chairperson is to be, or whether one part of a firm will secede (see e.g. Pfeffer 1992, pp. 289–90). In between, perhaps, there are issues that have some importance in themselves, but which are just the tip of an iceberg in terms of the other issues they are associated with: whether the Jews ought to pay taxes to Rome may have been in this category.

BELIEFS AND GROUPS

In calling attention to beliefs and commitments that are associated with group membership, influence tactics can make group membership more salient and bring forth the whole array of influence mechanisms that revolve around group membership, such as conformity effects and shared conceptions of what is legitimate. To that extent, such tactics may be assessed in the same way as other influence tactics we have considered. However, calling attention to group membership raises an array of other issues as well. For example, the association of group membership with particular positions generates expectations in others as well as group members. In particular, it affects others' evaluation of beliefs affirmed by group members. We may be inclined to set aside the content of people's affirmations when we take them merely to exhibit group membership and solidarity with other group members. Then, of course, there is the question which comes first, the belief or the group? Is it that people come first to different beliefs, and then form groupings around those beliefs, or is it that people first align themselves, and then embrace beliefs that distinguish them from others?

If we think about politics and group alignments in general, then the answer, of course, is that both occur, in various ways. Sometimes, respected individuals with positions on an issue gain followers who are committed primarily to them and only secondarily to the relevant position. Sometimes, aspiring leaders may choose positions, and espousals of belief, depending to some extent on the allegiance they believe that they can win from others if they commit themselves to those beliefs. Sometimes, a pre-existing group comes to espouse a belief on an issue which then becomes important to define its members. There is no reason to believe that every case is the same. In some, the content of the positions may be most important, and in others it may be personal or group allegiances.

We should note, therefore, that people's espoused commitments are not necessarily insincere, just because they are associated with group alignments. Sometimes, group membership may emerge from prior, sincere normative commitments, rather than the other way round. In that case, commitments associated with group membership can be genuine commitments.

When people do have sincere commitments to some principles, and those principles embody some group norms, and the members of the group also have personal commitments to one another, we may see again the sort of 'dirty hands' problem discussed in Chapter 3. There is a nice example in Kinnear's comment on the part played by Bonar Law in coalition government with Lloyd George:

> Bonar Law kept in close touch with the backbenchers, and up to his first retirement Lloyd George relied on him to keep the Conservative M.P.s quiet. His loyalties were undivided, and the M.P.s knew that he supported Lloyd George, but that if the premier presented a real threat to Conservative principles, he would put his party ahead of personal ties. (1973, p. 60)

Bonar Law's loyalties were undivided as between Asquith and Lloyd George, perhaps, and to the extent that they potentially were divided between Lloyd George, on the one hand, and the Conservative Party and its principles, on the other, it was clear what he would do. It may be that the lack of doubt about what he would do speaks well for Bonar Law's integrity and strength of character, but equally the forces contending for his allegiance show some of the complexity that can occur in real situations.

In such situations, the demands on us are complex partly because of the interplay of different sources of allegiance and obligation, but they are also complex because of the difficulty of evaluating people's affirmations and positions. Thus, to revert to our earlier example, when the Archbishop of Canterbury affirms that he believes in God, we may need to know more about him to decide whether he is truly committed to that belief. Without doubt, there have been many Archbishops of Canterbury who have been devout and sincere in their professions of faith, but it is not hard to find some historical examples of clergy and ostensibly committed lay people in various religions whose interests seem more to have been in the temporal than the spiritual benefits of faith, and whose affirmations of belief mainly signalled a political position. In Chapter 7 we discussed some of the ethical issues that arise around weighing evidence and drawing conclusions in organisational life. A related issue arises here as we evaluate affirmations of beliefs that are associated with group membership. It can be important to chart a way between the Scylla of undue cynicism and the Charybdis of uncritical naïveté.

How we should evaluate others' affirmations of belief will vary from cases to case, because the relationship between affirmation and group membership will vary from case to case. Religious beliefs provide vivid illustrations of complex interplay between belief and group alignment. Consider the negotiations between Catholics and Protestants at Regensburg in 1541, recounted in detail by Peter Matheson in his book *Cardinal Contarini at Regensburg* (1972).[3] The aim of the Regensburg meeting was to attempt a reconciliation between Catholics and Protestants. Central to that had to be agreement on some contested matters of doctrine, but intermingled with it also were issues to do with the political alignments of the day: 'by the time of the Diet of Regensburg in 1541 doctrinal and socio-political questions were inextricably bound up with one another' (p. 5). In describing the issue of the authority of Scripture in the Regensburg discussions, Matheson writes that

> If the principle of *sola scriptura*, with its ultimate basis in the absolute polarity of the divine will and human 'traditions' were sacrificed, the whole Protestant front could be rolled back and Catholic faith and practice defended at every critical point. Here there could be no retreat. Since, however, this applied equally to the Catholics, deadlock seemed imminent and the whole colloquy threatened to grind to a halt. For the moment a tactical rescue operation by the politicians saved the day. (p. 117)

Participants in the Regensburg discussions considered major issues of doctrine that separated Catholics and Protestants, and in doing so they focussed in great detail on the substance of the issues. But, at the same time, their deliberations were surrounded by implications of one position or another on party structures and alliances. The Emperor Charles V needed resolution of the religious schism to restore his political authority in Germany, the Papacy was concerned both about doctrine and about restoration of church lands, while German princes were concerned both about the religious principles that united their people and the preservation of a measure of independence. The religious and political issues were completely entwined. There is no need to assume that debate over doctrinal issues was simply a cloak for political bargaining, or that the debate would reach conclusions in an ivory tower remote from other considerations.

There are ethical dimensions both to how strongly participants in such conflict maintain their positions, and in how others evaluate participants' affirmations of belief. We shall comment further below on the fact that if parties affirm beliefs in order to continue or promote some political alignment, we may accuse them of insincerity and hypocrisy. At the other extreme, if they uncompromisingly maintained some beliefs at the expense of peace and harmony, we might call them stiff-necked or obstinate. However, for us as observers, it will not always be straightforward for us to make an evaluation: cases vary, and so will the motives of different individuals.

Whenever there is conflict between groups whose members have different beliefs, the question may arise to what extent people's positions are about the ostensible issue or about something that lies behind it. In Snow's case, there would not be much doubt, because no one was likely to be so naïve as to commit themselves simply on the issue of whether the Navy vote ought to be ten pounds more or less. To take a position on this issue would have to be very clearly to take a position on the issues that lay behind it. However, because of the ambiguous form of most of the contentious issues where people take positions to signify some group membership, doubt can arise about what actually is in contention.

In the Gospel case, the affirmation is of one or other belief with a normative element: whether taxes ought to be paid, or not. That it has a normative dimension may not be essential to the case. Many affirmations that have significance in a religious case are of descriptive beliefs. Readers of Terry Pratchett's novel *Small Gods* will recall the affirmation that unites adherents of the Great God Om: 'The Turtle Moves!'. In an organisation the beliefs might be to do with predictions about the new marketing plan, the safety of the new machines or products, possibilities of court action, or whatever. Any issue that may be the locus for dispute is potentially the content of beliefs that distinguish groups and parties. In many cases, though, the beliefs in question will have some normative element: about what ought to be done, about what is of value, or the like.

Matheson's description of these processes stands out only because of its clarity and detail. We can find similar interplay between religious doctrine and political positions throughout history, from the rise of Christianity in the Roman Empire down to the role of the Catholic church in communist Poland during the days of the Solidarity movement. Bar-Tal notes that 'group beliefs, which characterize the group, demarcate its boundaries with the out-groups' (1990, p. 106), and the corollary is that by professing such a belief one marks oneself as a member of the in-group.

Clear in the politics of nation-states and elsewhere, it is not surprising that such mechanisms are present also in modern corporate life. They are visible repeatedly in Jackall's exposition. The mechanisms for establishing group beliefs are in many respects comparable to those of religious organisations. Jackall says:

> The segmented, fragmented, and hierarchical structure of bureaucratic work lends itself more than other kinds of work situations to the manufacture of multiple ideologies and mythologies. These include not only the attempts of individuals to make sense of their world and lobby for their own positions with others, but also the semi-official viewpoints disseminated through the impressive communications apparatus common to all bureaucracies – I refer here to plant newsletters, monthly employee newspapers, newsbrief circulars, daily news sheet summaries for executives, magazines for managers, and so on – as well as official authoritative pronouncements that, of course, color all other views. (1988, p. 146)

Whether the views that managers accept are those promulgated through such official or semi-official views, or ones they arrive at through informal, less official exchanges, their acceptance is likely to be influenced by group allegiance as much as by the content of the belief. As a result, what they accept can depart widely from what might be reasonable according to evidence and logic. One of those whom Jackall interviewed said that managers 'end up going around believing in fairy tales that might have no relationship to reality at all' (1988, p. 147).

MULTIPLE FUNCTIONS

Problems can arise about interpreting others' affirmations, because of all the different motives people may have for their affirmations, and the different functions that such affirmations can have. We have noted earlier in other contexts how utterances can have multiple functions in organisational politics. For example, a comment may serve to give information but at the same time to distract attention from a different issue. It may conjure up one frame rather than another, or display trust, or friendship. Many of Jackall's descriptions illustrate how managers need to be aware of the full significance of what others do and say. The extent to which utterances can display group allegiance is often a crucial function, but a function which can be masked. Awareness of groupings, and their associated beliefs, can be important in all sorts of social and political life. Inviting an affirmation can be an invitation to disclose group membership, testing the person to whom the invitation is given. 'Knowing their hypocrisy', Jesus said to those who approached him, 'Why put me to the test?' Partly, the test was to know that it was a test. Because people's affirmations of belief sometimes have more to do with signalling membership of a particular party than with reflective commitment to the content of the belief, asking a question may ostensibly express interest in a particular issue, but also aim to lure the other party into some compromising response.

In organisational politics it is not uncommon for utterances to have dual functions, in various ways. Some of them are to do with group allegiances, but others are not, even though they have a tactical purpose. It can still be that the reason for the speaker to combine different functions is to put other parties off their guard, perhaps to respond in the way warranted by the ostensible purpose but inadvisable in the light of the ulterior purpose.

For example, the production manager may commend the marketing manager on increases in sales, asking whether the marketing department can keep up its good work. A natural answer – and perhaps a true one – may be that, yes, they expect they can. But the production manager's purpose may be to seek increased resources, perhaps even increases at the expense of the marketing department: after all, there may be no point to enhanced marketing without products to sell. Or the manager of a municipal rubbish dump may criticise new environmental guidelines, so that those who come to the guidelines' defence will be committed to offering greater resources to the dump. These are all instances of utterances or actions which have an ostensible purpose and one or more ulterior purposes. They all raise some similar ethical issues, potentially departing from the requirement that we treat one another as autonomous subjects and allow one another to make responsible decisions based on the best information available.

In some such cases, where a question or utterance has amongst its functions that of putting people off their guard, the ethical problem about attempted dissimulation may be treated as similar to the ethical problem with deception, in the sense that it tends to impair another's ability to make a responsible decision about what to do: in this case, about what to say as a response to the question. But there is a further issue in many cases, shown by the Gospel case. The charge of 'hypocrisy' made against the Herodians and Pharisees focuses on the aspect of their question which consists in their purporting to have a genuine interest in Jesus' answer to their question. Not only do they seek to lure him into a vexed position, at the same time they seek to display themselves in a favourable light, as earnest and humble seekers after truth.

In general, hypocrisy seems to consist in claiming moral purity or uprightness that one does not really have. In such a situation, apart from our claims to virtue, our behaviour may not be greatly evil. We may suffer from common shortcomings such as a degree of selfishness, or laziness, or short temper or other everyday failings that most of us struggle against with limited success. But in claiming rectitude we do not possess, we make worse what we do. We are like people who give counterfeit money in payment of a debt: not only have we failed to meet our obligations, what we do adds the further evil of undermining people's faith in the currency. As hypocrites, we not only fall short of virtue, we undermine people's belief in virtue as a goal. Further still, in some cases, we betray individuals who accept our expressions at face value. For these reasons at least, a charge of hypocrisy is a serious one. It may be all the more so in organisational politics, where assumptions of self-interested behaviour are common, and it is all the harder to sustain faith in virtue as a possible and worthwhile aspiration.

However, that is not all that is at issue here. Consider the Gospel case once more. The hypocrisy of Jesus' questioners lay in them purporting to have a genuine interest in the answer to their question, because if they did have such a genuine interest, that would show them to have worthy interests and concerns and aspirations towards good policy and right action. In fact, of course, their actual motivation was not a genuine interest in the answer to their question. They had their own views about that issue, and firm commitments, which Jesus' answer would not affect. Their actual motivation was to force Jesus into a difficult position. Their question, therefore, had several different functions. One was the surface function, of seeking information or opinion on the issue, for their guidance. A second was the ulterior function, of structuring a situation where any choice by Jesus would be problematic for him. A third was to put Jesus off his guard, perhaps to take less care with his answer than he might when he knew their intentions. Insofar as it is an attempt to put Jesus off his guard in a dangerous position, and lead him to expose himself to attack, the reasons to question it may not only be to do with hypocrisy and deception, but may be like reasons we have to question uses of force and violence.

That sort of tactic is especially likely in situations where group allegiances are in question. It is in such situations where an unwary utterance can most especially do someone harm, as it can signal their adherence to a particular group, with all the consequent sanctions that may follow from members of that and other groups. At the very least, such an utterance may contravene group norms and cast doubt on the person's reliability or integrity, with consequent harm in the future. But this point brings us back to the significance of group beliefs for the life of a group. Is it possible to avoid group beliefs having an important part in organisational life? It seems to some extent to be the differentiation of groups that promotes the variety of positions and group beliefs that can lead managers and others to end up, in the words of Jackall's manager, 'believing in fairy tales that might have no relationship to reality at all'. We may therefore ask if discouraging people's identification with groups might reduce the problems that accrue from espousal of group beliefs. Another way of asking this question is to consider how far it is possible to avoid party politics in organisations.

PARTIES AND POLITICS IN ORGANISATIONS

Jackall's manager referred to describing situations in ways that make them more palatable to 'some group that matters'. To some extent or other, any 'group that matters' constitutes a 'party'. In unitarist organisations, the 'group that matters' may be a party whose hegemony is great enough to obscure the existence of other parties, but in many there will be different parties identifiable at least by commitments on some specific issues, such as expansion into Asian markets, use of specific technologies, or strategies for environmental conservation. 'Party politics' is well known in the politics of nation-states, but we should not imagine that the discipline and organisation that is often associated with that process is necessary for the existence of a 'party': clearly enough, that term has a wider meaning that can refer to any group with a shared commitment on a particular issue.

In the context of organisational politics, there may be concern expressed about the idea that members of an organisation should form themselves into parties or factions. This raises the spectre of 'tribalism' which management writers have sometimes deplored. Is it not quite contrary to effectiveness for there to be groups with opposed political alignments within organisations? Surely an efficient organisation will have all members pulling in the same direction, working for a common goal, members of a united team, etc? The rhetoric is familiar and well-worn. It has some point, but is not in any way unique to modern Western organisations. Bailey comments on Bisipara, a village of India:

> '*Dolo*' and sometimes the English word 'party' are used by the people of Bisipara to refer to contending groups which we, in a loose way, would call 'factions'. As the word 'faction' carries a connotation of disapproval, so also does '*dolo*'. The scrapping (that word also has the right connotations) which goes on between *dolo* is called *doladoli*, and although it is entered into with zest and is a subject of burning interest both to those engaged and to those who merely watch, it is also deplored. 'The trouble with this village', they sometimes say, 'is that there is too much party.' They mean by this that so much time and energy is spent on disputing over minor issues and scoring points that the public interest is neglected. This, of course, happens at all levels. (1969, p. 88)

Undoubtedly, this sort of phenomenon is a problem in many places. It can impair the governments of countries, the effectiveness of organisations and even the peace of families. In the extreme, it can degenerate into hatred and war.[4] More often, though, it merely wastes time and resources that seem to all intents and purposes as though they could be better spent on productive activity.

Nevertheless, it is an over-simplification to condemn party formations and politics without further ado. It assumes that there is a straightforward choice between a situation with unity and harmony, and a situation riven by factionalism and dispute. That is implausible. In Chapter 1, it was noted that Mintzberg's conception of politics, as an activity outside of what is formally sanctioned, seems to forget that consideration and discussion are often needed before decisions are made. It is one thing to seek commitment and unity to a policy that has been decided on and endorsed by generally accepted processes. It is a different thing to expect unity beforehand. There are few organisations that are faced with internal processes and external environments so simple that no deliberation and thought is needed to arrive at decisions. In effective organisations, there will be many occasions where groups have to consider issues and work out the best course of action. Then, individuals will come to views partly on the basis of evidence and documentation, and partly on the basis of others' views and positions. Is that a bad thing? Can we avoid people taking account of others' views and positions in coming to their own? It is difficult to see how we could, and probable that we ought not. We know ourselves to be fallible, and often we can grasp only some detail of a complex issue. We rely on others to analyse other detail, and we rely on others' judgement to check our own.

Groups within organisations can emerge or form in a variety of ways. Many of the dynamics are similar to those that occur on a wider stage. We have considered the effect of 'group beliefs', and Bar-Tal notes that 'many groups contain subgroups that form their own subgroup beliefs, while at the same time accept the basic group beliefs of the group' (1990, p. 107). While they may sometimes be bound up with personal loyalties, they can also be oriented around issues or policies, and even around ways of seeing things. In discussing conflict at Ford Motor Company, Pfeffer says that 'the conflict at Ford (and at other automobile companies as well) between finance and engineering was, at its heart, a conflict about how to view the world' (1992, p. 43). We can imagine many situations where people in an organisation fall into two or more groups depending on their orientation to an issue. We also know that people in organisations are inevitably divided into groups, one way or another, whether it be the marketing department and the finance department, men and women, or those who work in the main headquarters and those in the regional office. Whether these groupings matter, and why, will depend on circumstances, but we know that there is at least a tendency for people to see themselves as members of such groups and for that self-identity to affect their behaviour.

The implication is that factionalism and political alignments in organisations are matters of degree which cannot usually be escaped entirely. It is difficult and perhaps a requirement of good management to discern the point at which they become counterproductive and to avoid reaching that point. For us, however, the point is that it is not inherently problematic any more than organisational politics is in general: like blood pressure, too much of it may be a bad thing, but so may too little.[5]

ETHICS, POLITICS AND PARTIES IN ORGANISATIONS

That often in fact there are 'parties' in organisational politics seems beyond question. The question for us is what the dynamics are of party politics in organisations, which have ethical implications.

One problem is just the extent to which group members espouse beliefs for reasons to do with group alignment and not to do with the intrinsic merits of the beliefs. Once again, the issue goes beyond organisational politics. Some of the theologians at Regensburg were undoubtedly moved by doctrinal reflection, but others may have been more concerned about orthodoxy and conformity with the dominant views of Protestantism or Catholicism. Members of the Finance group at Ford undoubtedly tended to emphasise different considerations and come to different conclusions because of their training, but sometimes they may also have been overcome by pressure to conform with the views of other group members. To do otherwise can lead to accusations of betrayal or disloyalty to the group.

It seems clear that there is sometimes an ethical problem with espousing beliefs for reasons to do with group membership rather than reasons to do with the beliefs' intrinsic merits. If we heed only consequences, we can see many possible problems: the tendency to accept beliefs that are misguided or poorly tested can in the extreme lead to events like the *Challenger* disaster or the Bay of Pigs episode. If we go beyond consequences, there are other considerations also. We have emphasised the importance of respect for human beings as responsible decision-makers, and coming to beliefs for reasons which are to do with the beliefs' intrinsic merits seems tied to responsible decision-making. To the extent that we accept our espousal of beliefs as a type of 'intellectual' activity, we can agree with Stocker that 'intellectual activities done for the goals and according to the criteria inherent in them are among the greatest human goods' (1980, p. 337). To arrive at beliefs for the reasons we can see for them, rather than because of the social pressures on us, is part of what it is for us to be responsible, autonomous agents. The implication seems to be that virtue requires us to try ourselves to espouse beliefs on merit and to allow others to do so. In practice, that may only imply some well-worn recommendations to foster an atmosphere of openness and free exchange of ideas within our organisations, but it is important that to do so is not just a requirement of organisational performance but also a matter of ethics.

However, the fact that there can be pressures on people to espouse beliefs for reasons of group alignment rather than the beliefs' inherent merit is not the only ethical issue that arises from the dynamics of groups and parties within organisations. Members of groups will often identify themselves as members of one group rather than another, in the ways that are depicted by social identity theory. And, of course, they will tend to favour members of their own group. In particular, for example, it seems reasonable to believe that they will tend to favour them with information. They will be more likely to confide in other members of the same group about matters of mutual concern, and they will be more likely to pass on information.

For example, go back to the case we considered earlier, about arrangement of a meeting. In a situation of party alignments, we might brief some prospective participants in the forthcoming meeting, but not others, about the items that are to arise, and what we anticipate the dynamics of the discussion to be.

Here, we return to the question we posed at the end of Chapter 6. If we accept that there is some principle that we ought not favour members of our own group over others, does that apply to information and communication as much as to distribution of goods and resources?

We might call on the principle we have put in terms of a general obligation to acknowledge other self-conscious subjects as beings like ourselves, to respect their need for an understanding of the world which is as accurate as our own, and to allow them to make morally responsible decisions. If we favour some with information that we do not impart to others, do we thereby fail in our respect for the latter? *Prima facie*, we are concealing information from them, and it is not immediately clear how to distinguish this from cases where we mislead them, for example by distracting their attention from something of importance. On the other hand, we know that there is not a general obligation to tell the same things to everyone, as is evident from the fact that some information is confidential, implying that some but not others have a right to it.

If we recall some of the considerations that emerged earlier in considering grounds for maintenance of confidentiality, some light may be shed on what is legitimate in this case. We noted several relevant considerations. These include the fact that some explicit or implicit promises had been given, or the inherent personal character of the information. However, they also include the fact that it may be inappropriate to associate positions with individuals as a result of discussions and processes that are still incomplete.

If this is correct, it at least suggests that principles of fairness can apply to communication as much as to distribution of goods and services. People can be treated unfairly by being misrepresented, as much as by having some benefit withheld. However, it also suggests that in the sort of case we are considering, about imparting information to some and not to others, the idea of people's 'positions' is important. In particular, to the extent that people have acknowledged positions on an issue, they and others will often have expectations about what is legitimate behaviour, to an extent that will affect what it is reasonable for them to expect in regard to information.

To the extent that I have a publicly acknowledged position on an issue, or to the extent that I am committed to membership of a group or party that has a publicly acknowledged position on an issue, that will generate expectations in others about what I believe ought to be done on certain policy issues, and they will not expect me to go out of my way to promote contrary policy. To that extent, at least, my failure to impart information to them about some kinds of matters will not mislead them. Of course, a number of different factors are also relevant, including the experience and sophistication of the other party, and how clear group membership is. Formal organisational structures can create group memberships, and so can shared beliefs and attitudes to policy issues. These will often be very salient, and to the extent that they are, they can shape people's expectations. If group memberships are less clear, that is something that needs to be taken account of when I am assessing others' expectations: if someone approaches me with a query that clearly discloses that they do not regard me especially as a member of a group with a specific alignment on a particular issue, that may be something that I need to take into account. It may mean that I ought to disclose my position and alignment as part of a group, or it may mean that I ought to be careful in what I say, not to give a misleading impression of detachment.

There are analogies elsewhere where similar factors are acknowledged in the ethics of communication. For example, radio commentators may be condemned for not disclosing that they have contractual arrangements with companies whose goods or services they refer to (see Turner 2001), advertising by political parties may be required by law to acknowledge its source, lawyers in discussing cases may need to disclose their affiliations with a client, and so on. These kinds of requirement seem to reflect the principle that people's group or party alignments and affiliations have important effects on how others interpret their communications, and on how others shape their own communications towards them.

That is the first implication for us of the interplay between group membership and affirmed beliefs: we may reasonably anticipate that others will take into account our group affiliations in their assessments of what we say, even though we need to take account of their knowledge and understanding, and the extent to which group structures are clear and salient. However, the way we take account of one another's group memberships as we give weight to the things they say, only reflects the more general way in which we tend to perceive our social world as a pattern of alignments, commitments and positions. We cannot separate issues to do with group commitments from other issues that we have already considered. When Baron de Rothschild and his acquaintance walk arm-in-arm across the floor of the stock exchange, others infer some mutual commitment between the two. When Walker's negotiator makes a suggestion, how others interpret it depends on group alignments and established positions. When Mason told Lund to take off his engineering hat and put on his management hat, he invited Lund to frame things in the light of one group alignment rather than another. Our group alignments affect our own cognitions, and also affect others' perceptions and understandings of us. The expectations others have of us, which often create some obligations for us, in many cases emerge from group alignments or commitments we show to people.

In this context, to make ethical decisions we have to take account of our commitments to other individuals, of the expectations others will have had of me on the basis of my publicly espoused positions and group alignments, and of the interpretations I can reasonably expect others to give to my words and actions. At the same time, I shall need to have regard for such other factors as what I and others regard as personal information, of others' capacities to attend to information and consider it, and the like. Other matters like fairness

and harmful consequences will also need to be considered, but those mentioned are especially relevant to the fact that ethical action requires us to take
realistic account of one another's actual situation in the world, including our
finite capacities and also the extent to which we live our lives largely as
members of a social world that includes alignments and commitments which
range from personal friendships to identification with abstract groups. How
much is morally required of us depends, as so often, on how much we can see
and understand, but it is clear at least that we ought to try to deal in a realistic
way with what we can see and understand.

HYPOCRISY: A FINAL WORD

Being realistic is not always easy. Self-deception and hypocrisy constantly
beckon. We have referred to 'hypocrisy' especially in connection with beliefs
and affirmations of belief which have as their real function some demonstration of group alignment more than anything else, but that is not the only form
of hypocrisy that can be very noticeable in the politics of groups. I argued
that friendship can give rise to genuine obligations. But the fact that friendship may give rise to obligations can allow the cultivation of real or simulated
friendship to be used for political purposes, just as the influence mechanism
of reciprocity can be used by a person who does a favour in order to get
something in return. Friendship and other close personal relationships can not
only be the source of genuine obligations, they can move people to action
from a sense of obligation or a sense of affection. To influence others through
such feelings as these can be problematic. Again, not always. To ask a friend
for help is unproblematic. But to cultivate someone's friendship for an ulterior purpose seems deceptive and reprehensible. Here, we start to enter into
complexities about interpersonal relationships that show many shades of grey
between the white of unselfish mutual regard and the black of conscious,
deliberate exploitation (see e.g. Blum 1973). In some cases, though, the
ethical implications seem clear-cut.

   There is a similar kind of ethical problem that arises when people feign
belief to demonstrate group membership. In each sort of case, there can be
more or less extreme instances, which can merit greater or lesser condemnation, but there is a similar underlying concern: that respect for genuine
commitments can be undermined by commitments that are feigned or
contrived for ulterior motives. Just as friendships can be cultivated or feigned
for ulterior motives, so can affirmations of belief or position. We may affirm
beliefs not only to demonstrate our own group alignments, but to influence
others'. 'Coalition building' is a significant tactic in many types of politics,
and often consists in defining or framing issues in ways that will bring people
into a particular group alignment, by definitions or framing that are consistent
with their other commitments or which show this alignment to be a natural

consequence of their other beliefs or positions. If our earlier argument was correct, there is not necessarily anything unethical about framing an issue in one way rather than another, or about focussing on some aspect of it rather than another, if it is done openly and frankly. But the case is different if we feign a commitment we do not really have, or if we deliberately give a false impression about our motives and intentions. Then we can be condemned for all the reasons that make deception unethical. To the extent that we simultaneously portray ourselves to have uplifting and virtuous commitments, we stand condemned also of hypocrisy.

This concern may arise in the context of the manipulations discussed in the previous chapter of people's expectations and the obligations associated with them. Individuals can base some manipulation of the local moral order by feigning regard for values or ends that others respect. They may advocate quality but really aim at control. They may claim concern for efficiency, but actually want to replace the current production manager. When individuals in organisations influence others by trading on the others' commitments, the same general type of criticism is often appropriate. In such cases, the perpetrators try to portray themselves in a good light, and to exploit others at the same time. In doing so, they act unfairly, they fail to treat others as responsible decision-makers, and they undermine people's confidence in normative commitments, including those that are worthwhile and important.[6]

Certainly, it can be hard to assess the motives of someone like Smith or the hypothetical Division Manager discussed in the previous chapter. On many occasions it may be contentious whether people's commitments are genuine. We know that pretences like hypocrisy are often opaque to their perpetrators. When we are self-deceiving about our hypocrisy, we obtain the benefit of a good opinion of ourselves as well as the other effects we contrive. It seems plausible to believe that many of people's efforts to involve others in some course of action are at least sincere, even though the extent to which they are self-serving or contrived might make us suspect that they embody substantial elements of self-deception. Once again, this seems to be an area where there is fertile scope for people to tell themselves that their efforts are well-meant, and that what they do is motivated by a sincere commitment to some important norms or values.

If we have made repeated allusions to hypocrisy in organisational politics, that is partly because hypocrisy tends most strongly to inhibit us from taking realistic account of one another's finite capacities and innate shortcomings. To the extent that hypocrisy is pretence at virtue that the pretender does not have, it is self-serving and tends to undermine our confidence in any appearance of virtue. But sometimes hypocrisy is not just a pretence at virtue that the pretender does not have: sometimes, it is pretence at virtue that individuals cannot reasonably be expected to have, and in that case it not only undermines our trust in a virtuous appearance, it also discourages us from realism about what is possible.

In particular, for example, a pretence at detachment from group commitments and a pretence at impartiality which is unaffected by party alignment or social identity can foster unrealistic expectations about the extent to which individuals in organisations can remove themselves from the dynamics of group interplay. This is not to say that we cannot ever distance ourselves from our commitments or try to act fairly to those with different alignments. However, it is to say that efforts at objectivity or fairness can only approach success to the extent that they are realistic about the influence that group alignments and social identity often have on us. Just as much as Cialdini's '*click*, and *whirr*' mechanisms like reciprocity, our social commitments can influence us strongly, and comprise an aspect of our nature that we need to be realistic about if we are to approach the degrees of autonomy and responsible decision-making we really are capable of.

SUMMARY

In the previous chapter we saw that it can be an ethically dubious tactic of organisational politics to manipulate people's obligations and the normative demands on them. In this chapter, we have noted that another tactic is to manoeuvre people into positions where they must amend either their normative commitments or their group alignments. An outstanding ethical problem with both these sorts of tactics is their tendency to involve their users in hypocrisy. In both sorts of case, there is potential for the user of the tactic to refer to moral or other normative commitments without genuinely caring about them, really caring only for the actions of others that the tactic seeks to elicit.

At the same time, and equally important in many ways, the association between group membership and positions or group beliefs, can lead to the espousal of beliefs for reasons to do with group membership rather than the intrinsic merit of the beliefs. It does not seem to be a solution to this to try to eliminate groups or parties in organisations, and the implication seems to be the importance once again of treating others as responsible decision-makers, in this context by allowing them to draw conclusions on the basis of evidence and reasoning, as far as possible mitigating pressure on them to espouse beliefs according to group membership.

Because group alignments are often a reality in organisations, we have to accept as an inevitable corollary the fact that people's communication and information exchange will to some extent favour their fellow group members rather than others. To some extent, this can be justified by the privacy of some information or the fact that others will expect it, and can make allowance for it in their decisions. But just as in other contexts, we ought to be realistic in our assessment of what others expect.

The need for realism is important. One problem with espousal of beliefs and values as ways of signalling group alignments is that it can undermine our respect for genuine commitments and our ability to be realistic about what is to be expected from others.

NOTES

1. Cf. Aristotle (1992), Book I, chap. ii, p. 60: 'Speech … serves to indicate what is useful and what is harmful, and so also what is just and what is unjust. For the real difference between man and other animals is that humans alone have perception of good and evil, just and unjust, etc. It is the sharing of a common view in *these* matters that makes a household and a state.'

2. The term 'wedge politics' has been used recently to refer to similar tactics.

3. For further discussion, considering how the episode shows the difficulty there can be distinguishing 'negotiation' from 'argument', see Provis (2004).

4. Some of the dynamics of how it may do so are analysed clearly in Hardin (1995).

5. In fact, the processes of group alignment and position formation can be governed by overriding norms that stop it from going too far. Sometimes in studies of group decision-making this is highlighted by distinguishing norms about task functions from norms about group maintenance: see e.g. Hoffman (1982), pp. 105–10. Bailey refers to 'the umbrella of normative restraint under the shade of which *doladoli* is conducted' (1969, pp. 90–91). Like nation-states and other communities, organisations may have sophisticated norms about what is and is not acceptable as part of the political process.

6. Cf. Kittay (2001). A related criticism that can be brought to bear on some processes of 'managing values' is the charge of inauthenticity: see Provis (1996b), pp. 481–3.

12. Conclusion

One dominant focus of this book has been how to participate in the life of organisations in an ethical way, while recognising our own and our colleagues' fallibility and susceptibility to influence. Another has been the fact that we have multiple sources of obligation, which may leave us in situations where we are subject to real ethical conflict. I have not tried to present simple answers or easy rules, but I have suggested that we can be on our guard against some mistaken answers and can hope for answers in concrete situations if we bear some general principles in mind.

The two chapters of Part One surveyed some general issues and identified a number of points that would be relevant to discussion in Parts Two and Three. In Chapter 1, the theme of our discussion was that organisational politics raises some important ethical issues which are distinctive and not always straightforward. One easy view we can set aside is that organisational politics is always bad. We cannot assume that participation in politics is always unethical, in organisations any more than anywhere else, and we cannot avoid specific questions about particular processes and tactics. Some of the issues are like analogous issues raised by the politics of nation-states, but there are some differences between the politics of nation-states and the politics of organisations. These include the facts that organisations often are to be found within nation-states and subject to them and that close personal relationships may have greater ethical implications in organisational politics. In Chapter 2 we then noticed aspects of human psychology that would prove to be relevant to discussion in later chapters. These included most especially the significance of schemas and scripts in our social cognition, our susceptibility to influence by Cialdini's '*click*, and *whirr*' mechanisms, and our strong tendency to identify with groups. Associated with our inclinations toward group identification and conformity is our susceptibility to influence by group norms and authority we perceive as legitimate. This point paves the way for some of the discussion to follow, about genuine sources of legitimacy for official organisational authority.

Part Two of the book revolves around Tricia's case. Central to the discussion are the conflicts we may face from different sources of obligation, and the question to what extent official organisational authority may be a legitimate source of obligation able to resolve such conflicts.

If the argument of those chapters is sound, our ethical obligations are more firmly based on relationships with individual persons than with abstractions like groups or organisations, and more firmly based on the expectations of concrete individual persons than on abstractions like group norms or official authority.

Certainly, organisations are important for providing people with goods and services they need. While I have acknowledged at several points that fulfilment of organisational purposes is a factor to be taken account of in coming to decisions, it may nevertheless appear to some readers that I have given disproportionate emphasis to other factors. If I have, that is because I believe that we all tend toward the contrary error, of reifying organisations and their purposes to a degree greater than justified by the goods and services they provide to individuals. Once more, this is in no way to deny the reality of those benefits, or the importance of organisations in providing them. It is merely to recognise the influence that group identity and perceptions of legitimacy can have on us, often giving them a weight beyond what is actually justified.

There seem in fact to be a number of considerations that might genuinely create obligations on us to comply with official organisational authority. Apart from benefits that organisational processes bring to other stakeholders, these include the transmission into organisations of the legitimate authority of a surrounding nation-state, or the fact that there are accepted internal norms that support organisational requirements, or the fact that individuals have expressly or tacitly consented to those requirements, or the fact that they are fair arrangements that people might reasonably consent to, whether or not they actually do. However, official organisational authority cannot always be assumed to have binding ethical force. Considerations like those will be relevant in some cases, but cannot be assumed to solve them all. Neither severally nor jointly do those considerations provide a general support for official authority in organisations, even though each of them may play some part in establishing such obligations on some occasions. We cannot ultimately avoid the need to scrutinise details of our own situation and the various considerations that may be relevant to ethical choice.

The discussion of legitimacy is related to a number of other issues that arise about ethics in organisational politics, including the issue that has been labelled the 'dirty hands' problem in discussions of the politics of nation-states, the idea that politics may require the violation of moral and ethical obligations.

The complexity of life in organisations means that we shall inevitably find ourselves confronted with conflicting obligations, and the need to make hard choices. We cannot rely on any straightforward routine to deal with those problems. In particular, we cannot partition issues into distinct categories – the ethical and the political, for example – and assume that the different sorts of issues can be given separate treatment. This is brought out most clearly when we have obligations to other individuals that clash with obligations of principle or of fairness and impartiality. Such conflicts may be especially salient in organisations because of the way that organisations occupy a sort of middle ground between personal relationships and the wider community. Obligations of friendship and loyalties to individuals confront organisational purposes and group expectations. There is no general presumption that either sort of requirement always takes precedence.

Admittedly, there is a strong argument that loyalties to individuals have more force for us as human subjects than loyalties to abstract entities like organisations. However, the discussion has still suggested that there is not necessarily any simple or straightforward way of resolving the dilemmas that arise. It is part of the moral dimension of human life that we must evaluate them when they arise for us in concrete terms. There have been a number of places in our discussion where we have been forced to conclude simply that ethical decisions will be difficult, either because of conflicting ethical demands or because of the moral complexity of the situation. Real decisions have to be made in situations where details matter, and sometimes the details may point a clear way to resolution. However, there is no presumption that they always make choices easy or straightforward.

The discussion thus gives deliberate emphasis to the dilemmas and quandaries that may confront us in organisational politics. It can be implicit in some discussions that it is easy to see what is ethical, and that our difficulties are primarily to support or encourage the ethical behaviour that is straightforwardly discernible. Sometimes, of course, it is easy to see. In those cases, the problem may be in doing what we see is right. Nevertheless, while it is undoubtedly true that how to support or encourage ethical behaviour is one major practical issue, it is also important to realise that it is not always straightforward to determine what ought to be done. Our discussion has alluded on several occasions to the potential for self-deception in organisational politics, and to the prospect of hypocritical behaviour. Self-deception and hypocrisy can be more likely if we neglect the various and conflicting factors that need to be taken account of in real situations. They may be less likely if we bear the complexities in mind and try to deal with them in a realistic way.

Part Three of the book builds on the idea that relationships with concrete individuals are a cornerstone of ethical action in organisations. The discussion revolves around the fact that ambiguity and uncertainty are ever-present, and so begins in Chapter 7 by considering some ethical issues about how we weigh evidence and come to conclusions. The central point is the need for us to be circumspect and realistic in assessing others' understandings and intentions. In some cases, others may still be exploring positions on an issue; alternatively, our own behaviour may be eliciting their intentions or attitudes.

The way in which our own behaviour interacts with others' expectations and behaviour can focus our attention on the need to be realistic in coming to beliefs about others, but there is the same need for realism in considering how we induce beliefs in others. Chapter 8 revolves around the way people can influence one another by affecting their beliefs. It considers issues about honesty in communication, and argues that once again it is important to be realistic about the effects we have on others and about their intentions toward us.

Ethical issues about communication raise principles to do with fairness and harm avoidance and rights of self-defence, and the principle that as far as possible we ought to treat others as autonomous subjects with a right to make responsible decisions. It is not always straightforward to say what is required in order to treat people as responsible decision-makers, since there are so many influences and factors that make us fallible and susceptible to influence. However, if we bear in mind those shortcomings and susceptibilities, it is often possible to discern ways of acting that are both realistic and ethical.

That principle of respect for others' autonomy can help to explain what is permissible by way of influencing others. It can help us specifically in regard to some of the considerations raised in Chapters 8 and 9, such as the ways of influencing others' decisions that have their effect not by any clear impact on others' beliefs, but through such processes as distraction or reframing. Some of these seem more acceptable than others, and the requirement that we allow others to make responsible decisions can help explain the difference.

The thrust of the discussion in much of the book is to analyse situations that recur in organisational politics, to consider ways in which widely accepted principles may be given application. Another principle which proves important in Chapter 10 is the requirement to meet obligations one has on account of others' expectations. When one has induced or maintained those expectations, the obligation is similar to the obligation one has to keep a promise, or to accept what one has consented to. In other cases, the obligation turns rather on the need to avoid harm to others where one can do so at little cost to oneself, emphasising the need to be realistic about circumstances; and in organisations the circumstances often include the actual expectations people have of one another.

Such expectations play a prominent part in the processes of social impression management first clearly described by Erving Goffman, where people's behaviour and expectations of one another are mutually sustaining. The earlier discussion of Chapter 5 rejected consent as a universal ground for respecting official authority in organisations. It is consistent with that that our consent to a process can sometimes generate obligations for us, and in Chapter 10 we see an example of this in the way that our eliciting or maintaining others' expectations can certainly do so. However, other obligations may stem from expectations others have of us even where we have no direct responsibility for those expectations, depending on such factors as the costs to them or others if the expectations are not met, and the costs to us of meeting them. Once again, in evaluating the obligations we may have as a result of others' expectations, we see the importance of being realistic and of having regard for the concrete individuals around us.

On the other side of the coin, the social pressures on us from people's expectations can be a potent source of influence, and others may trade on it by contriving that different people have expectations of us. Such contrivance may not be unethical, but it can be. To the extent that people's expectations of us can be not only a source of influence but a source of genuine obligation, unethical contrivance of such expectations may be especially problematic.

Such ethical problems become deeper because the sorts of mutual expectations to be found in social impression management may coalesce into group norms and create a local moral order which starts to have a life of its own, as people have interwoven obligations from which they cannot straight-forwardly free themselves. Individuals may find themselves in a dilemma, as others' expectations create real obligations for them. On occasion, they may avoid being exploited by exposing someone's contrivance and reaching a new set of mutual expectations with the others involved. In other cases, however, people can find themselves in a double bind, confronted by a dirty hands problem where any course of action is liable to involve forsaking something important.

To the extent that we accept the realities of organisational politics, we have to recognise that there can be ethical ways for people to influence one another, and unethical ways to do so. When others use unethical ways to influence us, that may not always free us from obligations to act as they wish us to. We can be alert to such techniques of influence, and can seek ethical ways to respond, but here as so often there are not routines or rules that will always provide a way out.

A particular problem with the form of influence that works by trading on people's obligations and commitments is that doing so may undermine our respect for such commitments. Such concerns emerge more fully in Chapter 11's discussion about means of influence that revolve around people's commitments to groups.

A commitment to a group may sometimes be associated with acceptance of a local moral order, a shared acceptance about what is right and proper, reflecting some shared scripts about social processes. The requirements of a local moral order may be invoked via background assumptions in discourse, like those we considered in Chapter 8. There we saw how negotiators' formulations of others' statements as offers or concessions may put the others in positions where they must either reject the formulation or accept its normative implications. Rejecting the formulation may involve questioning background assumptions or probing behind what is said, both of which carry costs, such as accusations of incompetence, madness or malice. But accepting the formulation may be accepting a position which entails obligations and requirements that serve the ends of the influencing party. In Chapter 11, we see how similar influence processes may trade on people's commitments to groups and to group positions. By accepting such a position, we effectively incur obligations which are based on expectations others now have of us.

Tendentious formulations are one way of manoeuvring others into situations where they have some obligations and commitments to particular lines of action. Questions of one sort or another can do so equally well, as shown by the question put to Jesus by the Pharisees and Herodians.

In that sort of case people are influenced by others trading on group alignments and the commitments that go with them. Special ethical problems arise in that case when people are led to avow beliefs in order to demonstrate their group allegiance, with little regard for the beliefs' justification. A gap may develop between reasons for avowing beliefs which are associated with group positions, and reasons which have to do with the possible truth of the beliefs. Those problems take us to Chapter 11's final note about hypocrisy, where it is contended that this can be a notable problem in organisational politics. It can be most especially so because of the way that group allegiances can be associated with espousals of belief: the need to espouse a belief to demonstrate continuing allegiance to the group can undermine people's trust in one another's avowals and ultimately our faith in ethical processes.

There is ample scope for self-deception and hypocrisy in organisational politics, since the absence of routines and rules about how to act ethically means that ethical decision-making in organisations is often demanding and often beset by error. The absence of routines and rules is compounded by the scope for conflicts of obligations. These may occur partly because our loyalty to individuals may conflict with requirements of fairness and impartiality, or with the achievement of organisational purposes. They may occur also because of conflicts between group expectations and other commitments. The absence of routines and rules is compounded also by the vagueness and ambiguity which are endemic to organisations, associated with difficulties in being sure about others' expectations and intentions. Despite the fact that most organisations involve a good deal of face-to-face interaction with specific individuals, the decisions we have to make often require us to deal with abstraction and uncertainty, just as those others do the same. The ambiguous flux of organisational politics makes it one of the most demanding contexts for ethical action. How we deal with it can have wider ramifications: the actions we take in organisations show our acceptance of certain values and principles that often are applicable in social life more generally, and what we show ourselves to accept in organisations will be that much more likely to be accepted outside them also.

References

Adams, D. (1979), *The Hitchhiker's Guide to the Galaxy*, London, Pan Books.

Aguilar, F.J. (1994), *Managing Corporate Ethics*, New York, Oxford University Press.

Anscombe, G.E.M. (1979), '"Under a Description"', *Noûs* **13**. Reprinted in G.E.M. Anscombe, *Metaphysics and the Philosophy of Mind* (vol. 2 of her *Collected Philosophical Papers*), Oxford, Basil Blackwell, 1981, pp. 208–19.

Anthony, P. (1994), *Managing Culture*, Buckingham, Open University Press.

Applbaum, A.I. (1998), 'Are Lawyers Liars? The Argument of Redescription', *Legal Theory* **4** (1), 63–91.

Argyle, M. (1983), *The Psychology of Interpersonal Behaviour*, 4th edition, Harmondsworth, Penguin.

Argyle, M. (1988), *Bodily Communication*, 2nd edition, London, Methuen.

Aristotle (1926), *The 'Art' of Rhetoric*, trans. J.H. Freese, Cambridge, Mass., Harvard University Press.

Aristotle (1934), *Nicomachean Ethics*, trans. H. Rackham, Cambridge, Mass., Harvard University Press.

Aristotle (1992), *The Politics*, trans. T.A. Sinclair, London, Penguin. Translation originally published 1962, revised by T.J. Saunders.

Atiyah, P.S. (1971), *The Sale of Goods*, 4th edition, London, Pitman.

Austin, J.L. (1975), *How to Do Things with Words*, Oxford, Clarendon Press. Edited by J.O. Urmson and Marina Sbisà.

Bacharach, S.B. and E.J. Lawler (1980), *Power and Politics in Organisations*, San Francisco, Jossey-Bass.

Baier, A.C. (1994), *Moral Prejudices*, Cambridge, Mass., Harvard University Press.

Baier, K. (1958), *The Moral Point of View*, Ithaca, NY, Cornell University Press.

Bailey, F.G. (1969), *Stratagems and Spoils*, Oxford, Basil Blackwell.

Bakhurst, D. (1992), 'On Lying and Deceiving', *Journal of Medical Ethics* **18**, 63–6.

Bandler, R. and J. Grinder (1975), *Patterns of the Hypnotic Techniques of Milton H. Erickson, M.D.*, Vol. 1, Cupertino, CA, Meta Publications.

Bandura, A. and R.H. Walters (1963), *Social Learning and Personality Development*, New York, Holt, Rinehart and Winston.

Baron, R.A. (1989), 'Impression Management by Applicants During Employment Interviews: The "Too Much of a Good Thing" Effect', in R.W. Eder and G.R. Ferris (eds), *The Employment Interview: Theory, Research, Practice*, Newbury Park, CA, Sage, pp. 204–15.

Baron, R.S., N.L. Kerr and N. Miller (1992), *Group Process, Group Decision, Group Action*, Buckingham, Open University Press.

Barry, B. (1980), 'Justice as Reciprocity', in E. Kamenka and A.E.-S. Tay (eds), *Justice*, New York, St. Martin's Press, pp. 50–78.

Bar-Tal, D. (1990), *Group Beliefs*, New York, Springer-Verlag.

Baumeister, R.F. (1989), 'Motives and Costs of Self-Presentation in Organizations', in R.A. Giacalone and P. Rosenfeld (eds), *Impression Management in the Organization*, Hillsdale, NJ, Lawrence Erlbaum, pp. 57–71.

Bell, D.V.J. (1975), *Power, Influence and Authority*, New York, Oxford University Press.

Benn, S.I. (1988), *A Theory of Freedom*, Cambridge, Cambridge University Press.

Benn, S.I. and R.S. Peters (1959), *Social Principles and the Democratic State*, London, George Allen & Unwin.

Bies, R.J. (1989), 'Managing Conflict before It Happens: The Role of Accounts', in M.A. Rahim (ed.), *Managing Conflict: An Interdisciplinary Approach*, New York, Praeger, pp. 83–91.

Bies, R.J. and S.B. Sitkin (1992), 'Explanation as Legitimation: Excuse-Making in Organisations', in M.L. McLaughlin, M.J. Cody and S.J. Read (eds), *Explaining One's Self to Others: Reason-Giving in a Social Context*, Hillsdale, NJ, Lawrence Erlbaum, pp. 183–98.

Bloch, M. (1965), *Feudal Society*, trans. L.A. Manyon, Vol. 1, London, Routledge & Kegan Paul.

Blum, L.A. (1973), 'Deceiving, Hurting and Using', in A. Montefiore (ed.), *Philosophy and Personal Relations*, London, Routledge and Kegan Paul, pp. 34–61.

Blum, L.A. (1980), *Friendship, Altruism and Morality*, London, Routledge and Kegan Paul.

Boatright, J.R. (1992), 'Morality in Practice: Dees, Crampton, and Brer Rabbit on a Problem of Applied Ethics', *Business Ethics Quarterly* **2** (1), 63–73.

Bok, S. (1978), *Lying: Moral Choice in Public and Private Life*, London, Harvester.

Bok, S. (1984), *Secrets: On the Ethics of Concealment and Revelation*, Oxford, Oxford University Press.

Bower, M. (1966), *The Will to Manage*, New York, McGraw-Hill.

Bowers, J.W., N.D. Elliott and R.J. Desmond (1977), 'Exploiting Pragmatic Rules: Devious Messages', *Human Communication Research* **3** (3), 235–42.

Bradshaw-Camball, P. and V.V. Murray (1991), 'Illusions and Other Games: A Trifocal View of Organizational Politics', *Organization Science* **2** (4), 379–97.

Branaman, A. (1997), 'Goffman's Social Theory', in C. Lemert and A. Branaman (eds), *The Goffman Reader*, Oxford, Blackwell, pp. xlv–lxxxii.

Broad, C.D. (1968), 'Conscience and Conscientious Action', reprinted in J.J. Thomson and G. Dworkin (eds), *Ethics*, New York, Harper & Row, pp. 492–511. First published 1952.

Brown, A.D. (1995), *Organisational Culture*, London, Pitman.

Brown, R.J. (1988), *Group Processes: Dynamics Within and Between Groups*, Oxford, Blackwell.

Buchanan, D. and R. Badham (1999), *Power, Politics, and Organizational Change*, London, Sage.

Bullock, A. (1962), *Hitler, A Study in Tyranny*, 2nd edition, Harmondsworth, Penguin.

Burawoy, M. (1979), *Manufacturing Consent*, Chicago, University of Chicago Press.

Button, G. (1992), 'Answers as Interactional Products: Two Sequential Practices Used in Job Interviews', in P. Drew and J. Heritage (eds), *Talk at Work: Interaction in Institutional Settings*, Cambridge, Cambridge University Press, pp. 212–31.

Cantor, N. and J.F. Kihlstrom (1987), *Personality and Social Intelligence*, Englewood Cliffs, NJ, Prentice-Hall.

Carnevale, P.J. and P.A. Keenan (1992), 'The Resolution of Conflict: Negotiation and Third Party Intervention', in J.F. Hartley and G.M. Stephenson (eds), *Employment Relations*, Oxford, Blackwell, pp. 225–45.

Carr, A.Z. (1968), 'Is Business Bluffing Ethical?' *Harvard Business Review* Jan–Feb, 143–53.

Carroll, J.S. and J.W. Payne (1991), 'An Information Processing Approach to Two-Party Negotiations', in M.H. Bazerman, R.J. Lewicki and B.H. Sheppard (eds), *Research on Negotiation in Organizations*, Greenwich, CT, JAI Press, Vol. 3, pp. 3–34.

Cartwright, D. and A. Zander (1960), 'Group Pressures and Group Standards: Introduction', in D. Cartwright and A. Zander (eds), *Group Dynamics*, London, Tavistock Publications, pp. 165–88.

Cavanagh, G.F., D.J. Moberg and M. Velasquez (1981), 'The Ethics of Organizational Politics', *Academy of Management Review* **6** (3), 363–74.

Chapman, R.A. (1993), 'Reasons of State and the Public Interest: A British Variation of the Problem of Dirty Hands', in R.A. Chapman (ed.), *Ethics in Public Service*, Edinburgh, Edinburgh University Press, pp. 93–110.

Churchland, P.M. (1995), *The Engine of Reason, the Seat of the Soul*, Cambridge, Mass., MIT Press.

Cialdini, R.B. (1987), 'Interpersonal Influence: Being Ethical and Effective', in S. Oskamp and S. Spacapan (eds), *Interpersonal Processes*, Newbury Park, Sage, pp. 148–65.

Cialdini, R.B. (1989), 'Indirect Tactics of Image Management: Beyond Basking', in R.A. Giacalone and P. Rosenfeld (eds), *Impression Management in the Organization*, Hillsdale, NJ, Lawrence Erlbaum, pp. 45–56.

Cialdini, R.B. (1993), *Influence: Science and Practice*, 3rd edition, New York, HarperCollins.

Coady, C.A.J. (1973), 'Testimony and Observation', *American Philosophical Quarterly* **10** (2), 149–55.

Coady, C.A.J. (1990), 'Messy Morality and the Art of the Possible', *Proceedings of the Aristotelian Society* Supp. Vol. **64**, 259–79.

Coady, C.A.J. (1991), 'Politics and the Problem of Dirty Hands', in P. Singer (ed.), *A Companion to Ethics*, Oxford, Blackwell, pp. 373–83.

Cocking, D. and J. Kennett (2000), 'Friendship and Moral Danger', *Journal of Philosophy* **97** (5), 278–96.

Connolly, W.E. (1993), *The Terms of Political Discourse*, 3rd edition, Oxford, Blackwell.

Cooper, J.M. (2001), 'Friendship', in L.C. Becker and C.B. Becker (eds), *Encyclopedia of Ethics*, New York, Routledge, Vol. 1, pp. 581–4.

Cox, G.E.P. (1952), *The Gospel According to St Matthew*, London, SCM Press.

Crick, B. (1964), *In Defence of Politics*, Revised edition, Harmondsworth, Penguin. Originally published 1962.

Crick, B. (1967), 'Freedom as Politics', in P. Laslett and W.G. Runciman (eds), *Philosophy, Politics and Society: Third Series*, Oxford, Basil Blackwell, pp. 194–214.

Cropanzano, R.S., K.M. Kacmar and D.P. Bozeman (1995), 'The Social Setting of Work Organizations: Politics, Justice and Support', in R.S. Cropanzano and K.M. Kacmar (eds), *Organizational Politics, Justice, and Support*, Westport, Conn., Quorum Books, pp. 1–18.

Cullity, G. (2002), 'Particularism and Presumptive Reasons', *Proceedings of the Aristotelian Society* Supp. Vol. **76**, 169–90.

Daniels, N. (ed.) (1989), *Reading Rawls*, Stanford, Stanford University Press.

Davies, B. and R. Harré (1999), 'Positioning and Personhood', in R. Harré and L. van Langenhove (eds), *Positioning Theory*, Oxford, Blackwell, pp. 32–52.

Davis, N. (1984), 'The Doctrine of Double Effect: Problems of Interpretation', *Pacific Philosophical Quarterly* **65** (2), 107–23.

de Callières, F. (1983), *The Art of Diplomacy*, Leicester, Leicester University Press. First published in 1716 as *De La Manière de Negocier avec les Souverains.*

de Tocqueville, A. (1961), *De la Démocratie en Amérique*, Paris, Gallimard. First published 1835.

de Waal, F. (1983), *Chimpanzee Politics: Power and Sex Among Apes*, London, Unwin.

Deal, T.E. and A.A. Kennedy (1988), *Corporate Cultures: The Rites and Rituals of Corporate Life*, Harmondsworth, Penguin.

Dees, J.G. and P.C. Cramton (1991), 'Shrewd Bargaining on the Moral Frontier: Toward a Theory of Morality in Practice', *Business Ethics Quarterly* **1** (2), 135–67.

Deighton, L. (1963), *Horse Under Water*, London, Jonathan Cape.

Deighton, L. (1977), *Fighter: The True Story of the Battle of Britain*, London, Jonathan Cape.

Donaldson, T. and T.W. Dunfee (1994), 'Toward a Unified Conception of Business Ethics: Integrative Social Contracts Theory', *Academy of Management Review* **19** (2), 252–84.

Drory, A. and T. Romm (1990), 'The Definition of Organizational Politics: A Review', *Human Relations* **43** (11), 1133–54.

Duncan, G. (1983), 'Political Theory and Human Nature', in I. Forbes and S. Smith (eds), *Politics and Human Nature*, London, Frances Pinter, pp. 5–19.

Dworkin, R. (1977), *Taking Rights Seriously*, London, Duckworth.

Ekman, P. (1991), *Telling Lies: Clues to Deceit in the Marketplace, Politics, and Marriage*, New York, W.W. Norton.

Elster, J. (1986), 'The Market and the Forum: Three Varieties of Political Theory', in J. Elster and A. Hylland (eds), *Foundations of Social Choice Theory*, Cambridge, Cambridge University Press, pp. 103–32.

Emmet, D. (1967), *Rules, Roles and Relations*, London, Macmillan.

Englehardt, E.E. and D. Evans (1994), 'Lies, Deception, and Public Relations', *Public Relations Review* **20** (3), 249–66.

Ewin, R.E. (1992), 'Loyalty and Virtues', *The Philosophical Quarterly* **42**, 403–19.

Ewin, R.E. (1993), 'Loyalties, and Why Loyalty Should Be Ignored', *Criminal Justice Ethics* **12** (1), 36–42.

Fairholm, G.W. (1993), *Organizational Power Politics*, Westport, Conn., Praeger.

Falk, W.D. (1965), 'Morality, Self, and Others', in H.-N. Castañeda and G. Nakhnikian (eds), *Morality and the Language of Conduct*, Detroit, Wayne State University Press, pp. 25–67.

Feinberg, J. (1983), 'Noncoercive Exploitation', in R. Sartorius (ed.), *Paternalism*, Minneapolis, University of Minnesota Press, pp. 201–35.

Feinberg, J. (1984), *Harm to Others*, Vol. 1 of *The Moral Limits of the Criminal Law*, New York, Oxford University Press.

Feinberg, J. (1986), *Harm to Self*, Vol. 3 of *The Moral Limits of the Criminal Law*, New York, Oxford University Press.

Ferris, G.R., J.F. Brand, S. Brand, K.M. Rowland, D.C. Gilmore, T.R. King, K.M. Kacmar and C.A. Burton (1993), 'Politics and Control in Organizations', in *Advances in Group Processes*, JAI Press, Vol. 10, pp. 83–111.

Finley, M.I. (1983), *Politics in the Ancient World*, Cambridge, Cambridge University Press.

Fisher, R., W.L. Ury and B. Patton (1991), *Getting to YES: Negotiating Agreement Without Giving In*, 2nd edition, New York, Penguin Books.

Fiske, S.T. and S.E. Taylor (1991), *Social Cognition*, 2nd edition, New York, McGraw-Hill.

Fiske, S.T., D.R. Kinder and W.M. Larter (1983), 'The Novice and the Expert: Knowledge-Based Strategies in Political Cognition', *Journal of Experimental Social Psychology* **19**, 381–400.

Fletcher, G. (1993), *Loyalty: An Essay on the Morality of Relationships*, New York, Oxford University Press.

Forster, E.M. (1965), *Two Cheers for Democracy*, Harmondsworth, Penguin. First published 1951.

Forsyth, D.R. (1990), *Group Dynamics*, Belmont, Wadsworth.

Fox, A. (1974), *Beyond Contract: Work, Power and Trust Relations*, London, Faber and Faber.

Frankfurt, H. (1986), 'On Bullshit', *Raritan* **6** (2). Reprinted in Harry Frankfurt, *The Importance of What We Care About: Philosophical Essays*, Cambridge University Press, 1988, pp. 117–33.

Freeman, R.B. and J.L. Medoff (1984), *What Do Unions Do?*, New York, Basic Books.

French, J.R.P. and B. Raven (1960), 'The Bases of Social Power', in D. Cartwright and A. Zander (eds), *Group Dynamics*, London, Tavistock Publications, pp. 607–23.

Friedman, R.A. (1994), *Front Stage, Backstage: The Dramatic Structure of Labor Negotiations*, Cambridge, Mass., MIT Press.

Gadlin, H. (1991), 'Careful Maneuvers: Mediating Sexual Harassment', *Negotiation Journal* **7** (2), 139–53.

Gilbert, D.T. and J. Cooper (1985), 'Social Psychological Strategies of Self-Deception', in M.W. Martin (ed.), *Self-Deception and Self-Understanding*, Lawrence, Kansas, University Press of Kansas.

Gillon, R. (1993), 'Is There an Important Moral Distinction for Medical Ethics Between Lying and Other Forms of Deception?' *Journal of Medical Ethics* **19** (3), 131–2.

Glazer, M.P. and P.M. Glazer (1989), *The Whistleblowers*, New York, Basic Books.

Gluckman, M. (1965), *Politics, Law and Ritual in Tribal Society*, Oxford, Basil Blackwell.

Goffman, E. (1955), 'On Face-Work', *Psychiatry* **18** (3). Reprinted in Erving Goffman, *Interaction Ritual: Essays in Face-to-Face Behavior*, Chicago, Aldine, 1967, pp. 5–45.

Goffman, E. (1956), 'Embarrassment and Social Organisation', *American Journal of Sociology* **62** (3). Reprinted in Erving Goffman, *Interaction Ritual: Essays in Face-to-Face Behavior*, Chicago, Aldine, 1967, pp. 97–112.

Goffman, E. (1970), *Strategic Interaction*, Oxford, Blackwell.

Goffman, E. (1971), *The Presentation of Self in Everyday Life*, Harmondsworth, Penguin. First published 1959.

Goffman, E. (1972), *Encounters*, Harmondsworth, Penguin. Original edition Bobbs-Merrill, 1961.

Graham, A. (1975), 'Impartiality and Bias in Economics', in A. Montefiore (ed.), *Neutrality and Impartiality*, London, Cambridge University Press, pp. 49–71.

Grant, R.W. (1997), *Hypocrisy and Integrity*, Chicago, University of Chicago Press.

Greenwald, A.G. (1980), 'The Totalitarian Ego: Fabrication and Revision of Personal History', *American Psychologist* **35**, 603–18.

Grice, H.P. (1957), 'Meaning', *Philosophical Review* **66**. Reprinted in *Studies in the Way of Words* (Cambridge, Mass., Harvard University Press, 1989), pp. 213–23.

Grice, H.P. (1989a), 'Logic and Conversation', in *Studies in the Way of Words*, Cambridge, Mass., Harvard University Press, pp. 22–40.

Grice, H.P. (1989b), *Studies in the Way of Words*, Cambridge, Mass., Harvard University Press.

Gundlach, G.T. and P.E. Murphy (1993), 'Ethical and Legal Foundations of Relational Marketing Exchanges', *Journal of Marketing* **57** (4), 35–46.

Habermas, J. (1976), *Legitimation Crisis*, trans. T. McCarthy, London, Heinemann. First published in German in 1973.

Hamm, R.M. (1988), 'Clinical Intuition and Clinical Analysis: Expertise and the Cognitive Continuum', in J. Dowie and A. Elstein (eds), *Professional Judgment*, Cambridge, Cambridge University Press, pp. 78–105.

Hampshire, S. (1982), 'Morality and Convention', in A. Sen and B. Williams (eds), *Utilitarianism and Beyond*, Cambridge, Cambridge University Press, pp. 145–57.

Hampshire, S. (1989), *Innocence and Experience*, London, Penguin.

Handy, C.B. (1985), *Understanding Organizations*, 3rd edition, Harmondsworth, Penguin.

Hardin, R. (1982), *Collective Action*, Baltimore, Johns Hopkins University Press.

Hardin, R. (1995), *One for All: The Logic of Group Conflict*, Princeton, Princeton University Press.

Harman, G. (1977), *The Nature of Morality*, New York, Oxford University Press.

Harré, R. and L. van Langenhove (1999), 'The Dynamics of Social Episodes', in R. Harré and L. van Langenhove (eds), *Positioning Theory*, Oxford, Blackwell, pp. 1–13.

Hart, H.L.A. (1961), *The Concept of Law*, Oxford, Clarendon Press.

Higgins, R.L. and C.R. Snyder (1989), 'The Business of Excuses', in R.A. Giacalone and P. Rosenfeld (eds), *Impression Management in the Organization*, Hillsdale, NJ, Lawrence Erlbaum, pp. 73–85.

Hirschman, A.O. (1970), *Exit, Voice and Loyalty: Response to Decline in Firms, Organizations and States*, Cambridge, Mass., Harvard University Press.

Hobbes, T. (1968), *Leviathan*, Harmondsworth, Penguin. Edited by C.B. Macpherson. First published 1651.

Hochschild, A.R. (1983), *The Managed Heart*, Berkeley, University of California Press.

Hodgson, D.H. (1967), *Consequences of Utilitarianism*, Oxford, Clarendon Press.

Hoffman, L.R. (1982), 'Improving the Problem-Solving Process in Managerial Groups', in R.A. Guzzo (ed.), *Improving Group Decision Making in Organizations*, New York, Academic Press, pp. 95–126.

Hume, D. (1897), *A Treatise of Human Nature*, 2nd edition, ed. L.A. Selby-Bigge, Oxford, Clarendon Press. First published 1739–40.

Hume, D. (1902), *Enquiries Concerning the Human Understanding and Concerning the Principles of Morals*, 2nd edition, ed. L.A. Selby-Bigge, Oxford, Clarendon Press. First published 1777.

Isaacson, W. and E. Thomas (1986), *The Wise Men*, London, Faber and Faber.

Jackall, R. (1988), *Moral Mazes*, New York, Oxford University Press.

Jackson, J. (1991), 'Telling the Truth', *Journal of Medical Ethics* 17, 5–9.

Jackson, J. (1993), 'On the Morality of Deception – Does Method Matter? A Reply to David Bakhurst', *Journal of Medical Ethics* 19, 183–7.

Jay, A. (1967), *Management and Machiavelli*, London, Hodder & Stoughton.

Jay, A. (1972), *Corporation Man*, London, Jonathan Cape.

Kacmar, K.M. and R.A. Baron (1999), 'Organizational Politics: The State of the Field, Links to Related Processes, and an Agenda for Future Research', in G.R. Ferris (ed.), *Research in Personnel and Human Resources Management*, Stamford, Conn., JAI Press, Vol. 17, pp. 1–39.

Kacmar, K.M. and G.R. Ferris (1991), 'Perceptions of Organizational Politics Scale (POPS): Development and Construct Validation', *Educational and Psychological Measurement* 51, 193–205.

Kahneman, D. (1992), 'Reference Points, Anchors, Norms, and Mixed Feelings', *Organizational Behavior and Human Decision Processes* 51 (2), 296–312.

Kahneman, D., J.L. Knetsch and R. Thaler (1991), 'The Endowment Effect, Loss Aversion, and Status Quo Bias', *Journal of Economic Perspectives* 5

(1), 193–206. Reprinted in Richard H. Thaler, *The Winner's Curse: Paradoxes and Anomalies of Economic Life*, Princeton University Press, 1992.

Kakabadse, A. and C. Parker (1984), 'Towards a Theory of Political Behaviour in Organizations', in A. Kakabadse and C. Parker (eds), *Power, Politics, and Organisations: A Behavioural Science View*, Chichester, John Wiley & Sons Ltd, pp. 87–108.

Kant, I. (1964), *Groundwork of the Metaphysic of Morals*, trans. H.J. Paton, New York, Harper & Row. First published in German in 1785.

Katz, D. and R.L. Kahn (1966), *The Social Psychology of Organizations*, New York, John Wiley & Sons.

Keller, M. (1989), *Rude Awakening: The Rise, Fall, and Struggle for Recovery of General Motors*, New York, William Morrow.

Kelley, H.H. and A.J. Stahelski (1970), 'Social Interaction Basis of Cooperators' and Competitors' Beliefs About Others', *Journal of Personality and Social Psychology* 16 (1), 66–91.

Kinnear, M. (1973), *The Fall of Lloyd George*, London, Macmillan.

Kipnis, D., S.M. Schmidt and G. Braxton-Brown (1990), 'The Hidden Costs of Persistence', in M.J. Cody and M.L. McLaughlin (eds), *The Psychology of Tactical Communication*, Clevedon, Multilingual Matters, pp. 160–72.

Kittay, E.F. (2001), 'Hypocrisy', in L.C. Becker and C.B. Becker (eds), *Encyclopedia of Ethics*, New York, Routledge, Vol. 2, pp. 819–24.

Kleinig, J. (1978), 'Crime and the Concept of Harm', *American Philosophical Quarterly* 15 (1), 27–36.

Kleinig, J. (1996), *The Ethics of Policing*, Cambridge, Cambridge University Press.

Krauss, R.M., S.R. Fussell and Y. Chen (1995), 'Coordination of Perspective in Dialogue: Intrapersonal and Interpersonal Processes', in I. Marková, C.F. Graumann and K. Foppa (eds), *Mutualities in Dialogue*, Cambridge, Cambridge University Press, pp. 124–45.

Kunz, P.R. and M. Woolcott (1976), 'Season's Greetings: From My Status to Yours', *Social Science Research* 5, 269–78.

Laing, R.D. (1969), *Self and Others*, 2nd edition, London, Tavistock Publications.

Laing, R.D. (1971), *The Politics of the Family and Other Essays*, London, Tavistock.

Lamb, R. and M. Lalljee (1992), 'The Use of Prototypical Explanations in First- and Third-Person Accounts', in M.L. McLaughlin, M.J. Cody and S.J. Read (eds), *Explaining One's Self to Others: Reason-Giving in a Social Context*, Hillsdale, NJ, Lawrence Erlbaum, pp. 21–39.

Laslett, P. (1956), 'The Face to Face Society', in P. Laslett (ed.), *Philosophy, Politics and Society: First Series*, Oxford, Basil Blackwell, pp. 157–84.

Lautenschlager, G.L. and V.L. Flaherty (1990), 'Computer Administration of Questions: More Desirable or More Social Desirability?' *Journal of Applied Psychology* **75**, 310–14.

Leidner, R. (1993), *Fast Food, Fast Talk: Service Work and the Routinization of Everyday Life*, Berkeley, University of California Press.

Lewicki, R.J., D.J. McAllister and R.J. Bies (1998), 'Trust and Distrust: New Relationships and Realities', *Academy of Management Review* **23** (3), 438–58.

Lewin, D. (1987), 'Dispute Resolution in the Nonunion Firm: A Theoretical and Empirical Analysis', *Journal of Conflict Resolution* **31**, 465–502.

Locke, J. (1980), *Second Treatise of Government*, Indianapolis, Hackett. Edited by C.B. Macpherson. First published 1690.

Lukes, S. (1974), *Power: A Radical View*, London, Macmillan.

Machiavelli, N. (1992), *The Prince*, trans. N.H. Thomson, New York, Dover. Originally 1513.

MacIntyre, A. (1985), *After Virtue*, 2nd edition, London, Duckworth.

MacNeal, K. (1939), *Truth in Accounting*, Philadelphia, University of Pennsylvania Press.

Manning, P. (1992), *Erving Goffman and Modern Sociology*, Stanford, Stanford University Press.

Margolis, H. (1987), *Patterns, Thinking, and Cognition*, Chicago, University of Chicago Press.

Marková, I., C.F. Graumann and K. Foppa (eds) (1995), *Mutualities in Dialogue*, Cambridge, Cambridge University Press.

Matheson, P. (1972), *Cardinal Contarini at Regensburg*, Oxford, Clarendon Press.

McCalman, J. (2001), 'But I Did It for the Company! The Ethics of Organisational Politics', *Reason in Practice: The Journal of Philosophy of Management* **1** (3), 57–66.

McDonnell, D.L. and J.G. Monroe (1952), *Kerr on the Law of Fraud and Mistake*, 7th edition, London, Sweet & Maxwell.

McLaughlin, M.L., M.J. Cody, R. Dickson and V. Manusov (1992), 'Accounting for Failure to Follow Advice: Real Reasons Versus Good Explanations', in M.L. McLaughlin, M.J. Cody and S.J. Read (eds), *Explaining One's Self to Others: Reason-Giving in a Social Context*, Hillsdale, NJ, Lawrence Erlbaum, pp. 281–94.

Messick, D.M. and M.H. Bazerman (1996), 'Ethical Leadership and the Psychology of Decision Making', *Sloan Management Review* (Winter), 9–22.

Milgram, S. (1974), *Obedience to Authority*, New York, Harper & Row.

Mill, J.S. (1952), *A System of Logic*, London, Longmans, Green & Co. First published 1843.

Miller, J.D.B. (1962), *The Nature of Politics*, Harmondsworth, Penguin.

Miner, J.B. (1992), *Industrial–Organizational Psychology*, New York, McGraw-Hill.

Mintzberg, H. (1983), *Power in and Around Organisations*, Englewood Cliffs, NJ, Prentice-Hall.

Moberg, D.J. (1989), 'The Ethics of Impression Management', in R.A. Giacalone and P. Rosenfeld (eds), *Impression Management in the Organization*, Hillsdale, NJ, Lawrence Erlbaum, pp. 171–87.

Morgan, T. (1985), *FDR: A Biography*, New York, Simon and Schuster.

Neale, M.A. and M.H. Bazerman (1985), 'Perspectives for Understanding Negotiation', *Journal of Conflict Resolution* **29** (1), 33–55.

Neisser, U. (1976), *Cognition and Reality*, San Francisco, W.H. Freeman and Co.

Nielsen, R.P. (1996), *The Politics of Ethics*, New York, Oxford University Press.

Nineham, D.E. (1969), *The Gospel of St Mark*, 2nd edition, Harmondsworth, Penguin.

Nisbett, R. and L. Ross (1980), *Human Inference: Strategies and Shortcomings of Social Judgment*, Englewood Cliffs, NJ, Prentice-Hall.

Oakeshott, M. (1989), 'Political Education', in T. Fuller (ed.), *The Voice of Liberal Learning*, New Haven, Yale University Press.

Offe, C. (1985), *Disorganised Capitalism*, Cambridge, Polity Press.

Okin, S.M. (1991), 'Gender, the Public and the Private', in D. Held (ed.), *Political Theory Today*, Cambridge, Polity Press, pp. 67–90.

Olson, M. (1965), *The Logic of Collective Action*, Cambridge, Mass., Harvard University Press.

O'Reilly, C. (1991), 'Corporations, Culture and Commitment: Motivation and Social Control in Organizations', in R.M. Steers and L.W. Porter (eds), *Motivation and Work Behavior*, 5th edition, New York, McGraw-Hill, pp. 242–54.

Pateman, C. (1970), *Participation and Democratic Theory*, Cambridge, Cambridge University Press.

Pateman, C. (1983), 'Feminist Critiques of the Public–Private Dichotomy', in S.I. Benn and G.F. Gaus (eds), *The Public and Private in Social Life*, London, Croom Helm, pp. 281–300.

Peters, E. (1955), *Strategy and Tactics in Labor Negotiations*, New London, CT, National Foremen's Institute.

Peters, R.S. (1958), 'Authority', *Proceedings of the Aristotelian Society* Supp. Vol. **32**. Reprinted in A. Quinton (ed.), *Political Philosophy*, Oxford University Press 1967, pp. 83–96.

Pettigrew, A.M. (1975), 'Towards a Political Theory of Organisational Intervention', *Human Relations* **28** (3), 191–208.

Pettit, P. (1988), 'The Paradox of Loyalty', *American Philosophical Quarterly* **25** (2), 163–71.

Pfeffer, J. (1981), *Power in Organizations*, Boston, Pitman.

Pfeffer, J. (1992), *Managing with Power*, Boston, Mass., Harvard Business School Press.

Phillips, A. (1993), *Democracy and Difference*, Cambridge, Polity Press.

Porter, J.A. (1991), 'Complement Extern: Iago's Speech Acts', in V.M. Vaughan and K. Cartwright (eds), *Othello: New Perspectives*, Cranbury, NJ, Associated University Presses, pp. 74–88.

Pratchett, T. (2000), *The Truth*, London, Doubleday.

Prentice, D.A., D.T. Miller and J.R. Lightdale (1994), 'Asymmetries in Attachments to Groups and to Their Members: Distinguishing Between Common-Identity and Common-Bond Groups', *Personality and Social Psychology Bulletin* **20** (5), 484–93.

Provis, C. (1996a), 'Interests *vs* Positions: A Critique of the Distinction', *Negotiation Journal* **12** (4), 305–23.

Provis, C. (1996b), 'Unitarism, Pluralism, Interests and Values', *British Journal of Industrial Relations* **34** (4), 473–95.

Provis, C. (2000a), 'Ethics, Deception and Labor Negotiation', *Journal of Business Ethics* **28** (2), 145–58.

Provis, C. (2000b), 'Honesty in Negotiation', *Business Ethics: A European Review* **9** (1), 3–12.

Provis, C. (2001), 'Why Is Trust Important?' *Reason in Practice: The Journal of Philosophy of Management* **1** (2), 31–41.

Provis, C. (2004), 'Negotiation, Persuasion and Argument', *Argumentation* **18** (1), 95–112.

Provis, C. and S. Stack (2004), 'Caring Work, Personal Obligation and Collective Responsibility', *Nursing Ethics* **11** (1), 5–14.

Provis, C., J. McKay and J. Tomaino (1998), 'Whistleblowing and Organisational Strategy', *Journal of Contemporary Issues in Business and Government* **4** (1), 43–51.

Pruitt, D.G. (1981), *Negotiation Behavior*, New York, Academic Press.

Punch, M. (1996), *Dirty Business: Exploring Corporate Misconduct*, London, Sage.

Quine, W.V.O. (1960), *Word and Object*, Cambridge, Mass., M.I.T. Press.

Rachels, J. (1995), *The Elements of Moral Philosophy*, 2nd edition, New York, McGraw-Hill.

Ralston, D.A., R.A. Giacalone and R.H. Terpstra (1994), 'Ethical Perceptions of Organizational Politics: A Comparative Evaluation of American and Hong Kong Managers', *Journal of Business Ethics* **13**, 989–99.

Rawls, J. (1972), *A Theory of Justice*, Oxford, Clarendon Press.

Ridgeway, C.L. (1993), 'Legitimacy, Status, and Dominance Behaviour in Groups', in S. Worchel and J.A. Simpson (eds), *Conflict Between People and Groups*, Chicago, Nelson-Hall, pp. 110–27.

Riker, W.H. (1986), *The Art of Political Manipulation*, New Haven, Yale University Press.

Robbins, S.P. and N.S. Barnwell (1994), *Organisation Theory in Australia*, 2nd edition, Sydney, Prentice Hall.

Robbins, S.P., T. Waters-Marsh, R. Cacioppe and B. Millett (1994), *Organisational Behaviour: Concepts, Controversies and Applications; Australia and New Zealand*, Sydney, Prentice Hall.

Rojot, J. (1991), *Negotiation: From Theory to Practice*, London, Macmillan.

Rosenfeld, P. (1997), 'Impression Management, Fairness, and the Employment Interview', *Journal of Business Ethics* **16** (8), 801–8.

Rothschild, J. and T.D. Miethe (1994), 'Whistleblowing as Resistance in Modern Work Organizations', in J.M. Jermier, D. Knights and W.R. Nord (eds), *Resistance and Power in Organizations*, London, Routledge, pp. 252–73.

Rousseau, D.M. (1995), *Psychological Contracts in Organizations*, Thousand Oaks, CA, Sage.

Rousseau, J.J. (1947), *The Social Contract*, trans. C. Frankel, New York, Hafner. First published in French in 1762.

Ryan, A. (ed.) (1973), *The Philosophy of Social Explanation*, Oxford, Oxford University Press.

Scanlon, T.M. (1982), 'Contractualism and Utilitarianism', in A. Sen and B. Williams (eds), *Utilitarianism and Beyond*, Cambridge, Cambridge University Press, pp. 103–28.

Scanlon, T.M. (1998), *What We Owe to Each Other*, Cambridge, Mass., Harvard University Press.

Schank, R.C. and R.P. Abelson (1977), *Scripts, Plans, Goals and Understanding*, Hillsdale, NJ, Lawrence Erlbaum.

Scheffler, S. (ed.) (1988), *Consequentialism and Its Critics*, Oxford Readings in Philosophy, Oxford, Oxford University Press.

Schein, V.E. (1977), 'Individual Power and Political Behaviour in Organizations: An Inadequately Explored Reality', *Academy of Management Review* **2** (1), 64–72.

Schiffer, S.R. (1972), *Meaning*, Oxford, Clarendon Press.

Schumpeter, J.A. (1954), *Capitalism, Socialism and Democracy*, Revised edition, London, George Allen & Unwin.

Sen, A. and B.A.O. Williams (eds) (1982), *Utilitarianism and Beyond*, Cambridge, Cambridge University Press.

Sheffrin, S.M. (1996), *Rational Expectations*, 2nd edition of *Cambridge Surveys of Economic Literature*, Cambridge, Cambridge University Press.

Sherif, M. (1936), *The Psychology of Social Norms*, New York, Harper & Row.

Shklar, J.N. (1984), *Ordinary Vices*, Cambridge, Mass., Harvard University Press.

Sidgwick, H. (1907), *The Methods of Ethics*, 7th edition, London, Macmillan.

Simmons, A.J. (1979), *Moral Principles and Political Obligation*, Princeton, Princeton University Press.

Simon, H. (1957), *Models of Man*, New York, John Wiley & Sons.

Sinclair, T.A. (1992), 'Translator's Introduction', in Aristotle, *The Politics*, London, Penguin. First published 1962.

Smart, J.J.C. and B.A.O. Williams (1973), *Utilitarianism: For and Against*, Cambridge, Cambridge University Press.

Snow, C.P. (1961), *Science and Government*, London University Press, Oxford.

Snow, C.P. (1962), *Postscript*, London University Press, Oxford.

Snow, C.P. (1972a), *The Affair*, Omnibus edition, Macmillan. First published 1960.

Snow, C.P. (1972b), *Corridors of Power*, Omnibus edition, Macmillan. First published 1964.

Snow, C.P. (1972c), *The Masters*, Omnibus edition, Macmillan. First published 1951.

Snow, C.P. (1972d), *The New Men*, Omnibus edition, Macmillan. First published 1954.

Solomon, R.C. (1992), *Ethics and Excellence*, New York, Oxford University Press.

Solomon, R.C. (1994), *Above the Bottom Line: An Introduction to Business Ethics*, 2nd edition, Fort Worth, Harcourt Brace.

Solso, R.L. (1995), *Cognitive Psychology*, 4th edition, Boston, Allyn and Bacon.

Spector, P.E. (2000), *Industrial and Organizational Psychology*, 2nd edition, New York, John Wiley & Sons.

St. Augustine (1847a), 'Lying', in *Seventeen Short Treatises*, Oxford, John Henry Parker, pp. 382–425.

St. Augustine (1847b), 'To Consentius: Against Lying', in *Seventeen Short Treatises*, Oxford, John Henry Parker, pp. 426–69.

St. Ignatius Loyola (1951), *The Spiritual Exercises of St. Ignatius*, trans. L.J. Puhl, Chicago, Loyola University Press.

Stanton, K.M. (1994), *The Modern Law of Tort*, London, Sweet & Maxwell.

Steinberger, P.J. (1993), *The Concept of Political Judgment*, Chicago, University of Chicago Press.

Stocker, M. (1980), 'Intellectual Desire, Emotion, and Action', in A.O. Rorty (ed.), *Explaining Emotions*, Berkeley, University of California Press.

Stocker, M. (1981), 'Values and Purposes: The Limits of Teleology and the Ends of Friendship', *Journal of Philosophy* **78** (12), 747–65.

Stocker, M. (1990), *Plural and Conflicting Values*, Oxford, Clarendon Press.

Strudler, A. (1995), 'On the Ethics of Deception in Negotiation', *Business Ethics Quarterly* **5** (4), 805–22.

Strutton, D., J.B. Hamilton, III and J.R. Lumpkin (1997), 'An Essay on When to Fully Disclose in Sales Relationships: Applying Two Practical Guidelines for Addressing Truth-Telling Problems', *Journal of Business Ethics* **16**, 545–60.

Swann, W.B., Jr., T. Giuliano and D.M. Wegner (1982), 'Where Leading Questions Can Lead: The Power of Conjecture in Social Interaction', *Journal of Personality and Social Psychology* **42** (6), 1025–35.

Thompson, L. (1990), 'An Examination of Naive and Experienced Negotiators', *Journal of Personality and Social Psychology* **59** (1), 82–90.

Thompson, L. and G. Loewenstein (1992), 'Egocentric Interpretations of Fairness and Interpersonal Conflict', *Organizational Behavior and Human Decision Processes* **51**, 176–97.

Thomson, D. (1966), *Europe Since Napoleon*, Revised edition, Harmondsworth, Penguin.

Treitel, G.H. (1995), *The Law of Contract*, 9th edition, London, Sweet & Maxwell.

Trevelyan, G.M. (1909), *Garibaldi and the Thousand*, London, Longmans, Green and Co.

Treviño, L.K. and K.A. Nelson (1995), *Managing Business Ethics: Straight Talk About How To Do It Right*, New York, John Wiley & Sons.

Turner, G. (2001), 'Ethics, Entertainment, and the Tabloid: The Case of Talkback Radio in Australia', *Continuum: Journal of Media & Cultural Studies* **15** (3), 349–57.

Tversky, A. and D. Kahneman (1981), 'The Framing of Decisions and the Psychology of Choice', *Science* **211**, 453–8.

Tversky, A. and D. Kahneman (1986), 'Judgement under Uncertainty: Heuristics and Biases', in H.R. Arkes and K.R. Hammond (eds), *Judgment and Decision-Making: An Inter-Disciplinary Reader*, Cambridge, Cambridge University Press.

Van Maanen, J. and S.R. Barley (1985), 'Cultural Organization: Fragments of a Theory', in P.J. Frost, L.F. Moore, M.R. Louis et al. (eds), *Organizational Culture*, Newbury Park, CA, Sage, pp. 31–53.

Vaughn, D. (1996), *The Challenger Launch Decision*, Chicago, University of Chicago Press.

Vedung, E. (1987), 'Rational Argumentation and Political Deception', in F.H. van Eemeren, R. Grootendorst, J.A. Blair and C.A. Willard (eds), *Argumentation: Across the Lines of Discipline*, Dordrecht, Foris, pp. 353–64.

Velasquez, M.G. (2002), *Business Ethics: Concepts and Cases*, 5th edition, Upper Saddle River, NJ, Prentice Hall.

Velasquez, M.G., D.J. Moberg and G.F. Cavanagh (1983), 'Organizational Statesmanship and Dirty Politics: Ethical Guidelines for the Organizational Politician', *Organizational Dynamics* **12** (2), 65–80.

Walker, E. (1995), 'Making a Bid for Change: Formulations in Union/Management Negotiations', in A. Firth (ed.), *The Discourse of Negotiation*, Oxford, Pergamon, pp. 101–40.

Wallbott, H.G. (1995), 'Congruence, Contagion, and Motor Mimicry: Mutualities in Nonverbal Exchange', in I. Marková, C.F. Graumann and

K. Foppa (eds), *Mutualities in Dialogue*, Cambridge, Cambridge University Press, pp. 82–98.

Walters, R. (1974), 'What Did Ziegler Say, and When Did He Say It', *Columbia Journalism Review* **13**, 30–37.

Walton, R.E. and R.B. McKersie (1991), *A Behavioral Theory of Labor Negotiations*, 2nd edition, Ithaca, NY, ILR Press. Original edition New York: McGraw-Hill, 1965.

Walzer, M. (1973), 'Political Action: The Problem of Dirty Hands', *Philosophy and Public Affairs* **2** (2), 160–80.

Watzlawick, P., J.H. Beavin and D.D. Jackson (1967), *Pragmatics of Human Communication*, New York, Norton.

Werhane, P.H. (1991), *Adam Smith and His Legacy for Modern Capitalism*, New York, Oxford University Press.

Werhane, P.H. (1998), 'Moral Imagination and the Search for Ethical Decision-Making in Management', *Business Ethics Quarterly* (The Ruffin Series: Special Issue No. 1), 75–98.

Werhane, P.H. (1999), *Moral Imagination and Management Decision-Making*, New York, Oxford University Press.

Werhane, P.H. (2000), 'Business Ethics and the Origins of Contemporary Capitalism: Economics and Ethics in the Work of Adam Smith and Herbert Spencer', *Journal of Business Ethics* **24**, 185–98.

Werhane, P.H. (2002), 'Moral Imagination and Systems Thinking', *Journal of Business Ethics* **38**, 33–42.

White, J.J. (1980), 'Machiavelli and the Bar: Ethical Limitations on Lying in Negotiation', *American Bar Foundation Research Journal*, 926–38.

Williams, B.A.O. (1985), *Ethics and the Limits of Philosophy*, London, Fontana Press.

Williams, G.R. (1983), *Legal Negotiation and Settlement*, St. Paul, Minn., West Publishing Co.

Willmott, H. (1993), 'Strength Is Ignorance; Slavery Is Freedom: Managing Culture in Modern Organizations', *Journal of Management Studies* **30** (4), 515–52.

Wilson, J.R.S. (1978), 'In One Another's Power', *Ethics* **88** (4), 299–315.

Wollheim, R. (1962), 'A Paradox in the Theory of Democracy', in P. Laslett and W.G. Runciman (eds), *Philosophy, Politics and Society: Second Series*, Oxford, Basil Blackwell, pp. 71–87.

Young, H. (1976), *The Crossman Affair*, London, Hamish Hamilton and Jonathan Cape.

Young, J., C.J. Thomsen, E. Borgida, J.L. Sullivan and J.H. Aldrich (1991), 'When Self-Interest Makes a Difference: The Role of Construct Accessibility in Political Reasoning', *Journal of Experimental Social Psychology* **27** (3), 271–96.

Young, R. (1991), 'The Implications of Determinism', in P. Singer (ed.), *A Companion to Ethics*, Oxford, Blackwell, pp. 534–42.

Zebrowitz, L.A. (1990), *Social Perception*, Buckingham, Open University Press.

Zeckhauser, R.J. and D.V.P. Marks (1996), 'Sign Posting: The Selective Revelation of Product Information', in R.J. Zeckhauser, R.L. Keeney and J.K. Sebenius (eds), *Wise Choices*, Boston, Harvard Business School Press, pp. 22–41.

Index